THE
VANCOUVER
GUIDE

Revised and Updated

1991-1992 Edition

Chronicle Books ● San Francisco

Thanks to Barbara Tuepah and Jill Bain
for their assistance.

Second Chronicle Books edition published in the United States in 1991.

Published in Canada by Douglas & McIntyre, Vancouver/Toronto

Library of Congress Cataloging-in-Publication Data
Wershler, Terri.
The Vancouver guide.—Rev. & updated ed.
p.   cm.
Includes index.
ISBN 0-87701-880-4
1. Vancouver (B.C.)—Description—Guide-books. I. Title.
F1089.5.V22W47 1991
917.11'33044—dc20   90-27586
CIP

Text design: Robert MacDonald/MediaClones
Cover design: Alex Hass
Photographs by Rosamond Norbury (except where noted)
Maps by David Gay and Barbara Hodgson
Map assistance by Brenda Code
Cover photograph by Jurgen Vogt
Printed and bound in Canada by D. W. Friesen & Sons Ltd.

10 9 8 7 6 5 4 3 2 1

Chronicle Books
275 Fifth Street
San Francisco, California
94103

CONTENTS

LIST OF MAPS 6

1. ABOUT VANCOUVER 7
The Look of the City, Getting Oriented,
History, Population,
Weather, Major Industries

2. ESSENTIAL INFORMATION 19
Emergency Phone Numbers, Major Hospitals,
Motor Vehicles, Travel Information,
Public Holidays, Lost and Found,
Foreign Visitors, Banking, Sales Taxes,
Post Office, Late Night Services,
Baby-sitting, Liquor/Beer/Wine,
Dry Cleaning, Shoe Repairs,
Radio, Television, Newspapers

3. WHERE TO STAY 27
Hotels, Alternative Accommodation,
Bed and Breakfast,
Trailer Parks/Campgrounds

4. RESTAURANTS 41
Breakfast/Brunch, Lunch,
Seafood, Pizza, Vegetarian, Late Night,
Outdoors, With a View, Espresso Bars,
By Nationality, By Location

5. GETTING AROUND 67
Public Transit, Coach Lines,
Cars, Taxis, Trains, Ferries,
Vancouver International Airport,
Flights to Victoria and Seattle

6. SIGHTSEEING 83
The Sights, Granville Island,
The Royal Hudson/M.V. *Britannia* Excursion,
Chinatown, Touring Vancouver,
Calendar of Events

7. PARKS/BEACHES/GARDENS 101

Ambleside Park, Capilano River Regional Park,
Dr. Sun Yat-sen Garden, Grouse Mountain,
Jericho Beach to Spanish Banks,
Lighthouse Park, Lynn Canyon Park, Mount Seymour,
Nitobe Garden/UBC Botanical Garden,
Queen Elizabeth Park/Bloedel Conservatory,
Reifel Bird Sanctuary,
Seymour Demonstration Forest, Stanley Park,
Pacific Spirit Park (University Endowment Lands),
VanDusen Gardens

8. MUSEUMS/ART GALLERIES 125

Museum of Anthropology, Vanier Park Museum Complex,
Science World, Vancouver Aquarium, Other Museums,
Public Art Galleries, Vancouver Art Gallery, Major Private Galleries,
Artist-Run Galleries, Photo Galleries, Indian or Inuit (Eskimo) Galleries,
Print Galleries, Craft Galleries

9. ENTERTAINMENT/CULTURE 139

At the Movies, Theatre,
Classical Music, Dance

10. NIGHT LIFE 147

Jazz, Rhythm 'n' Blues, Comedy,
A Nice Quiet Bar, Lively Pubs and Bars,
Neighbourhood Pubs, Supper Clubs,
Discos, Rock Clubs, Gay Clubs

11. SPORTS/RECREATION 153

Auto Racing, Bicycling, Camping,
Canoeing/Kayaking/Rowing,
Cruising, Fishing, Fitness,
Golf, Hiking/Mountaineering, Horseback Riding,
Horse Racing, Professional Sports,
River-Rafting, Sailing, Scuba Diving, Skating
Skiing, Swimming, Tennis, Windsurfing

12. SHOPPING 185

Shopping Areas, Accessories, Art Supplies,
Auctions, Antiques and Oriental Rugs,
Books and Magazines, Books (Used),
Clothing for Men, Clothing for Women,
Maternity Wear, Clothing for Men and Women,
Consignment Clothing Stores, Home Furnishings,
Kitchenware, Marine Supplies,
Photo Supplies/Film Processing, Records
Shoes, Souvenirs, Sports Equipment, Food Stores

13. WITH THE KIDS 209

Kids and Animals, Day Trips,
Museums, Baby-sitting,
Entertainment, Restaurants, Shopping

14. EXCURSIONS FROM VANCOUVER 219

Gulf Islands: Galiano/Mayne/Salt Spring,
Whistler

INDEX 234

LIST OF MAPS

Southwestern British Columbia 9
Greater Vancouver 11
Hotel Locations 28
Restaurant Locations 65
Downtown Vancouver 69
The West End 71
Ferry Routes 77
Airport Location 80
Granville Island Area 84
Granville Island 86
Chinatown/Gastown/Japantown 92-93
Vancouver Harbour 97
Stanley Park 114-15
Pacific Spirit Park/University of British Columbia 121
Vanier Park/Kitsilano Beach 128
Howe Sound 160
Ski Locations 176
Gulf Islands 220

ABOUT VANCOUVER

THE LOOK OF THE CITY **8**

GETTING ORIENTED **10**

HISTORY **12**

POPULATION **16**

WEATHER **16**

MAJOR INDUSTRIES **18**

THE LOOK OF THE CITY

Vancouver's greatest asset is the beauty of its natural surroundings, that perfect combination of sea and mountains. The sea plays a major role in the city's economy and so defines much of people's work – and leisure. The mountains of the Coast Range form a breathtaking panorama and provide ski slopes just a short drive away. They also protect the city from biting north winds and create a mild, wet climate.

In many large cities the downtown core is a place of business where people work and shop by day, but avoid at night. The suburbs lure with their open spaces and convenient shopping malls. Not so in Vancouver. Downtown is vital because people live there; inhabitants of the nearby, densely populated West End keep the streets alive at almost any hour. The best shopping is downtown, with the Pacific Centre underground mall and Robson St. drawing people out of their suburban homes.

Vancouver has the features of a young city – in fact, it is just over 100 years old. Visitors will notice differences between Vancouver and eastern cities. In the East many buildings are brick or stone, but on the West Coast, where quality lumber is abundant, houses are built of wood. This does not give the city a feeling of history, and sometimes Vancouver has the semblance of a frontier town that shot up overnight. Also, styles of architecture parallel those of California more than those of eastern Canada. And although the downtown core has little greenery, residential areas abound with flowers and lush landscaping.

A 20-year urban redevelopment project, the largest in North America, is about to begin construction on the Expo 86 site, and this will change the look of Vancouver.

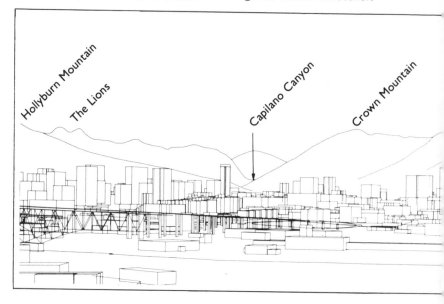

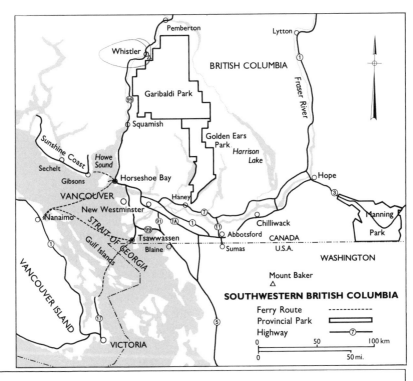

SOUTHWESTERN BRITISH COLUMBIA

Ferry Route ----------
Provincial Park
Highway

0   50   100 km
0   50 mi.

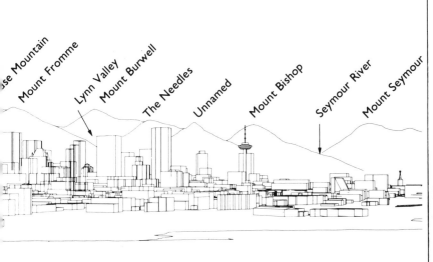

H.A. Simon (International) Ltd.

GETTING ORIENTED

The city centre is encompassed by water on three sides. Burrard Inlet, which separates the North Shore (both North and West Vancouver) from the city proper, is spanned by two bridges. The Lions Gate Bridge connects downtown with the North Shore; one end is in Stanley Park and the other between West and North Vancouver. The Second Narrows Bridge runs between the East End of Vancouver and North Vancouver.

False Creek juts into the heart of the city, and is crossed by three bridges connecting the West End and downtown to the rest of Vancouver. From east to west, there is the Cambie St. Bridge by the stadium at B.C. Place, the Granville St. Bridge and the Burrard St. Bridge.

The Fraser River, which marks the southern limit of the city, is spanned (from west to east) by the Arthur Laing Bridge, the Oak St. Bridge, the Knight St. Bridge, the Alex Fraser Bridge, the Pattullo Bridge and the Port Mann Bridge.

South of the city is Vancouver International Airport, located on an island at the mouth of the Fraser River.

Most of Vancouver's streets form a grid, laid out by surveyors who had only utility in mind. The grid makes finding your way around quite simple. The area south of False Creek is especially easy, since east-west roads are numbered avenues. The dividing line between east and west is roughly Main St. To avoid confusion, be sure to check whether avenues are preceded by a "W" for West or "E" for East.

Highway One, the Trans-Canada, goes through east Vancouver and crosses the Second Narrows Bridge to the North Shore, ending at Horseshoe Bay. From there, ferries run to Nanaimo on Vancouver Island and Langdale on the Sechelt Peninsula.

Highway 99 runs south and goes under the south arm of the Fraser River via the George Massey Tunnel. Past the tunnel, Highway 17 branches off for Tsawwassen and the terminal for ferries sailing to Victoria, Nanaimo and the Gulf Islands. Highway 99 itself continues on to the U.S. border, about an hour's drive from downtown.

Highway 99 also runs northward to the ferry terminal at Horseshoe Bay, then on to Squamish and points beyond.

Highway 91 runs from the border to the eastern municipalities such as Burnaby, New Westminster and Port Coquitlam.

Greater Vancouver consists of the city of Vancouver and a number of communities. Across Burrard Inlet are Lions Bay, West Vancouver and North Vancouver. South of the city, across the Fraser River, are Richmond, Delta, Surrey and White Rock. East and northeast are Burnaby, New Westminster, Port Moody, Port Coquitlam, Coquitlam, Ioco-Buntzen and Belcarra. In many of these communities, avenues run east-west and streets run north-south. Often, the names of both avenues and streets are numbers, so take careful note of addresses.

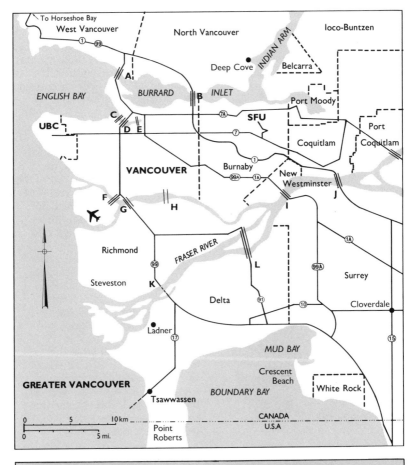

A Lions Gate Bridge	**I** Pattullo Bridge
B Second Narrows Bridge	**J** Port Mann Bridge
C Burrard St. Bridge	**K** George Massey Tunnel
D Granville St. Bridge	**L** Alex Fraser Bridge
E Cambie St. Bridge	**UBC** University of British Columbia
F Arthur Laing Bridge	**SFU** Simon Fraser University
G Oak St. Bridge	✈ Vancouver International Airport
H Knight St. Bridge	—⑨①— Highway

HISTORY

NATIVE PEOPLE

The Coast Salish inhabited approximately 10 villages on the shores of Burrard Inlet and Point Grey. Their ancient culture was highly developed; they were master carpenters and canoemakers and exquisite craftsmen.

Coast Salish baskets made from cedar root, cherry bark and reeds. Drawings by Hilary Stewart from her book, *Cedar.*

EXPLORATION

1791 A Spanish navigator, José Narváez, was the first white man to arrive in the immediate area. He anchored off Point Grey but missed the entrance to Burrard Inlet.

1792 Capt. George Vancouver arrived and claimed the land for Britain while searching for a northwest passage to the Orient. He spent only one day on the site of the city named after him 100 years later. While charting Burrard Inlet, he had an amicable meeting with a Spanish explorer, Dionisio Alcalá Galiano.

Although the Spanish did not play a large part in the history of this area, they left their mark on place names: Alberni, Galiano, Cordova, Langara, San Juan, Saturna and Juan de Fuca.

1808 Explorer and fur trader Simon Fraser of the North West Company reached the Pacific overland by a river he thought was the Columbia. It was not, and the river was later named after him. He did not reach Burrard Inlet.

SETTLEMENT

"By all accounts, from the present Granville Street to the tip of Point Grey grew one of the most magnificent stands of virgin timber the world has ever seen." Alan Morley, *Vancouver: From Milltown to Metropolis*

1827 The Hudson's Bay Company set up a fur-trading post, Fort Langley, 48 km (30 mi.) east of Vancouver on the Fraser River. It was the first settlement in the Lower

Mainland, but homesteaders were not encouraged since land-clearing would drive away fur-bearing animals.

1858 Gold was discovered up the Fraser River and the valley was flooded with 25,000 prospectors, mostly from the depleted gold mines of California. To provide law and order among the gold seekers, and to secure the land from encroachment by the United States, the area was declared the Crown Colony of British Columbia.

1859 New Westminster, a town on the Fraser River, was named the capital of British Columbia.
A British survey ship discovered coal on the shores of Burrard Inlet. (This bay at the entrance to Stanley Park is still called Coal Harbour.)

1862 Unable to find gold, three British prospectors acquired 200 ha (500 acres) of land on the south shore of Burrard Inlet to start a brickworks. (It failed . . . who wanted bricks with all that wood?) Their land, now the entire West End, is some of the most expensive real estate in Canada, but was then valued at $1.01 per acre.

1867 John Deighton, called "Gassy Jack" because he was so talkative, opened a saloon near the Hastings Sawmill on Burrard Inlet. As liquor was prohibited on company land, business boomed for Jack; he was so successful that a community known as Gastown grew around his saloon.

Towering Douglas-firs on Granville St. in the 1880s.

1869 Gastown was officially incorporated as the town of Granville.

1884 The Canadian Pacific Railway decided on Coal Harbour, at the mouth of Burrard Inlet, as its transcontinental terminus. This decision was crucial to the subsequent rapid development of Vancouver.
For a time the CPR controlled the town. It was, in fact, the president of the CPR who chose the name Vancouver.

Vancouver Public Library

VANCOUVER AS A CITY

1886 The town of Granville, population 1000, became the City of Vancouver. On 13 June the entire city was wiped out in less than an hour by a clearing fire gone wild. Fewer than half a dozen buildings remained.

Despite the chaos of rebuilding, the inaugural City Council showed remarkable foresight by turning the First Narrows Military Reserve into a park. It was named Stanley Park after Governor General Lord Stanley. (The Stanley Cup is also named after him.)

After the fire, the city grew at a rapid rate. By the end of the year there were 800 buildings.

After the Great Fire of 1886 the first City Hall was in a tent.

LATER LANDMARK YEARS

1887 The first CPR train chugged into Vancouver. The transcontinental railway was complete!

1889 The original Granville St. Bridge was built, the first to span False Creek.

1893 The Hudson's Bay Company opened its first department store at Granville and Georgia, the same site as the present store.

1908 The University of British Columbia was founded.

1925 The original Second Narrows Bridge opened, connecting Vancouver with the North Shore.

Vancouver Public Library

1936 Vancouver's City Hall was completed in the popular art deco style of the time.

1938 The Lions Gate Bridge opened.

1939 The Hotel Vancouver (the third and existing one) was completed. Construction was suspended during the Depression, so the hotel was eleven years in the making.

1950 Park Royal, Canada's second shopping centre, was built in West Vancouver.

1964 The B.C. Lions football team won the Grey Cup.

1965 Simon Fraser University, designed by architect Arthur Erickson, opened for classes.

1970 The Vancouver Canucks hockey team made its NHL debut.

1979 The Vancouver Whitecaps won the North American Soccer League championship.

1983 B.C. Place Stadium, the state-of-the-art in inflated domes, opened.

1986 Vancouver's centennial. The city hosted Expo 86, a world transporation exhibition.

Vancouver's art-deco style City Hall, shortly after its completion in 1936.

POPULATION

In just over 100 years Vancouver has grown to be the third-largest city in Canada, after Toronto and Montreal. According to the latest census in 1986, the population of the City of Vancouver was 431,000 and Greater Vancouver was 1.3 million.

The main ethnic groups in Greater Vancouver are:

British	392,000
Chinese	100,000
German	60,000
Indo-Pakistani	46,000
French	29,000
Italian	29,000
Dutch	25,000
Scandinavian	24,000
Ukrainian	23,000
Filippino	14,000
Japanese	12,000
Native Indian	11,000
Jewish	11,000
Greek	6000

Chinese. There have been three major waves of immigration: in 1858 for the Fraser Valley gold rush, in the 1880s to construct the Canadian Pacific Railway and since the 1960s because of unrest in Hong Kong. Today the Chinese community is the second largest in North America, after San Francisco.

German, Dutch, Jewish, Scandinavian and Ukrainian. Although these form sizable groups, they have integrated into Vancouver life and are not highly visible ethnic communities.

Indo-Pakistani. Many came from the Himalayas because of their logging skills. They have a community on Main St. between 49th and 51st avenues.

French. The French community has its own church, newspaper, and radio and television stations. There is a large community called Maillardville in Coquitlam.

Italian. The Italians also publish their own newspaper, available in "Little Italy" on Commercial Dr. north of Broadway. Many Italians arrived at the turn of the century, and a second wave arrived after World War II.

Filippino. Many Filippinos are women who came to Vancouver in the 1960s because of a severe shortage of nurses.

Japanese. Many emigrated at the turn of the century to fish, farm, work in sawmills or build the railroad. Japantown, along Powell St. east of Main, was much larger before the war. Steveston, south of Richmond, still has remnants of its heritage as a Japanese fishing village.

Native Indian. The Coast Salish originally inhabited this area. Three bands (Burrard, Squamish and Musqueam) now live on two large reserves in Greater Vancouver.

Greek. Most Greeks arrived after World War II, opening restaurants and shops or working in construction. Their community is centred on Broadway west of Macdonald.

WEATHER

When people talk about Vancouver, the subject of weather invariably arises. Vancouverites are either pitied because of the rain or envied because of the balmy climate.

Summers are warm and winters are mild with little snow, while the rest of Canada experiences hot, humid summers and cold, snowy winters. Temperatures below -13°C (0°F) have only been recorded once in Vancouver.

One reason for the balmy climate is that weather systems move from west to east. So when the rest of Canada is submerged in cold air from the mountains and the prairies, Vancouver basks in warm Pacific airstreams.

Vancouver is blessed with mild temperatures but is cursed with rain.

While the picturesque mountains protect the city from wind, they also latch onto rain clouds, so the closer people live to the mountains, the more they get rained on. For ex-ample, the annual level of precipitation on Grouse Mountain is 3500 mm (140 in.), while downtown Vancouver receives 1400 mm (55 in.) and sunny Richmond only 1000 mm (40 in.). Rain has its advantages, however; the grass stays green and the air is usually fresh and clear.

If you visit between May and September bring a sweater, a raincoat and an umbrella. In winter months, you'll need a warm raincoat, an umbrella and waterproof boots.

For a recorded weather forecast, phone 664-9010. For an air quality report call 436-6767.

WEATHER CHART	Daily Mean Temperature		Average High Temperature		Average Number Days of Precipitation	Average Monthly Precipitation		Average Number Hours of Sunshine
	°C	°F	°C	°F		cm	in.	
January	2	36	5	41	20	21.8	8.6	55
February	4	40	7	44	15	14.7	5.8	93
March	6	43	10	50	16	12.7	5.0	129
April	9	48	14	58	13	8.4	3.3	180
May	12	54	18	64	10	7.1	2.8	253
June	15	59	21	69	10	6.4	2.5	243
July	17	63	23	74	6	3.1	1.2	305
August	17	63	23	73	8	4.3	1.7	255
September	14	58	18	65	9	9.1	3.6	188
October	10	50	14	57	16	14.7	5.8	116
November	6	43	9	48	18	21.1	8.3	70
December	4	39	6	43	20	22.4	8.8	44

MAJOR INDUSTRIES

Industry has developed in Vancouver largely because of two factors: the province's wealth of natural resources and the city's great natural harbour.

Throughout the province, industry is based on mining, fishing and forestry, and Vancouver is active in the processing and shipping of these raw materials. Mills, canneries and oil refineries are common on the outskirts of the city. Commercial fishboats dock throughout city waterways, unloading their catches of salmon, herring, sole and halibut.

Burrard Inlet is one of the world's largest natural harbours; it is deep, sheltered and ice-free all year. Vancouver is a major North American port because of the harbour and because it is the western terminus for two transcontinental rail lines. With nearby Roberts Bank, it handles more tonnage than any other port on the West Coast and is second only to that of New York City in the western hemisphere. Freighters anchored in Burrard Inlet are as much a part of the city's panorama as the mountains that form their backdrop. Outgoing cargoes include grain, fish, lumber, pulp, coal, potash, sulfur, asbestos, iron ore and copper.

A FUTURISTIC CONCEPTION OF VANCOUVER

Tourist — Shipping — Manufacturing — Lumber — Mining

ESSENTIAL INFORMATION

EMERGENCY PHONE NUMBERS 20

MAJOR HOSPITALS 20

MOTOR VEHICLES 21

TRAVEL INFORMATION 21

PUBLIC HOLIDAYS 22

LOST AND FOUND 22

FOREIGN VISITORS 22
Interpreter Services, Customs Regulations, Metric Conversion

BANKING 22
Currency Exchanges

SALES TAXES 23

POST OFFICE 23

LATE NIGHT SERVICES 23
Pharmacies, Restaurants

BABY-SITTING 24

LIQUOR/BEER/WINE 24

DRY CLEANING 25

SHOE REPAIRS 25

RADIO 25
AM Radio Stations, FM Radio Stations

TELEVISION 25
Network and Cable TV, Pay TV

NEWSPAPERS 26

EMERGENCY PHONE NUMBERS

Police, Fire, Ambulance
Call 911 in Greater Vancouver.

Doctors and Dentists
Side by side on the lower level of the Bentall Centre, Dunsmuir and Burrard are drop-in medical and dental clinics: Medicentre (683-8138) and Dentacentre (669-6700).

Opticians
Same-day service is available at Granville Mall Optical (683-4716) at 807 Granville at Robson or Image Contact Lens Centre (681-9488) at 815 W. Hastings at Howe.

Poison Control Centre
Call 631-5050.

Crisis Centre
For persons in emotional crisis, call 733-4111 any time.

Rape Relief
Call 872-8212.

Aids Hotline
Call 687-2437.

Alcoholics Anonymous
Call 434-3933.

Veterinarians
The Animal Emergency Clinic (734-5104) at 4th and Fir is open 24 hours every day.

Legal Services
For a referral, phone 687-3221; for free general legal information, phone 687-4680. These services are offered by the B.C. branch of the Canadian Bar Association.

Marine and Aircraft Emergencies
Call the Canadian Coast Guard at 666-4302.

RCMP Tourist Alert
The RCMP attempts to contact travellers with urgent messages via radio, television, newspapers, B.C. Travel Infocentres and provincial campgrounds. Call the closest RCMP office.

MAJOR HOSPITALS

Vancouver General Hospital
855 W. 12th near Oak
875-4111

St. Paul's Hospital
1081 Burrard near Davie
682-2344

Grace Hospital (Obstetrics)
4490 Oak at 29th
875-2424

University Hospital: Shaughnessy
4500 Oak at 29th
875-2222

Children's Hospital
4480 Oak at 29th
875-2345

University Hospital: UBC
2211 Wesbrook Mall, UBC
228-7121

Lions Gate Hospital
15th and St. Georges, east of Lonsdale, North Vancouver
988-3131

MOTOR VEHICLES

Seatbelts are compulsory in B.C.; motorcyclists must wear helmets. Children under five must be secured in infant restraint systems. Right turns on red lights are allowed after you have come to a complete stop. Speed limits and road distances are posted in kilometres, and gas is sold only in litres.

Emergency Road Service
The BCAA offers 24-hour emergency road service to its members and members of other auto clubs. Call 293-2222. (Be patient, as it is often difficult to get through.)

Towing
If you've been towed from the street, call Unitow at 688-5484. Their lot at 1410 Granville at Pacific is open 24 hours. You can pay the towing charge ($15.50) with cash, Visa or Mastercard.

If you were towed from a private lot, call Buster's at 685-8181. Their lot at 104 E. 1st near Quebec is open 24 hours. The $55 charge can be paid with cash, Visa or Mastercard.

Road Conditions
Call the Department of Highways at 660-9775.

TRAVEL INFORMATION

Vancouver Travel Infocentre
1055 Dunsmuir near Burrard
683-2000
Will book accommodation, tour reservations, car rentals and restaurant reservations. Stamps, souvenirs, maps, brochures and B.C. Transit tickets, schedules and passes are available here. Summer hours from May to Labour Day are 8-6, seven days a week; winter hours are Mon to Sat, 9-5.

A Vancouver Travel Infocentre booth operates from the end of May to Sept at the aquarium parking lot in Stanley Park 10-6 daily. Another booth in Pacific Centre mall is open all year. In the summer, hours are Mon to Sat, 9-5; Sun, noon-5. In winter they are closed Sundays.

Tourist information booths are also located during the summer months on the main floors of two department stores, Eaton's and The Bay, at Georgia and Granville.

TRAVEL INFOCENTRES

These are run by the provincial government.

White Rock Travel Infocentre
1554 Foster and North Bluff
536-6844
Open seven days a week in July and August, Mon to Fri in winter.

Richmond Travel Infocentre
Highway 99 at the George Massey Tunnel
271-5323
Open seven days a week in summer; in winter, Mon to Sat, 10-4.

North Vancouver Travel Infocentre
131 E. 2nd St. near Lonsdale
987-4488
Open Mon to Fri, 9-5.

New Westminster Travel Infocentre
New Westminster Quay Public Market
810 Front Street at 8th St.
526-1905
Open daily 9:30-6:30.

Tsawwassen Infocentre
Ferry Terminal Causeway
943-3388 (seasonal)
Open May 24 to Labour Day, Mon
to Fri, 9-5.

Delta Infocentre
Highway 10 at Highway 99
(on Chevron lot)
590-3666 (seasonal)
Open May 24 to Labour Day, seven
days a week.

PUBLIC HOLIDAYS

New Year's, January 1
Good Friday, date varies
Victoria Day, third Monday in May
Canada Day, July 1
B.C. Day, first Monday in August
Labour Day, first Monday in
September
Thanksgiving, second Monday in
October
Remembrance Day, November 11
Christmas, December 25
Boxing Day, December 26

Traffic at border crossings and on
the ferries is very high around a
holiday weekend; avoid both if
possible.

LOST AND FOUND

B.C. Transit
682-7887

Police (Property Room)
665-2232

FOREIGN VISITORS

There are about 35 consulates in
Vancouver but no embassies. Check
The Yellow Pages.

INTERPRETER SERVICES

The Society of Translators and
Interpreters of B.C. (684-2940) will
provide names of accredited translators.
The College of Physicians and
Surgeons (733-7758) provides a list
of doctors speaking second languages.

CUSTOMS REGULATIONS

After a 48-hour visit, U.S. citizens
can take home $400 (U.S.) worth of
goods every 30 days. This may
include 1 litre of alcohol, 200
cigarettes and 100 cigars (not
Cuban). Only $25 worth of goods is
allowed after a visit of less than 48
hours.

METRIC CONVERSION

Metric conversion charts are at the
back of *The Yellow Pages.*

BANKING

There are over 25 foreign banks in
Vancouver. Check *The Yellow Pages.*

CURRENCY EXCHANGES

American Express
1040 W. Georgia near Burrard
669-2813
Open Mon to Fri, 8:30-5:30, Sat 10-4.
American Express also has an office
on the 4th floor of The Bay department store at Granville and Georgia,
hours are Mon to Fri 9:30-5, Sat
9:30-4.

Thomas Cook Foreign Exchange
617 Granville near Dunsmuir
687-6111
Open Mon to Sat, 9-5.

International Securities Exchange
1169 Robson near Thurlow
683-9666
1036 Robson near Burrard
683-4686
Summer hours are 9-9, seven days a week. Winter hours are Mon to Wed and Sun, 9-6; Thurs to Sat, 9-9.

Bank of America
Vancouver International Airport
273-8808
Open daily 6:15 AM-8 PM.

Many banks are open on Saturdays. The main downtown branches of banks all have foreign exchange departments.

SALES TAXES

A provincial sales tax of 6% is applied to most purchases with the noteable exception of groceries, books and magazines. A new 7% federal tax called the Goods and Services Tax will also be added to virtually everything you purchase except groceries. Non-Canadians can apply for a rebate of the portion of this tax paid on accommodation if it is at least $20. Ask for details at your hotel.

POST OFFICE

The main post office at Georgia and Homer is open Mon to Fri, 8-5:30. A substation is at 757 W. Hastings at Granville and is open Mon to Fri, 8:30-5. Eaton's and The Bay downtown stores also have post offices.
Basic postal services are available at designated drugstores and convenience stores Mon to Sat. Look for the Canada Post sign in the front window.

LATE NIGHT SERVICES

PHARMACIES

Shopper's Drug Mart
1125 Davie and Thurlow
685-6445
Open Mon to Sat, 9-midnight; Sun 9-9.

Pharmacies in the following Safeway supermarkets are open 8-midnight every day:
2733 W. Broadway at Trafalgar
4440 E. Hastings at Willingdon
1780 E. Broadway at Commercial

RESTAURANTS

The Bread Garden
812 Bute and Robson
688-3213
1880 W. 1st at Cypress
738-6684

The Naam
2724 W. 4th near Stephens
738-7151
A health food restaurant with beer, wine and espresso.

Hamburger Mary's
1202 Davie at Bute
687-1293
Open 24 hours on Fri and Sat.

BABY-SITTING

Most major hotels can arrange for baby-sitters if notified in advance.

Neighbourhood Babysitters
737-2248
Same day booking, adult sitter comes to you for $10/hour. Mastercard accepted.

Over-the-Rainbow Drop-in Playcare Centre
1508 Anderson, Granville Island
683-2624
Will take children 2-5 years. Reservation required 2 days in advance. Open 9-5, Mon to Fri. Will take 2 year olds until 1 PM only.

LIQUOR/BEER/WINE

In B.C. you must be at least 19 to purchase or consume alcohol. Spirits are sold only in government liquor stores, which are also the main outlet for beer and wine.

Private beer and wine stores sell their products at slightly higher prices than government stores, but are convenient because they are generally open seven days a week and sell chilled wine and beer.

Pubs have "off-license sales" whereby they are allowed to sell cold beer to be consumed off the premises.

Vancouver police are tough on drinking drivers. Don't do it.

Centrally located government liquor stores are:

1120 Alberni near Thurlow
Mon to Sat, 10-9.

1716 Robson near Denman
Mon to Sat, 9:30-11.

1155 Bute near Davie
Mon to Thurs and Sat, 9:30-6, Fri 9:30-9.

1655 Davie near Cardero
Mon to Sat, 9:30-9.

2020 W. Broadway at Maple
Mon to Sat, 9-11.

2933 Granville and 13th
Mon to Thurs and Sat, 9-6, Fri 9:30-9.

5555 Cambie and 39th
Mon to Sat, 9:30-9. The largest liquor store in the province; wine consultants on staff.

Some centrally located private wine and beer stores are:

Bimini
2010 W. 4th at Maple
738-3411
Open daily 11-11.

Granville Island Brewing Co.
1441 Cartwright, Granville Island
688-9927
Open Sun to Thurs, 9-7; Fri and Sat, 9-9. Beer and wine.

Marquis Wine Cellar
1034 Davie off Burrard
685-2446
Open Mon to Sat, noon-8; Thurs to Sun, noon-9. Wine only and a selection that is quite different from the government liquor stores.

DRY CLEANING

Woodman's
567 Hornby near Dunsmuir
684-9235

The Valetor
The Bay (concourse)
Georgia and Granville
681-6211 (local 2522)

Scotty's One Hour Cleaners
834 Thurlow near Robson
685-7732

SHOE REPAIRS

J.R. Donald
Bentall Centre, lower level
Dunsmuir and Burrard
688-0538

Sinclair Shoe Repair
Sinclair Centre
Hastings and Granville
662-7505
Repairs while you wait.

RADIO

Cable stations are in brackets.

AM RADIO STATIONS

600 CHRX, classic rock (90.9)
650 CISL, '50s-to-contemporary hits (91.3)
690 CBU-CBC, news, talk, classical music, no commercials (93.1)
730 CKLG, top 40 (94.7)
800 CKST, adult contemporary (not on cable)
980 CKNW, news, talk, MOR music, sports (95.5)

1040 CKXY, top 40 (96.7)
1130 CKWX, country (97.1)
1320 CHQM, easy listening (97.5)
1410 CFUN, soft rock (100.1)
1470 CJVB, multilingual news, talk (103.3)

FM RADIO STATIONS

93.7 CJJR, country (91.7)
96.9 CKKS, soft rock (103.9)
97.7 CBUF-CBC, French (102.3)
99.3 CFOX, adult rock (99.7)
101.1 CFMI, light rock (105.3)
101.9 CITR, university station, alternative music (101.9)
102.7 CFRO, community radio (102.9)
103.5 CHQM, easy listening (106.1)
105.7 CBU-CBC, classical music, talk, no commercials (107.1)

TELEVISION

This is a list of TV channels showing where they appear on cable dial. If you are on the North Shore, check the local TV listings because many channels are different there.

NETWORK AND CABLE TV

2 KING Seattle NBC (also on cable 16)
3 CBUT Vancouver CBC
4 Community TV Vancouver
5 Knowledge Network Vancouver
6 CHEK Victoria CTV
7 CBUFT Vancouver CBC, French
8 KIRO Seattle CBS (also on cable 15)
9 KCTS Seattle PBS
10 KOMO Seattle ABC
11 BCTV Vancouver CTV
12 KVOS Bellingham
13 CKVU Vancouver

14 **Home Shopping**
17 **KCPQ** Tacoma FOX
18 **Real Estate Listings**
20 **KSTW** Tacoma
21 **Rogers TV Listings Guide**
24 **The Sports Network**
25 **YTV,** youth
26 **CBC Newsworld**
27 **House of Commons/Broadcast News**
28 **Vision,** multireligious
29 **MuchMusic,** rock music
30 **WeatherNow**
31 **Transportation/Weather,** includes airline departure and arrival information
32 **Financial/Multicultural TV**

Before 9 AM, the weather, ferry schedules and news are printed continuously on Cable 4.

PAY TV

33 **Superchannel**
34 **Family Channel**
35 **Cathay TV,** Asian languages station
36 **Chinavision,** Chinese language station
37 **Cable News Network**
38 **Cable News Network: Headline News**
39 **Arts and Entertainment**
40 **The Nashville Network**
43 **Financial News Network**

NEWSPAPERS

The Vancouver Sun
Published every afternoon except Sunday. Complete entertainment listings on Thursday, weekly *TV Times* on Friday.

The Province
Published every morning except Saturday. Entertainment and TV listings on Friday.

Georgia Straight
A free entertainment weekly. Published on Thursday, available at newsstands and corner stores.

Business in Vancouver
Excellent weekly in tabloid format, published on Friday.

Vancouver Child
Free monthly paper with family-related events. Available at libraries, children's retail outlets and community centres.

Out-of-Town Newspapers
The best selection downtown is at Mayfair News in Royal Centre, Burrard and Georgia.

WHERE TO STAY

HOTELS 28
Downtown, Robson Street, West End, Granville Island and Kitsilano,
Near the Airport, Kingsway, North Shore

ALTERNATIVE ACCOMMODATION 38

BED AND BREAKFAST 39

TRAILER PARKS/CAMPGROUNDS 39
In and Near Vancouver, Near Tsawwassen, White Rock, Surrey

Only recommended hotels are listed. Comments may seem overly enthusiastic, but these are a few selected from many. The hotels are grouped by location and then listed by price in each section. (Prices quoted are for a standard double in high season.) After the hotels are listings for Alternative Accommodation, Bed and Breakfast and Trailer Parks/Campgrounds.

If you are planning an extended stay, you may want to book through **Executive Accommodations (522-6669)**, which can find you an apartment, townhouse or family home. Accommodation can include a fully-equipped kitchen, maid service, a fireplace, plants – whatever makes you feel at home. Minimum stay is one week; children and pets require advance notice. For a long-term stay, this can represent a substantial saving over hotel rates. Prices start at $465/week.

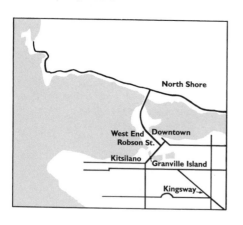

HOTELS

DOWNTOWN

Le Meridien Hotel
845 Burrard near Robson
682-5511
(800) 543-4300 toll free
Fax (604) 682-5513

The Meridien, an Air France chain, is Vancouver's finest hotel and is one of three in the city to receive a five-star rating from AAA. (Only 45 hotels in North American received this top award.) Luxury envelops as you step into the lobby: thick carpets, extravagant floral arrangements, French provincial furniture and an air of tranquility. The exquisite furniture is continued in the rooms — with detailed moldings, silk bedspreads and marble bathrooms, you feel like you're in a grand European home.

Although the Meridien is large, it is not a convention hotel and has maintained an intimate feeling. Amenities include a business centre, a private dining room, downtown limousine service, pool and sundeck and health and beauty centre.

Gérard is the formal French dining room. Café Fleuri is known for its chocolate buffet on Fri and Sat evenings and for the best Sunday brunch in town (see Restaurants, Breakfast/Brunch). The hotel bar is extraordinarily comfortable – dark and warm with lots of maple, soft leather and a fireplace.

The location is perfect for shopping and restaurants and is a five-minute walk from the business district. Doubles $240.

Delta Place

645 Howe near Georgia
687-1122
(800) 268-1133 toll free
Fax (604) 689-7044
When Delta took over this ultra-deluxe hotel built for the Mandarin chain, they changed very little. The luxurious surroundings and the location are still the attractions. The elegance is quiet but pervasive: marble everywhere, handcarved oak desks and silk-covered coat hangers. One floor is set aside for a health centre (racquet courts, lap pool, sundeck, exercise room, whirlpool, massage, saunas with television) and a business services centre. Unfortunately the restaurant does not match the surroundings. Excellent location. Doubles $204.

The Four Seasons Hotel

791 W. Georgia and Howe
689-9333
(800) 268-6282 (Canada)
(800) 332-3442 (U.S.)
Fax (604) 684-4555
Stay at the Four Seasons if you want to be pampered. Some of the niceties are bathrobes, hair dryers, free shoeshine (just leave your shoes outside the door overnight), 24-hour valet service, a year-round indoor-outdoor pool and a rooftop garden. The hotel is connected to Pacific Centre shopping mall which makes it a handy location but unfortunately turns the lobby into a thoroughfare. Above the lobby level the Four Seasons regains that tranquil feeling of a luxurious hotel.

Chartwell is one of the best dining rooms in the city (see Restaurants, Lunch). The bright and airy Garden Lounge is worth a stop for a drink or a light lunch even if you're not staying at the hotel. Another five-star AAA rating here. Location handy to everything. Doubles $190.

Pan Pacific Vancouver

999 Canada Place, foot of Burrard
662-8111
(800) 663-1515 toll free (Canada)
(800) 937-1515 toll free (U.S.)
Fax (604) 685-8690
A convention hotel de luxe that is built on the Canada Place cruise ship pier. An eight-storey atrium with totem poles draws you into the spacious lobby where the lounge and cafe have 12-m (40-foot) glass walls and a panorama of the harbour. Japanese influence is present everywhere in the decor: grasscloth wall coverings, subdued earth tones and graceful rattan furniture. All rooms have views (so do the bathrooms in rooms 10 and 20 on each floor) and every convenience for travellers; even more amenities are offered on the exclusive Pacific Floors.

A heated outdoor pool is open all year. There's an extra charge for the health club but you'll see why immediately: state-of-the-art exercise equipment and weights, a low-impact running track, trainers on duty, racquetball and squash courts, a video aerobics room and a Sports Lounge with a wide screen TV make it the best hotel health club in Canada. The Pan Pacific is in the business district and is about a 10-minute walk from shopping on Robson Street. A five-star hotel according to the AAA. Doubles $189.

Hotel Vancouver

900 W. Georgia and Hornby
684-3131
(800) 268-9420 (Quebec and
Ontario)
(800) 268-9411 (other provinces)
(800) 828-7447 (U.S.)
Fax (604) 662-1929

This Vancouver landmark is one of the chateau-style hotels built by the Canadian National and Canadian Pacific railways. These French chateau structures with gargoyles, ornate chimneys, steep copper roofs, and carved Indian chiefs (on the Hornby Street exterior) were built as a romantic enticement to visitors across Canada.

The decor of the rooms is traditional. Complimentary morning coffee and newspapers on each floor is a nice touch. Perhaps because this is a convention hotel, the lobby does not do the hotel justice but it is soon to be renovated to its original thirties style.

An entire floor is designated Entré Gold, with deluxe rooms and premium service that includes a reception desk and concierge on that floor, a continental breakfast and afternoon canapés served in a lovely private lounge, an adjoining board room at the disposal of Entré Gold guests, secretarial services, and fresh flowers, plants and crystal glasses in your room – all included in the Entré Gold rate. This is what the grand old Hotel Vancouver was meant for and it's worth every penny.

The health club provides a skylit lap pool, jacuzzi, exercise room and an intriguing indoor golf system. You hit a special golf ball and optical sensors monitor your swing and the angle of the club. A video, programmed to replicate the Banff Springs golf course, shows where your ball lands along the course.

Staying at a grand old place like this is a special experience and a brush with history. The location is excellent for business or shopping. Doubles $175.

Wedgewood Hotel

845 Hornby near Robson
689-7777
(800) 663-0666 toll free
Fax (604) 688-3074

The Wedgewood is the best medium-priced hotel in Vancouver. The place exudes elegance and charm and the staff really seems to care. This is probably because the manager of the hotel, Eleni Skalbania, is also the owner. It is a small and intimate hotel — only 94 rooms, each with a large balcony — and you won't find any tours or conventions here. Some of the extras are: dark-out drapes, flowers growing on the balcony, afternoon ice delivery, a daily sheet of menu specials, turn down service and twice-daily maid service.

The restaurants and bar are outstanding. The Bacchus Ristorante and Lounge is decorated like some marvelous Tuscan inn (terra cotta, faux marble) and the food is excellent. A great location for shopping and restaurants and a five-minute walk from the business district. Doubles $140.

Hotel Georgia

Hotel Georgia
801 W. Georgia and Howe
682-5566
(800) 663-1111 toll free
Fax (604) 682-8192
Other cities have several of these distinguished stone high-rises built in the thirties that are now good medium-priced hotels. In Vancouver the Georgia is one of a kind. The small lobby has oak panelling and ornate brass elevators. The rooms are larger than in modern hotels and have retained some of their old-fashioned charm, although furnishings are contemporary. Rooms on the south side have a view of the Art Gallery gardens.

There's no health club and the hotel restaurant is nothing to get excited about but there's no shortage of restaurants close by. The hotel has two popular bars: the Night Court Lounge and an English pub, the George V, an after-work stop for the Vancouver Law Society. Doubles $119.

Days Inn
921 W. Pender and Burrard
681-4335
(800) 663-1700 toll free (Canada)
(800) 325-2525 (U.S.)
Fax (604) 681-7808
This small stone-faced hotel has just been renovated. Rooms have standard hotel furnishings but, like other old hotels, they are very large. Rooms 9 and 10 on most floors have views of the harbour. Prices are less than half what you'd pay elsewhere in the business district. The area is quiet after 6 PM but the Days Inn is such a bargain that it's worth the short walk to more lively neighbourhoods. The Bombay Bicycle Club, a lunch spot and after-work bar, is very popular with the office crowd. Doubles $85.

YWCA Hotel
580 Burrard and Dunsmuir
662-8188
(800) 663-1424 toll free (western Canada and northwest U.S.)
Fax (604) 684-9171
"Ys" are often listed in the "if you're desperate" section of guidebooks. Not so with this one. First of all, it is co-ed (though a man must be accompanied by a woman), and families are welcome. Secondly, it is a modern high-rise in the heart of the business area. The 169 rooms are basic but clean. Some rooms need a facelift, others are more attractive and some even have a view of the harbour. Room sizes range from miniscule singles to those large enough for families. Some have private baths but most share with the unit next door or have the bathroom down the hall. Telephones are in some units. Kitchen facilities

(no utensils) are on odd-numbered floors, TV lounges on even-numbered floors and there is a coin-op laundry room. Women staying at the hotel have free use of Y's superb fitness centre: pool, gym, weight room, classes, etc. There is no other central location with modern facilities that is this cheap. A cafeteria is in the basement. Credit cards accepted. Monthly rates available. Doubles $49–53.

Kingston Hotel
757 Richards near Robson
684-9024

Approaching the Kingston, you realize immediately that it's not a typical cheap hotel. Cheap, but not average. Care has been taken to give this small hotel a warm atmosphere – more like a European hotel, complete with continental breakfast. Rooms are very small but immaculate. Prices are reasonable because they've eliminated extras such as room service, televisions, and private baths. (Of the 60 rooms, 7 have private baths.) The Kingston is four storeys and has no elevator. Laundry, sauna, pay parking and TV rental available. A real bargain. Doubles $30–55, weekly and monthly rates available.

ROBSON STREET

Robson St. is the perfect spot to stay – it's close to downtown, Stanley Park and the beaches. The numerous small shops and restaurants make it lively all the time and provide alternatives to hotel food. Also, accommodation on Robson is reasonable. Here are some of the best bets.

O'Doul's Hotel
1300 Robson and Jervis
684-8461
(800) 663-5491 toll free
Fax (604) 684-8326

O'Doul's is a small, modern hotel that has the amenities associated with the big chains: 24-hour room service, indoor pool and exercise room, sophisticated security systems and secretarial services. Each room has three telephones, remote control TV, hairdryer, mini-bar, individual temperature control and windows that open. The decor in the rooms and public areas is very west coast – bright and airy in blues and greens and with lots of plants. Electronic locks are reprogrammed after each visit and the elevator has an additional security system. The Robson Street location makes it great for shopping, eating, getting to Stanley Park. Doubles $140.

Riviera Motor Inn
1431 Robson and Broughton
685-1301
Fax (604) 685-1335

A converted 11-storey 1960s apartment building with 13 large studios and 27 one-bedrooms. All have balconies and well-equipped kitchens. Furnishings are of the rumpus room variety but the Riviera is clean (unlike some nearby). The view of the harbour and the North Shore mountains from the back of the building is terrific. Free parking, small pets allowed. The location is very good for tourists – about a 10-minute walk to the park and the same to shopping and restaurants – but a little out of the way for business travellers. Doubles $98.

Barclay Hotel

1348 Robson near Broughton
688-8850
Fax (604) 688-2534

Two three-storey walk-ups have been joined to form the Barclay Hotel. Renovations have just been completed and the place has that clean, freshly painted look. Rooms vary considerably – see another if you're not happy with the first. Furnishings are quaintly psuedo French provincial. Avoid a room above the noisy bar. Limited free parking. Doubles $89.

WEST END

Westin Bayshore Hotel

1601 W. Georgia and Cardero
682-3377
(800) 228-3000 toll free
Fax (604) 687-3102

One big advantage of the Bayshore is its scenic harbour site next to Stanley Park. It combines the amenities of a resort with all the features of the city.

Rooms are available in a tower and a low-rise built around a large outdoor pool and garden, with a marina and the ocean at your feet. The view of the North Shore mountains is terrific (on the north or west side of the tower). The rooms are not extraordinary but those in the tower are larger, more modern and have views and balconies.

Stay at the Bayshore if you want to take advantage of the resort atmosphere. It's definitely more relaxing than staying downtown. A shuttle bus takes you to the heart of downtown in five minutes. Avoid Trader Vic's, the dining room. Doubles $143–199 depending on view.

Rosellen Suites

2030 Barclay and Chilco
689-4807
Fax (604) 684-3327

The plain exterior of this three-storey apartment hotel makes the black, beige and peach designer furniture seem even more striking. The Rosellen caters to the film industry and executive travellers and their families. Minimum stay is three nights and prices go down the longer you stay. Amenities in the large one- and two-bedroom units include microwaves, remote control TVs, tape decks, twice-weekly maid service, free washers and dryers and fully equipped kitchens with juice, tea and coffee to get you started. Each unit has a private telephone line with free local calls. Some have fireplaces and dishwashers. Free health club facilities are in the neighbourhood.

In a quiet residential spot right beside Stanley Park, a 20-minute walk from dowtown and lots of restaurants nearby. In short, a home-away-from-home kind of place. Doubles $125.

English Bay Inn

1968 Comox and Chilco
683-8063

The English Bay Inn will be open by the time you read this. The five-room bed and breakfast is in a 1939 house that has been smartly renovated in a British private club style. It occupies a quiet corner of the West End, a block from the beach and Stanley Park. All rooms have private baths. Rates will be about $110 for doubles.

Sunset Inn

1111 Burnaby (near Davie and
Thurlow)
684-8763
Fax (604) 669-3340

The Sunset Inn is the best of several
West End apartment buildings that
have been converted into hotels. The
units, studios and one-bedrooms,
have kitchens and balconies. The
one bedrooms have sofabeds and
sleep four. Furnishings are standard
but the hotel is fairly well maintained. Laundry facilities and under-

One of the many popcorn vendors who
are a familiar sight at English Bay.

ground parking. Located in a residential area close to shops and
buses, a 10-minute walk to downtown. Particularly recommended for
families and/or long stays. Doubles
$98.

West End Guest House

1362 Haro near Jervis
681-2889

While only one block from the action
and glitz of Robson St., this small
guest house suggests another time
and place. It is a carefully restored
Victorian house with period furniture
and dozens of wonderful framed old
photographs of Vancouver. The main
floor has a parlour, piano, breakfast
room and a guest pantry where you
can help yourself to snacks. The
seven guest rooms are small but
bright and very charming with brass
beds with feather mattress pads,
exotic linen and fresh flowers. Each
room has a private bathroom, telephone and remote control TV.
Guests are served afternoon tea and
evening sherry. Breakfast is included and can be served in bed.
The hosts, George and Charles, are
determined to do everything
possible to make your stay memo-
rable – and they are succeeding won-
derfully. I can't imagine staying
anywhere else in this price range.
No smoking in the building. Doubles
$80–100.

Buchan Hotel

1906 Haro (near Robson and
Denman)
685-5354

A small inexpensive hotel, the
Buchan is located in one of the
quietist residential sections of the
West End. Rooms are spotless,
though small; those on the east side

are brighter and overlook a minipark. The staff is friendly, but at these prices there are none of the usual hotel services. Parking is on the street, which in the West End can be frustrating. A laundry room is available.

Stanley Park is at your doorstep, and so are the shops and restaurants on Robson or Denman. English Bay beach is five minutes away and downtown is a 15-minute walk. In the basement a popular restaurant, Delilah's, serves dinner. Doubles $65, weekly rates available.

Sylvia Hotel
1154 Gilford and Beach
681-9321

The eight-storey Sylvia Hotel has long been a Vancouver landmark. This ivy-covered brick structure, built in 1912, was declared a heritage building in 1975. A new low-rise wing was added to the hotel in 1986, but they blend so well you can't really tell. There are 116 rooms, all with bathrooms, 25 with kitchens. Rooms on the south side overlook English Bay and the beach across the street. The rooms are plain and some could use a little sprucing up but it's hard to complain considering the price. It's a 20-minute walk through the lovely residential West End to downtown. The location and view are as perfect as you get in this city. At these prices it is necessary to book well in advance during the summer. Doubles $50–70.

GRANVILLE ISLAND AND KITSILANO

Granville Island Hotel
1253 Johnston
683-7373
(800) 663-1840 toll free
Fax (604) 683-3061

This stylish waterfront hotel has been designed with hi-tech details inside and out. The hotel is small, 54 rooms, and so are the basic rooms, but many have balconies and a view of False Creek. There are some nice touches: wooden venetians, bidets, tape decks and skylights. A hotel marina will arrange the charter of almost any kind of boat. The advantage of this hotel is the relaxed

The Sylvia Hotel on English Bay is a landmark heritage building.

resort atmosphere that is only 10 minutes by car from downtown. A problem may arise if you are staying Thursday through Saturday when the popular bar, Pelican Bay, turns into a disco. If you're not in the quiet wing, you may need the earplugs that the hotel supplies. Because of the dense weekend traffic at the nearby market, don't count on making hasty exits. Doubles $130.

Kenya Court Guest House
2230 Cornwall near Yew
738-7085
Only a 10-minute drive from the heart of the city, this small apartment building facing Kitsilano Beach is a great alternative to staying downtown. This lovely 1920s guest house has three units: large one- and two-bedroom apartments (that sleep up to six) with tasteful period furnishings and gleaming hardwood floors. ("Immaculate" is taken to new heights at Kenya Court.) The units on the second and third floor have the most character and best views. All units have kitchens for preparing snacks but cooking meals is discouraged. A complimentary breakfast is served in a cheery rooftop solarium that has a breath-taking view of English Bay and the North Shore mountains. No smoking in the building. Run by a friendly couple who speak Italian, French and German. On street parking. Book well in advance for the summer. No credit cards. Doubles $85.

NEAR THE AIRPORT

Delta River Inn
3500 Cessna, Richmond
278-1241
(800) 268-1133 toll free
Fax (604) 276-1975
This 418-room hotel in a quiet location on the Fraser River is geared to business travellers. All rooms have views – the south side is best – and some have balconies. Unfortunately even the renovated rooms have a bit of a dowdy feel to them. The hotel marina has boat charters. Outdoor pool, jogging route along the river plus full use of the exceptional facilities at the nearby Delta Airport Inn. Shuttle available to and from the airport, Airport Inn and Lansdowne Shopping Centre. Most convenient hotel to the airport. Doubles $145.

Delta Airport Inn
10251 St. Edwards, Richmond
278-9611
(800) 268-1133 toll free
Fax (604) 276-1122
Two towers and a low-rise on 5 ha (12 acres) make up this 464-room convention hotel resort. The rooms in the low-rise open onto a grassy area and outdoor pool, perfect for families. The large and comfortable rooms are a bit plain but it is the facilities that are the drawing card: indoor tennis courts with instructors (and partners if you wish), squash courts, two outdoor pools and one indoor, volleyball court, golf practice range, equipment rentals, outdoor exercise circuit, aquacise classes, poolside barbecues, and a complete business centre. There is a playground and children receive special attention at the Creative Centre

where they can play for two hours without you. Transportation to the airport and the local mall. Doubles $145.

KINGSWAY

2400 Motel
2400 Kingsway and Nanaimo
434-2464
The 2400 is a marvellous looking motel, with a dozen little white bungalows and a two-storey building of connected units. The bungalows are the best, just like smaller versions of home, with kitchens and front and

Lonsdale Quay Market

back doors. Landscaped grounds, pets allowed. A playground, park and good Chinese restaurants nearby. If you have a choice, get a unit at the rear of the complex. Three-star AAA rating. Doubles $40–60.

NORTH SHORE

While the North Shore, particularly West Vancouver, is a delightful place, it is difficult to recommend staying there because of the horrendous rush-hour traffic around Lions Gate Bridge. If you do stay there, plan your day to avoid the bridge at rush hours.

Lonsdale Quay Hotel
123 Carrie Cates Court,
North Van
986-6111
Fax (604) 986-8782
Situated immediately beside the SeaBus (a 13-minute ferry trip to downtown Vancouver, see Getting Around), this is the North Shore's most convenient hotel. Most of the rooms take advantage of the waterfront location and the fabulous view, with either a full balcony or French doors. The rooms are modern and pleasantly decorated in cool pastel tones; facilities include a restaurant, lounge (with a dance floor), pub and fitness centre. Parking available. An added bonus is that the hotel is perched directly on top of the Lonsdale Quay Market, where you can spend hours browsing through the fresh food stalls and the various boutiques and eateries. Doubles $110–155.

The hotel and public market at Lonsdale Quay are connected to downtown by a short SeaBus ride.

Park Royal Hotel

540 Clyde off Taylor, West Van
926-5511
Fax (604) 926-6082
Call to check, but don't count on the Park Royal unless you have made a reservation months in advance.

The ivy-covered building is tudor in style, and the atmosphere is British country inn, with beams, stone fireplaces and a pub. The hotel is tucked away on the banks of the Capilano River. From the patio and gardens you can sit and enjoy the view of the river (great for salmon and steelhead flyfishing) and the surrounding woods, or you can go for a stroll along the riverbank. It's hard to believe that Park Royal Shopping Centre is just minutes away.

The hotel is difficult to find; go over the Lions Gate Bridge, head into West Vancouver and take the first right onto Taylor Way, then turn right immediately at Clyde Ave. Doubles $93–138.

ALTERNATIVE ACCOMMODATION

La Grande Résidence

845 Burrard and Smithe
682-5511
(800) 543-4300 toll free
Fax (604) 682-5513
La Grand Résidence is a luxury apartment building connected to and run by the Meridien Hotel. It has maid service, 24-hour switchboard, front desk, concierge, plus all of the other services of the five-star Meridien. A home-away-from-home where staff will change a flat tire, sew on a button, organize a party or buy your groceries. This new 18-storey building has 162 completely equipped one- and two-bedroom apartments. An outstanding feature is the exceptional quality and good taste shown in the furnishings. Kitchens have dishwashers and Royal Doulton china. Some units have VCRs and microwaves and each has a balcony. Spa facilities are shared with the Meridien Hotel, where the indoor pool opens onto a sunny deck. Minimum stay is 30 days; rates start at $2600.

Walter Gage Residence

Sub Boulevard at Wesbrook Mall
University of British Columbia
228-2963
The residence consists of three towers, each with 1200 rooms. Six single bedrooms are clustered around a kitchen (with limited cooking facilities), bathroom and living room to form self-contained units.

Single accommodation is provided in these rooms for $28. Self-contained studios and one-bedroom suites are available for single or double accommodation at $45–60 for the room. Some larger suites at $60 are usually reserved for families.

Free visitor parking is next to the residence, and meals are available at the Student Union Building across the street (and the food is not bad). UBC is a 20-minute drive from downtown. During fall and winter a very limited number of rooms (suites only) are available, for which reservations are necessary.

Vancouver Hostel

1515 Discovery near 4th
224-3208
Fax (604) 224-4852
Despite its origin as an air force barracks, the newly renovated hostel

building is far from bleak. Located beside Jericho Park, it is adjacent to tennis courts, a sailing club and one of the finest beaches in the city. While the setting is perfect, the location is not, about a 30-minute bus ride to downtown.

Food at the hostel is good and cheap. Breakfast and dinner are served, or you can cook meals. Separate sleeping accommodation for men and women is dormitory style, but rooms are available for families. Bring a sleeping bag or rent sheets and blankets. No accommodation is available for children under five or for pets. Mountain bikes are for rent at the cheapest rates in town. The hostel also has a coin-op laundry, storage facilities.

Although the capacity is 285, you may need a reservation (including one night's deposit) from June to Sept. An adult Canadian Hostelling Association membership is $21 a year. Members stay for $10 a day, and nonmembers for $15. Mastercard or Visa accepted.

BED AND BREAKFAST

Bed and breakfast agencies represent homes throughout the city (and sometimes the province) that provide a basic room or a luxury suite. Most accept children, some have facilities for the handicapped and some take pets. Meals in addition to breakfast can sometimes be arranged. Discounts may be available for long stays. Major credit cards are generally accepted.

A Home Away From Home
873-4888

Best Canadian Bed and Breakfast
738-7207

Old English
986-5069

Town and Country
731-5942

WestWay
273-8293

TRAILER PARKS/ CAMPGROUNDS

Prices listed here are for a trailer and two people in high season, with a full hook-up if available.

IN AND NEAR VANCOUVER

Capilano Mobile Park
295 Tomahawk, West Van
987-4722
Underneath the north foot of the Lions Gate Bridge, beside the Capilano River. Trailers, tents and RVs on 208 sites. Newly renovated facilities include showers, jacuzzi, games room, pool, laundry room and supervised playground. Sani-station, propane. Surprisingly quiet considering the location. Adjacent to shopping centre, beach and park. Five minutes from downtown. $25.

Cariboo Motel and Trailer Park
2555 Kingsway near Nanaimo
435-2251
Trailers and RVs only, 34 sites. Showers. $21.

Mount Seymour Provincial Park

North Vancouver

929-1291

Parking lots 2 and 3 can be used for trailers and RVs, no hook-ups. Some tenting accommodated. Washrooms, cafeteria, water, wood. Full facilities available July through Sept only. $10.

Burnaby Cariboo RV Park

8765 Cariboo Place

Cariboo exit from Hwy. 1

Burnaby

420-1722

This highly rated RV park offers a heated indoor pool, jacuzzi, store, sani-station, laundry, free showers, cablevision, RV wash and shuttle bus. RVs, trailers and tents; 217 sites. Adjacent to Burnaby Lake Regional Park. $25.

Richmond RV Park

Hollybridge and River Rd.

Richmond

270-7878

Open Apr 15 to Oct 15. Free showers, laundry, sani-station, propane, games room, playground and mobile septic service. Tents, trailers, RVs; 200 sites. Central location. $20.

NEAR TSAWWASSEN

ParkCanada Recreational Vehicle Inn

4799 Hwy. 17,

exit north on 52nd St., Delta

943-5811

Near the ferry terminal. RVs, tents and trailers; 150 sites. Laundry, free showers, sani-station, heated outdoor pool, store. Near golf course and water park. $18.

WHITE ROCK

Sea Crest Motel and RV Park

880 – 160th St.

531-4720

RVs only, 36 sites. Showers, laundry, close to beach and golf course. $15.

Hazelmere RV Park and Campground

18843 – 8th Ave. at 188th St.

538-1167

In forest setting on the Campbell River. Tents, RVs and trailers; 154 sites. Showers, laundry, propane, sani-station, store. $16.

SURREY

Dogwood Campgrounds

15151 – 112th Ave.

583-5585

Take the 160th Ave. exit from the Trans-Canada Hwy. RVs, tents and trailers; 350 sites. Showers, laundry, store, propane, outdoor pool, jacuzzi, playground, salmon bakes and bus tours. Natural treed setting. $20.

Tynehead RV Camp

16275 – 102nd Ave.

589-1161

Tents, trailers and RVs; 117 sites. Heated outdoor pool, showers, laundry, store, games room, mini-golf. Adjacent to forest and near shopping centre. $21.

Fraser River RV Park

11940 Old Yale Rd.

580-1841

Beside the Fraser River. Tents, trailers and RVs; 135 sites. Showers, laundry, sani-station, dock, boat ramp and pub. $18.

RESTAURANTS

BREAKFAST/BRUNCH **42**

LUNCH **44**

SEAFOOD **45**

PIZZA **46**

VEGETARIAN **47**

LATE NIGHT **47**

OUTDOORS **47**

WITH A VIEW **48**

ESPRESSO BARS **49**

BY NATIONALITY **50**

Chinese, Contemporary, Continental, East Indian, Ethiopian, French, Greek, Italian, Japanese, Jewish, Korean, Mexican, Portuguese, Spanish, Thai, Vietnamese/Cambodian, West Coast

BY LOCATION **65**

Broadway (between Main and Granville), Chinatown, Downtown, East Side, Granville Island, Kitsilano, North Shore, South of 33rd Avenue, West End

Cooks quit, restaurants close, menus change, and so do hours: restaurant guides are written on sand. But two things can be said with certainty about Vancouver's restaurants.

A new ethnic group has arrived, and it's us: West Coast. A hundred years after the city's founding, we have finally turned our attention to what we can do with local ingredients. Some of the most interesting food in Vancouver is being served up in self-consciously West Coast restaurants. It's long overdue.

The old ethnic groups have multiplied. Chinese and Japanese restaurants were, and still are, some of the city's best culinary bets. Now they've been joined by Vietnamese, Cambodian, Thai and Korean restaurants, growing as quickly as Pacific Rim immigration and business ties. Meanwhile, Greek, Italian, East Indian and even Ethiopian restaurants are going strong.

If you're on a budget, you'll find the best value in Chinese, Japanese, Vietnamese and Thai restaurants.

The restaurants listed here are all recommended, some more highly than others. Each one has been chosen because, whatever its price range it reliably gives good value.

A standard tip is 10 to 15 per cent. Provincial sales tax of 10 per cent is levied on alcohol served in restaurants. A new federal Goods and Services Tax of 7% is applied to restaurant meals.

Restaurants marked with one $ are inexpensive; a generous dinner for one, excluding alcohol and tip, costs $15 or less. In a moderate ($$) restaurant, expect to pay between $15 and $30; in an expensive ($$$) restaurant, over $30.

BREAKFAST/BRUNCH

Cafe Fleuri $$$
Le Meridien Hotel
845 Burrard and Robson
682-5511
If you're downtown, need a gentle entry to the day, and don't mind spending money to get it, then eat breakfast at Cafe Fleuri. Classical music, muted browns, soft surfaces absorbing discordant sounds, coffee and orange juice poured just before the menu is presented — it's a cocoon of discreet service.

You can order the usual run of pancakes and eggs, wake up over crepes, or venture into a Japanese breakfast: miso soup, raw egg, rice and broiled salmon. Open every day for breakfast, lunch and dinner. Chocolate dessert buffet on Fri and Sat, 6-11 PM.

Caffe Barney $$
2975 Granville near 13th
731-6446
The best place to eat in South Granville on a Sunday morning. A narrow, cheerful restaurant, vinyl tablecloths in primary colors, and usually a line out the door for reasonably priced eggs and an imaginative specials menu. Eggs Barney is eggs Benedict, with smoked salmon and mushrooms standing in for the ham. The back deck is shaded by a giant-sized canvas and wood umbrella. Breads, muffins and desserts baked on site. Open daily, breakfast, lunch and early dinner. Closes 8 PM Mon to Sat, 5 PM Sun.

Capers $$

2496 Marine Drive and 25th
West Vancouver
925-3316
Hidden in the back of a lavishly
handsome health food store, Capers
serves traditional breakfasts made
from free-run eggs and nitrate-free
bacon, along with excellent blueberry pancakes, yogurt, meusli and
fruit. Somehow 70s in feeling – you
might say laid back – with wood
tables, houseplants and a partial view
of the water. Service can be slow and
forgetful. Open at 7:30 weekdays, 8
on weekends, breakfast, lunch and
dinner daily, except no dinner Sun.

Danann Mondial Cafe $

1809 W. 1st and Cypress
732-4656
Want to feel modern and urban over
brunch? Danann is a big, high-
ceilinged room with rough concrete
walls, all the pipes out in full view
and a rotating show of work by local
artists, on one of the most intensely
developed single-block stretches in
the city. Brunch is weekends only.
Skillet eggs are the best buy; coffee
is very good here. Lunch is antipasto
plates, homemade soups, a daily
quiche and salad. Decadent baked
goods and desserts. Open lunch and
dinner, Mon to Fri; breakfast, lunch,
dinner, Sat and Sun.

Fresgo Inn $

1138 Davie and Thurlow
689-1332
If it has to be bacon and eggs, no
matter what time of day you first find
yourself out on the surface of the
planet, keep the Fresgo in mind:
classic, standard breakfasts, big
servings at reasonable prices, orange
vinyl, cafeteria service, a sometimes
seedy clientele as a result of its
spleen-of-the-West-End location.
Open Mon to Sat, 8 AM-3 AM;
Sundays and holidays, 9 AM-
midnight.

Isadora's $$

1540 Old Bridge
Granville Island
681-8816
Isadora's is the best place in
Vancouver to take children for
breakfast. Windows on one side
overlook the Granville Island
waterpark. There's an indoor play
corner, children's servings and
change tables in both washrooms.
Isadora's has good cappuccino, well-
done versions of brunch classics,
and a sunny, glad-to-greet-the-day
atmosphere. The rest of the day's
menu is modern eclectic: samosas,
stuffed croissants, salads and
burgers – including a nutburger.
    Open at 7 weekdays and 9 on
weekends. Very popular for weekend brunches; go early if you don't
want to wait in line. Reservations for
six or more. Breakfast, lunch and
dinner daily, no dinner Mon, Sept to
May.

The Scanwich $

551 Howe near Dunsmuir
687-2415
The Scanwich is a haven for anyone
who wants to eat a good breakfast
downtown without paying hotel
dining room prices. To the usual
selection of eggs, ham, bacon and
sausages (from $2.75 to $4.25), the
Scanwich adds a choice of nine
omelettes, French toast, variations
on eggs Benedict, and cold cereals,
including Alpen. Good coffee arrives
almost at once; service is speedy.

But don't sleep in – breakfast service ends at 10:30. For lunch, the Scanwich serves open-faced sandwiches, 30 varieties of Scandinavian *smørrebrød* including gravlax, steak tartare, shrimp and dill, house pâté and roast pork with red cabbage and prunes.

Sit at a table in the mezzanine and you'll have a good view of this thoroughly European looking room with its high ceilings, dark wood chairs, white tablecloths and wall of antique posters. Airmailed copies of *Politiken* and *Svenska Dagbladet* are there for those who can read them. Open Mon to Fri, 7-4.

The Tomahawk $
1550 Philip near Marine Drive
North Vancouver
988-2612
The Tomahawk serves gigantic breakfasts at good prices. It started out as a hamburger stand 65 years ago, when North Vancouver was mostly trees, and is still run by the son of the original owner. The decor is kitsch museum, with portraits of royalty, Indian baskets and carvings, settler's tools and placemats with a 50s-style tourist map of the province. Yukon breakfast is five slices of back bacon, two eggs, hash browns, and toast; muffins are gigantic. No reservations, no alcohol. Breakfast, lunch, dinner every day.

Also
Bacchus, see Lunch
Teahouse, see Outdoors
Bread Garden, see Espresso Bars
See Chinese, Dim Sum

LUNCH

Bacchus $$$
Wedgewood Hotel
845 Hornby and Robson
689-7777
Bacchus, the lounge and informal restaurant in the Wedgewood Hotel, is for days when lunch is the main event. You need time to loll about in one of those deep armchairs – near the gas fireplace if it's a rainy day – and soak up the relaxed charm. There's an excellent antipasto plate, a seafood chowder with tomato, dill and sour cream, plenty of pasta choices, grilled fish, and a very pleasant chicken and Brie frittata.

Bacchus serves breakfast until 11:30: hazelnut waffles and French-toasted brioche, along with the more standard offerings. Breakfast, lunch and dinner daily.

Chartwell $$$
The Four Seasons Hotel
791 West Georgia and Howe
689-9333
Serious power lunchers choose Chartwell, named after Winston Churchill's country estate, and decorated on the model of an upper-class British men's club: floor-to-ceiling dark wood panelling, deep leather armchairs, barons of beef under brass domes. Chef Wolfgang Von Weiser, formerly of the Toronto Four Seasons, makes a salad of smoked loin of wild boar sprinkled with hazelnuts; seafood pot au feu is served with fennel bread and aioli. Very good desserts and pastries; port and Stilton available, of course. Lunch Mon to Fri, dinner daily.

Gallery Cafe $
Vancouver Art Gallery
Robson and Howe
688-2233
A sharp, clean, modern restaurant in the sharp, clean, modern Arthur Erickson re-design of the Vancouver Art Gallery, the Gallery Cafe is an upscale cafeteria. Now run by the people who own the Bread Garden, it shares the same high standards of display – the food here always looks superb. The fare is light meals, lots of salads, a limited selection of wine and beer, and killer desserts. Sit on the terrace overlooking Robson on sunny days. Open daily 9-5, Thurs 9-9.

Japanese Deli House $
381 Powell and Jackson
681-6484
The best place for an early lunch if you're browsing the remains of Vancouver's pre-war Japantown is also one of the city's least expensive sushi outlets. Sushi is made in advance for the 11:30 AM opening; eat close to noon and you'll have it at its freshest. The appetizer menu is worth exploring, especially the ginger squid appetizer, served hot.

Truck stop meets Japanese restaurant decor, made restful by the graceful, high-ceilinged room, the main floor of a turn-of-the-century commercial building. No credit cards. Lunch and dinner daily except Mon. Closes at 8 weeknights, 6 Sat and Sun.

Also
Scanwich, see Breakfast/Brunch
Danann, see Breakfast/Brunch
Isadora's, see Breakfast/Brunch

Marineview Cafe, see Seafood
Olympia Oyster and Fish Co., see Seafood
Settebello, see Outdoors
Teahouse, see Outdoors
Pink Pearl, see Chinese
Kirin, see Chinese
Le Crocodile, see French
Il Barino, see Italian
Piccolo Mondo, see Italian
Chiyoda, see Japanese
Ossu, see Japanese
Kaplan's, see Jewish
Cafe Mercaz, see Jewish
Topanga, see Mexican
Raintree, see West Coast
See Chinese, Dim Sum, Noodles

SEAFOOD

Chesa Seafood House $$
2168 Marine Drive and 22nd
West Vancouver
922-3312
Vancouver has always been low on good seafood restaurants – at least ones that call themselves seafood restaurants. Much of the time, seafood desires can be best satisfied by going to a Cantonese restaurant and ordering crab.

Chesa is a bit of a hike into West Vancouver, but it's worth it, a comfortable seafood restaurant with exceptionally good value for money, an adventuresome menu and superb daily specials. Fish and chips, yes, but much more: filet of smoked trout on braised leek with a saffron butter sauce, or spinach fettuccine with crab, black beans and tomatoes. Prices are at the low end of moderate. Open for dinner daily.

Steamers and Stews $$

900 Pacific and Hornby
682-6661

Downstairs from Kettle of Fish, its bigger, more expensive, and not so good sibling, Steamers and Stews is an engaging spot to eat raw oysters, fish and chips, steamed clams and chowders. Decor details are vaguely reminiscent of the glory days of steamship travel. Lunch Mon to Fri, dinner daily.

Marineview Coffeeshop $

611 Alexander and Princess
253-0616

The Marineview used to be a fishermen and dock workers' cafe, perched above the Campbell Avenue docks, with a great view of fishboats and mountains and legendary crab sandwiches. The building was demolished and the Marineview moved. The new location – in the old American Can Building, renovated and filled with architects' offices — doesn't have a view. Even though the counter is from the old restaurant, the fishermen and dockworkers are gone. The crab sandwich (and the shrimp, for that matter) is still one of the great examples of its kind. Don't order anything else on the menu, and get there before noon if you don't want to wait. Open Mon to Fri until 4 PM.

Olympia Oyster and Fish Co. Ltd. $

1094 Robson and Thurlow
685-0716

Fish and chips, to eat in, on a stool at the counter, or take out and eat while window-shopping Robson. The fish and chips counter is at the back of the store. Check out the fish on crushed ice as you go in: what's featured in the fish store is usually the special fish of the day. Halibut, cod, prawns, calamari, served with genuine, unfrozen, french fries. No reservations, no cards. Open lunch, dinner daily, to 7 PM.

Also
The Cannery, see With a View
The Accord, see Late Night
Kirin Seafood House, see Chinese
Shijo, see Japanese
Tojo's, see Japanese

PIZZA

Flying Wedge $

1937 Cornwall and Cypress
732-8840
1175 Robson and Bute
681-1233

Pizza-by-the-slice is a relative newcomer to Vancouver. Flying Wedge has two well-placed locations: one on Robson, one close to Kits Beach. A whole-wheat herb crust and trendy toppings — Broken Hearts is artichoke hearts, onions, tomatoes, mushrooms; Deep Purple is marinated eggplant, onions, mushrooms, asiago cheese. Hot Licks – pepperoni, mushrooms, green peppers, spicy sauce – is hot enough to bring tears to your eyes. $3 for a big slice. Open daily to midnight, 1 AM Fri and Sat.

Passionate Pizza $

1387 W. 7th and Hemlock
733-4411

Pizza takes a leap past ham and pineapple. The Wolfgang Puck has smoked bacon, eggplant, sweet red pepper, mozzarella, asiago and goat cheese and red onions. Provençal is tomato sauce, goat cheese, mozzarella, eggplant, green olives and caramelized onions; a Classic is fresh tomatoes, mozzarella, Parmesan and fresh basil. Passionate? The boxes are kissed with a red-lips stamp, and at their fresh best these are pizzas worth being passionate about. Expect to wait an hour for delivery. Mon to Sat, 5-midnight, Sun, 5-11.

Also
Simpatico, see Greek

VEGETARIAN

The Naam $
2724 W. 4th and Stephens
738-7151
A landmark of counterculture history, the Naam has been serving vegetarian food in the same location since the 1970s. Lately the herbal tea has been joined by cappuccino and beer, and there are some killer chocolate desserts on the menu, but the Naam is still a safe place for people who don't eat animals. Best bets are ethnic specialties, particularly if you get scary flashbacks at the sight of a plate of stewed vegetables. Decor is homey, with wood tables, kitchen chairs, and in the back, an outdoor courtyard that's a fine, leafy place to be on a warm day. No reservations. Open 24 hours.

LATE NIGHT

The Accord $$
4298 Main and 26th
876-6110
Behind the Accord's formidable white venetian blinds, is a haven for anyone with a late-night need for

good Chinese food. Tanks full of live lobster, crab, shrimp and rock cod ensure freshness. Less opulent than the most expensive of the new Cantonese pleasure palaces, more comfortable than the old Chinese-Canadian greasy spoons, the Accord has a minimally decorated, but comfortable dining room.

Try prawns steamed in their shells, to be peeled and dipped in a brown vinegar, soy, and hot-pepper sauce, or beef tenderloin teppan with peppercorn sauce. Dinner daily, open to 2 AM Sun to Thurs, 3 AM Fri and Sat.

Also
Bread Garden, see Espresso Bars
Bridges Bagels, see Espresso Bars
Danann, see Breakfast/Brunch
Fresgo Inn, see Breakfast/Brunch
The Naam, see Vegetarian
Simpatico, see Greek

See also Essential Information, Late Night Services.

OUTDOORS

Dundarave Concession $
Dundarave Pier in West Vancouver
Foot of 25th Street
The smell hits when you round the corner of the little wooden concession building: equal parts hamburger and nostalgia. Vera Hochstader doesn't make the city's biggest burger, but it may be the best: good meat, fresh iceberg lettuce, a fresh bun – heaven in one handful. Walk your burger to the beach and find a log to sit on. No french fries, no alcohol, no credit cards, no side issues. Open May to Oct, 10 AM to dusk.

Settebello $$

1131 Robson near Thurlow, upstairs
681-7377
Settebello is a great place to regroup
after heavy shopping. The large patio
is one of the prettiest in the city, and
if the food isn't superb, it's at least
adequate. The menu is pasta, salads
and brick-oven pizzas, washed down
with wine, and if all goes well,
sunshine. Lunch and dinner daily.

Teahouse at
Ferguson Point $$

Stanley Park
669-3281
Patio tables under the trees on the
front lawn are a civilized addition to
what was already the best place to
eat in Stanley Park. The glassed-in
conservatory wing is pleasant on
colder days, and is stuffed to the gills
on Mother's Day and Easter.

Cream of carrot soup, duck in
cassis, perfectly grilled fish,
brunches with the usual variations
on eggs in Hollandaise, and, for
giddy desserts, baked Alaska. Drive
through the park to Ferguson Point,
breathe country air, see squirrels,
get all the benefits of eating at a
country inn without having to brave
a freeway. Reservations required at
brunch and weekend dinners.
Dinner every day, lunch Mon to Fri,
brunch Sat and Sun.

Also
Caffe Barney, see Breakfast/Brunch
Isadora's, see Breakfast/Brunch
Gallery Cafe, see Lunch
The Naam, see Vegetarian

WITH A VIEW

The Cannery $$$

2205 Commissioner near foot of
Victoria
254-9606
This refitted cannery with its
industrial view of the Burrard Inlet
waterfront may be the perfect
marriage of great seafood and an
absorbing view. Tugs hustle by
against a backdrop of the North
Shore mountains, the grain elevators, the view of Lion's Gate bridge
off in the west. The menu has clam
chowder and Caesar salad for people
who want to concentrate on the view,
and live lobster, a good choice of
east coast oysters, a shopping list of
fish to grill, and a strong wine list for
those who want to eat well.

Choose the upstairs for cosy,
cluttered romance, the downstairs if
you like a more spacious seaside dal-
liance. To find the restaurant, travel
east on Hastings to Victoria Drive,
turn left on Victoria then right on
Commissioner. Dinner every day,
lunch Mon to Fri.

Seasons $$

Queen Elizabeth Park
33rd and Cambie
874-8008
A big, comfortable restaurant with
light wood and deep carpeting,
Seasons has an unmatchable view of
city and mountains from the highest
point inside city limits. Grilled
salmon with fresh mint, roast duck
with Bing cherry sauce, and a few
favourites drawn from the menu of
the Teahouse at Ferguson Point (see
Outdoors), which is also managed
by Brent Davies. Outdoor seating on
the patio. Dinner daily, lunch Mon to
Fri, brunch Sat and Sun.

English Bay Cafe $$
1795 Beach and Denman
669-2225
The noisy downstairs bar serves the usual variety of international grazing food, from Oriental noodles to Cajun chicken strips. Upstairs it's a more restrained restaurant, given to racks of lamb and venison. Both levels share the same classic view: across two lanes of traffic on Beach to English Bay, the Pacific and the setting sun. Downstairs there's a large choice of imported beers, upstairs you can get a jalapeno-pepper martini. Walk, take public transit, or use the valet parking service. Dinner every day, lunch Mon to Sat, brunch Sun.

Also
Tojo's, see Japanese

ESPRESSO BARS

The Bread Garden $
1880 W. 1st and Cypress
738-6684
812 Bute at Robson
688-3213
Trashing the Bread Garden is a favourite sport in Kitsilano. It's too slow; people have gone into trance states while waiting in line to order a muffin and never made it back out, that sort of thing.
  It's all true: even the separate Bread Garden To Go can be infuriating if you're in a hurry, or even running at normal speed. But the Bread Garden's food not only is good, it looks good. This is the most riotously plentiful looking deli in the city: salads, smoked salmon pizzas, quiches, elaborate cakes and pies, giant muffins and a great sunflower seed loaf.

Once you have your food, the view is endlessly absorbing. Beamers and Miatas double-parked outside, power breakfasters, the girls at coffee, after-the-movie crowds (the line can stretch out the door at midnight). Take a number when you get into line or you may never get out again. Open 24 hours.

Bridges Bakery & Bagels $
1595 W. 6th and Pine
736-3651
A bagel bakery that's taken the Bread Garden path and branched out into sit-down deli food and late hours. Lox and bagels, Thai salad, cajun chicken breasts – it's a modern Jewish deli with international influences and good coffee. Outdoor tables in good weather. Service by numbers, dispenser on the counter. Open daily, 7 AM-2 AM.

Starbucks $
1100 Robson and Thurlow
688-5125
811 Hornby near Robson
685-3695
1116 Denman near Pendrell
685-9332
102-700 W. Pender and Granville
685-7373
Seattle-based Starbucks seems to be bent on putting espresso within walking distance of anyone, anywhere in downtown Vancouver. The mood is designer Italian: pop in for a quick jolt of coffee and drink it standing up, leaning against the bar – there are never enough seats to go around. The menu is sandwiches and pastries, including biscotti to soften in your latte, and you can buy Starbucks' excellent coffees by the pound.

Open daily from early to late at 1100 Robson and 1116 Denman. Open Mon to Fri, 5:30 AM-5:30 PM at 700 W. Pender. Open Mon to Fri, 6:30-6, and Sat, 9-5:30 at 811 Hornby.

The sleek Starbucks espresso bar on Robson Street has the best cup of coffee downtown.

BY NATIONALITY

CHINESE

Keeping up with Chinese restaurants in Vancouver could occupy all your waking hours if you let it. New ones open every week, each one more opulent than the last. People who felt relatively sure of themselves while ordering crab with ginger and green onion in some homely family restaurant on East Hastings now have to consider whether or not a soup with birdsnest and sharks fin is actually worth $32 per person, and what effect a tastefully appointed dining room and waiters in uniforms whisking away plates as soon as they collect a single crab shell has on the enjoyment of dinner.

Furthermore, the old signs that marked a good Chinese restaurant are no longer reliable. It used to be that a truck stop decor, the absence of the phrase "Chinese and Canadian cuisine" and a location outside of Chinatown were solid indicators. Anything that looked like money was spent on the interior was a hint that sweet and sour spareribs in neon hues awaited inside.

The new signs? They're so new that I don't know them yet. You can find wonderful food in some of the new, glossy Hong Kong-style palaces, often at prices that aren't all that much higher than the ones charged in more modest surroundings.

One style to look for: the self-effacing Chinese restaurant that turns a blank face of vertical venetian blinds to the street. If you poke your head in and the place has live fish tanks and is reverberating with the Cantonese wall of sound, it's worth trying.

Pink Pearl $$
1132 East Hastings and Glen
253-4316
The Pink Pearl is an old Vancouver-style Cantonese restaurant. It's in a run-down section of town, in a spruced up but unpretentious building that doesn't look nearly as big as it is – 650 seats. But the edges are still a little rough, the waiters haven't got time to discuss the menu and probably would rather not anyway, and prices are low. Bring the kids. Pink Pearl has a comfortable, family feel, and no one can possibly be bothered by a crying baby in the midst of the bustle. Live seafood tanks near the door hold crab, shrimp, geoduck, oysters, abalone, rock cod, lobsters and scallops – all offered in a dozen or so ways.

Try clams in black bean sauce as a first course, and crab sautéed with five spices as a main course. The crispy-skinned chicken will please everyone from the most adventurous palate to the most discerning critic of Chinese food. Arrive early for dim sum if you don't want to wait in line. Lunch and dinner daily.

Kirin Mandarin Restaurant $$
1166 Alberni and Bute
682-8833
The Kirin was one of the first restaurants to serve Chinese food in style. It was all a bit disconcerting at first: white linen tablecloths and a trendy postmodern decor, waiters who were fluent in English and trained to do more than slap dishes on the table with the aplomb of the old-style Chinese waiter. Stay out of the sharks fin and abalone sections of the menu and you can eat very well for a reasonable price.

Peking duck does not have to be ordered in advance here; the menu is a mix of Szechuan, Shanghai and pan-regional party food, with a few Cantonese favourites, such as scallops in black bean sauce – the scallops from the live tank, served still in their shells. Lunch and dinner every day.

Dynasty $$$
New World Harbourside Hotel
1133 W. Hastings and Thurlow
689-9211
There are those who would argue that the Dynasty is the best Chinese restaurant in the Pacific Northwest. It has to be one of the most beautiful – rosewood chairs with curved arms and backs, chopstick rests in the form of silver plated Chinese lions, lazy Susans made from thick slabs of glass, etched glass panels and waiters in uniform who apologize profusely if the kitchen runs out of the dessert you ordered.

And the food? It is delicate, subtle, refined, and expensive, the sort of food you might find in an Asian big-city hotel. Try hot and sour seafood soup if you want to see what the rough customer you've met in Szechuan restaurants can turn into, given the benefit of finishing school – a delicately hot, delicately sour broth, pale, golden, full of long threads of ginger. Dinner daily, lunch daily except Sun.

Szechuan Chongqing $

2495 Victoria and Broadway
254-7434

This unpretentious white-tablecloth
restaurant in a revamped fried-
chicken franchise serves the best
Szechuan food in the city. Two
dishes to try: fried green beans
Szechuan style, steamed and tossed
with spiced ground pork and
Chongqing chicken, boneless
chicken on a bed of fried spinach
that has the crispness of dried
seaweed and a taste that is salty,
rich, and nutty all at once. Food here
is hearty Northern-style, plenty of
garlic and red peppers. Order
steamed buns – plain or deep-fried
so the outside sixteenth of an inch is
golden brown and sweet – instead of
rice, and use them to mop up the
sauces. Lunch, dinner daily.

One of the Expo 86 gates now sits
outside the Chinese Cultural Centre in
Chinatown.

Won More Szechuan Cuisine $

1944 W. 4th at Maple
737-2889
1184 Denman near Davie
688-8856

The one on Denman is the old Won
More, the Fourth Avenue Won More
is newer, fancier, and just a tiny bit
more expensive. Both follow the
same pattern. The cooks work up
front in a glassed-in kitchen, so you
can watch them while you wait for a
table; the functional dining room is
in the back.

Good, gutsy, food, heavy on meat
and even heavier on garlic – there's a
vampire-free zone for several

Serving steaming dim sum in Chinatown.

hundred yards around the Won More. You can get *mu shu* shrimp, beef and chicken here, but the classic shredded pork stirfry, wrapped in thin mandarin pancakes and flavoured with hoisin sauce is still best. The fried dumplings are good, and so is the green onion pancake – a flat, six-inch round of flaky pastry with flecks of green onion. Don't miss the eggplant with minced pork in hot garlic sauce – the best in Vancouver, and the leftovers make exotic filling for omelettes the next day. Lunch and dinner daily.

DIM SUM

Ming's Restaurant $
147 E. Pender and Main
683-4722
Start a day's exploration of Chinatown here, but arrive before 11 on weekends if you don't want to wait in line. If the line has formed when you get there, give your name to the host at the top of the stairs and wait for your number to be called. Dim sum is served in a cavernous upstairs room. The best seats are near the kitchen, where the trolleys emerge laden with several of the more than 60 varieties of dim sum made daily. Look for *ye zup go* in the summer, a cool, white cube of gelled coconut cake. Lunch and dinner daily.

Kirin Seafood House $$
555 W.12th and Cambie
879-8038
Owned by the people who own Kirin Mandarin Restaurant, Kirin Seafood House is the Cantonese variation on an equally elegant theme. Dim sum waitresses pushing carts, voicing plaintive cries of *har kow...siu mai...cha siu bao...*, can't even be imagined here. For one thing, the

wheels would get bogged down in the carpet.

Instead there's a dim sum menu, small, but exotic and sure to offer something you've never eaten before – shark's fin dumplings, perhaps, or Chinese sausage and spinach dumplings, or fried leek and shrimp pastry. For once, all of the noodle dishes are on the menu, accessible even to people who don't speak Cantonese. Highly recommended: the stewed vermicelli noodles with shredded duck and salted vegetables. North-facing windows have a spectacular view of the mountains. Service is attentive. Expect to pay $10 each – more expensive than regular dim sum, but far from exorbitant. Lunch and dinner daily.

Also
Pink Pearl, see Chinese

NOODLES

Landmark Seafood House $$
3338 Cambie and 17th
873-3338
The first Vancouver outlet for a chain that operates four restaurants in Hong Kong, the Landmark is a glossy new restaurant with a full lunchtime menu of noodles. You can watch the cook work inside a little glassed-in island, and choose from 70 kinds of noodles in soup, congee, fried noodles, steamed rice and fried rice, with a few side dishes thrown in for good measure. Lunch and dinner daily.

Hon's Wun Tun House $
268 Keefer and Main
688-0871
Hon's Wun Tun House on Main Street had been there forever, great

DIM SUM

Dim sum originated in Canton, so most dishes are subtle and lightly cooked, usually steamed. (Northern restaurants serve their own version of dim sum.)

Carts piled with bamboo steamers of hot food are wheeled around the tables. A steamer usually contains a plate with two or three dumplings of some sort. Savoury dishes are on the top of the carts, and sweet ones below; the Chinese intermingle the sweet and the savoury during the meal. After eating your fill, signal a waiter, and he will tally your bill

by counting the number of dishes on the table. Average cost is $8 per person.

Dim sum is a family affair; the more friends, children and grandparents the better. It is served from about 10 AM to 2 PM every day.

The laws of dim sum are:
1. Go to a busy restaurant where the selection is varied and freshly steamed.
2. Don't sit in a corner or you'll be watching most of the carts pass you by.
3. Keep in mind that after 1 PM the selection shrinks.

cauldrons of chicken stock steaming up the windows, cooks at work on noodles in soup, fried noodles, fried rice, steamed and fried dumplings, arborite tables and minimal service. But Hon's has moved now, into a new and plusher building around the corner on Keefer Street. It's the old menu, although prices are a little higher.

You'll want to try shrimp and meat dumpling with noodle (noodles and dumplings in a clear broth), potstickers (meat- or shrimp-filled dumplings fried to a golden crisp on their sweet little bottoms) and *gai lan* a kind of Chinese broccoli, stir-fried and topped with oyster sauce. Lunch and dinner daily.

CONTEMPORARY

Bishop's $$$
2183 W. 4th and Yew
738-2025

For six years now, this modest little restaurant on Fourth Avenue has had a major reputation for what owner John Bishop likes to call contemporary home cooking. That means a mixture of Northern Italian, nouvelle cuisine and East-West crossover with a fine eye for dramatic presentation. The daily specials are always worth ordering, or try penne with grilled eggplant, roasted peppers and basil, or marinated loin of lamb with ginger and sesame.

Everything about the restaurant – all white except for Jack Shadbolt's vibrant expressionist paintings – is simple, stripped down, and in very good taste, the better to focus your attention on the food. Team service is friendly and professional; a "dessert technician" will visit your table after dinner and rhyme off an astonishing list of choices.

Bishop's has one flaw: you can arrive with dinner reservations and still not get seated for an hour. Best insurance: reserve for no later than 7:30. Dinner daily, lunch Mon to Fri.

Delilah's $$
1906 Haro and Gilford
687-3424

The statuesque Delilah, who gave her name to this pleasant spot on the ground floor of the old Buchan Hotel, is gone. But the martinis remain, and so does the fresh, innovative food. Portions are modest, but so are the prices, which means you can eat both corn and crab chowder with bourbon and wild-rice pancakes with chicken in an apricot-rosemary demi-glace.

The decor is 19th century bordello – overstuffed red velvet banquettes, cherubs on the ceiling. Your menu is your bill; check off what you want. Reservations only for groups of six or more. Dinner daily.

Santa Fe Cafe $$
1688 W. 4th and Pine
738-8777

The first restaurant in Vancouver to serve California-Southwestern food is still the best. Pan-fried linguini with jalapeno, black beans and smoked chicken or prawns is a signature dish; so is the Caesar salad made from whole, untorn Romaine leaves. There's also a crab enchilada, a Sante Fe burger, plenty of choice in grilled fish, and desserts by local dessert specialist Leslie Stowe. A small, white room with a changing display of local art, the Santa Fe is close to both Granville Island and Fourth Avenue shopping. Dinner daily, lunch Mon to Fri.

CONTINENTAL

William Tell $$$
Georgian Court Hotel
765 Beatty and Robson
688-3504
The ultimate luxurious, coddling restaurant in Vancouver is now heading into its second quarter century under the amiable hand of owner and maitre d' Erwin Doebeli. At dinner the tables gleam with silver plate liners and the flower vases are silver too.

Chef Lars Trolle Jorgensen, a member of the Canadian gold medalist team at the Culinary Olympics, cares enough about the quality of ingredients to keep a Fraser Valley farmer growing organic vegetables for the restaurant. Try pheasant with glazed grapes and red wine sauce, sautéed veal sweetbreads with red onion marmalade and marsala sauce, and

Martinis are the specialty of the house at Delilah's.

the Swiss specialty *buendnerfleisch*, paper-thin slices of air-dried beef. A glorious place for a self-indulgent lunch or a big-occasion dinner. Jacket required in the evening. Lunch and dinner daily.

EAST INDIAN

Noor Mahal $
4354 Fraser and 27th
873-9263
A *dhosa* is a light, lacy pancake made of bean flour, rice flour and semolina, mixed into a batter and fermented overnight. Cooked and rolled around fillings – onions, green chilies and spices; cauliflower and potatoes; shrimp – it's the most popular street snack in southern India.

Paul and Susan Singh, the entire staff of Noor Mahal, make a dozen or so dhosas, all hearty and substantial, all but two of them priced around $5. Prices are equally modest on the rest of the menu – a good broad range of breads and curries.

East Indian videos, elaborate beaded chandeliers, framed arrangements of tropical butterflies, red vinyl tablecloths – it's truck-stop simple decor with cross-cultural touches. A superb value for the money. Dinner daily, lunch daily except Mon and Tues.

Rubina Tandoori $$
1962 Kingsway and Victoria
874-3621
Rubina Tandoori is an utterly reliable restaurant, the first place I would choose to indulge myself with a feast of East Indian food. Yes, it's worth the drive. The Jamal family owned a restaurant in London before coming to Vancouver, son Shaffeen is the maitre d', and has a phenomenal memory for faces.

Walk in past the display cases of desserts and *chevda*, a nuts-and-bolts salty snack you can buy by the pound. The non-smoking room at the back is funkier; the smoking section, to the left as you walk in, is a more polished affair of upholstered banquettes.

The menu covers the range of sub-continental cuisines, from South Indian seafood to meat dishes from the north. Rubina's menu also suggests a series of duet meals – set menus for two with themes like tandoori, vegetarian, Punjabi. Dinner daily, lunch Mon to Fri.

ETHIOPIAN

Nyala Ethiopian Restaurant $
2930 W. 4th and Macdonald
731-7899
Whether or not you find Ethiopian food to your taste generally comes down to a question of bread. Made from a grain called *tef*, the staple food of Ethiopia, *injera* is a flat, spongy bread served cold. You get it in two ways: as a plate, on which all of the main dishes are served, and on the side, folded up like napkins. Ethiopian food is food to eat with your fingers: tear off a little piece of injera and use it to pick up a bit of whatever you're eating. Lots of choices here for vegetarians. If you want to try the national dish of Ethiopia, order *yedoro watt*, chicken in a spicy red sauce. Dinner daily.

FRENCH

Chez Thierry $$
1674 Robson and Cardero
688-0919
The West End's best neighbourhood restaurant is a 35-seat storefront on Robson serving French country food. Thierry Damilano, windsurfing enthusiast and sabreur – he slices the corks off champagne bottles with a sabre – is the host; Pierre Launoy is the chef. Damilano brushes cheeks with repeat clients (zeez Frenchmen!), and keeps a wine list with at least one choice from every major French growing region. You can always get a simple piece of grilled fish, and if you don't like the way the day's catch is offered, you can get it prepared your way. Chocolate desserts, of the dark, bittersweet variety, are not to be missed. Dinner daily.

Le Crocodile $$$
818 Thurlow and Robson
669-4298
The Vancouver French restaurant
that leads the pack in critical acclaim
is a pleasant bistro that serves
simple food, superbly and at reasonable prices. It can feel claustrophobic
on a busy night – the tables are too
close together for even a pretence of
privacy. Be sure to try the sweet
onion tart appetizer – a reminder of
chef-owner Michel Jacob's Alsatian
origins. Always make reservations:
Le Crocodile has a loyal following.
Closed Sun, no lunch Sat.

Le Gavroche $$$
1616 Alberni and Cardero
685-3924
I can't think of a better place for a
romantic dinner: a turn-of-the-
century house, a bit of a view over
Coal Harbour, ever-so-slightly-
superior Gallic service, and rich,
subtle, inventive, passionate food,
food along the lines of smoked
pheasant breast on a purée of
celeriac, shallots and wine with a
light truffle sauce. Should you feel
nostalgic, you can always get owner
Jean-Luc Bertrand to mix a Caesar
salad by your table – and perhaps remember why everyone made such a
big fuss of Caesars before the advent
of salad bars. Le Gavroche handles
seafood particularly well, so pay
attention to the daily specials. If it's a
special occasion with a big budget,
ask for the reserve wine list. Closed
Sun, no lunch Sat.

GREEK

Simpatico Ristorante $
2222 W. 4th and Vine
733-6824
Simpatico has been a fixture on 4th
Avenue since 1969, an enduring
source of nourishing meals at low
prices. Order one of the wholewheat
crust pizzas – every table has a black
metal pizza stand – or venture off
into the Greek menu. Cornish game
hen with rice, potatoes and Greek
salad is a hearty, robust meal. Decor
is generically Greek, with pathos
plants, white walls, wood floors and
tables, blue-and-white checked
tablecloths. Students eat here, and
young families, and the rest of that
vast army of us with more appetite
than cash. Lunch and dinner daily.

Vassilis Taverna $$
2884 W. Broadway near Macdonald
733-3231
Greek food is simple. What distin-
guishes Vassilis is fresh food,
generous portions, reasonable prices
and an amazing consistency. Years
go by, and apart from the passing of
Dino, the restaurant canary, nothing
changes.
　　Vassilis' *kotopoulo* – a chicken
pounded flat, rubbed with herbs and
grilled – is the standard other
Vancouver Greek restaurants can be
measured by. *Skordalia*, a velvety,
sinful potato and garlic puree is
served cold as an appetizer. Don't
miss the homemade *navarino*, a
creamy custard square topped with
whipped cream and ground nuts.
Lunch Tues to Fri, dinner Tues to
Sat.

ITALIAN

Il Barino $$$
1116 Mainland and Helmcken
687-1116
Yaletown is an old warehouse
district newly flourishing as a centre
for fashion and interior design, and Il
Barino, a handsome, sunny, sophisticated northern Italian restaurant, is
the neighbourhood's perfect expression. It's a long narrow room,
painted pale gold, with a bit of faux
scenery ever so tastefully painted on
the walls. The cold kitchen is open to
view, and bursting with fresh herbs
still planted in flats, strings of dry
red peppers, platters of grilled
eggplant and zucchini, roasted red
peppers and a case full of rich
desserts. A few wines by the glass
every day, some brilliant ways with
grilled shiitake and oyster mushrooms, a great veal scaloppine, and
at lunch time, the sounds of people
discussing the purchase of leather
sofas. Lunch Mon to Fri, dinner
daily.

Piccolo Mondo $$
850 Thurlow and Robson
688-1633
Don't let the modern brute ugliness
of the outside of Piccolo Mondo put
you off. Inside it's an elegant brown-
and-beige room, walls covered with
framed menus, candles winking,
silver gleaming.
Expect to spend a while with the
menu. It's as long as some novels,
and equally fraught with serious
decisions. If you get the grilled
raddichio salad, will it go with the
homemade tortellini in mustard
cream sauce? Or is the idea of veal
chops with balsamic vinegar sauce
and grilled fennel simply too

tempting? Maybe you should change
that appetizer to grilled seasonal
vegetables with foccacia? Or how
about the earthy splendour of celery
root braised in red wine and
sprinkled with rich little gobbets of
marrow? Now that's definitely too
heavy to pair with the calf liver in
Marsala sauce – and so it goes. The
choice of Italian wines is the city's
best. If you aren't tempted by angel
hair pasta with vodka Parmesan
sauce and caviar ($33), food prices
are remarkably moderate. Dinner
daily except Sun, lunch Mon to Fri.

Arriva $$
1537 Commercial and Grant
251-1177
Commercial Drive was once the
centre of Vancouver's Italian
community. Little Italy is making
room for little Vietnam and little
Nicaragua right now, but the Italian
delis are still on the Drive and so are
a number of good Italian restaurants.
My favourite is Arriva, for its
uncluttered design and its commit-
ment to authentic Italian food.
If you must have spaghetti and
meatballs, you can, but there's also
ziti with spicy squid sauce and fusili
with wild game. The antipasto plate
is heaped with octopus, shrimp,
roasted red peppers, cheese,
sausage, and fat lima beans in a
herby marinade. Order orange
sherbet served in a hollowed-out
orange for dessert. Dinner daily,
lunch Mon to Fri.

JAPANESE

Tojo's $$

777 W. Broadway and Willow
872-8050

The best Japanese food Vancouver money can buy is made by Hidekazu Tojo, a meticulous, demanding, inventive artist among sushi makers. If you'd like your knowledge of Japanese food enlarged, pick a slow night, sit at the sushi bar, and ask Tojo to feed you something different.

He always can. Tatami rooms are blond wood with kimonos hung on the walls for decoration. Seats by the north facing windows have a splendid view of False Creek and the North Shore mountains. Prices reflect the quality of the food, which means they are higher than in other Japanese restaurants – but still far from expensive, gauged against prices people called Pierre or Luigi feel justified in charging. Dinner daily except Sun.

SUSHI

I can't imagine finding better sushi anywhere in Canada. If you're new to sushi, imagine fish – the freshest you've ever had – with a delicate rather than a fishy taste.

There are three kinds of sushi. One kind is a small patty of rice that is covered with a thin slice of raw tuna, salmon or mackerel, etc., and is called *nigiri*. Another is a *maki,* or roll of rice covered with a paper-thin sheet of crisp seaweed and filled with tuna, salmon, salmon roe or cucumber, etc. The third is crisp seaweed rolled into a cone and filled with rice and fish.

If you are trying sushi for the first time, order just enough for an appetizer – an assorted sushi plate will do for two to four people. If you're more adventurous or experienced, wait for a seat at the sushi bar where you can be part of the

congeniality and watch the sushi master at work. At the bar you can order particular types of sushi, one or two pieces at a time.

After sitting down you will be presented with a hot towel for your hands, because sushi is eaten with the fingers or chopsticks. Sake, green tea or beer are all appropriate and should be ordered from the waitress, though you order your sushi directly from the sushi chef. You can also order soup (to be drunk from a bowl) from your waitress, but traditionally nothing else is eaten at the bar.

Pick up a piece of sushi and dip it fish-side down into the little dish of soy sauce, then pop it into your mouth (still fish-side down). The taste is clean, pure and delicious. The hotness comes from a thin layer of green horseradish called *wasabi* between the rice and the fish. Refresh your palate in between courses of sushi with a piece of shaved pickled ginger.

Shijo Japanese Restaurant $$
1926 W. 4th and Cypress
732-4676
Shijo is the chic sushi bar, a convivial place one flight up from Kitsilano's main artery, light-filled and thoroughly modern, with a team of sushi and robata chefs cracking jokes behind the bar. Jazz plays discreetly in the background. Handsome lamps with patinated bronze finishes, lots of black wood: this is the esthetic of modern Japan – oddly enough evoked by Vancouver designer Tony Robins, who has gone on to design a string of restaurants for Japanese clients. Ask for Japanese eggplant cooked on the robata, and, if they're available, shiitake mushrooms cooked in foil. Lunch Mon to Fri, dinner daily.

Chiyoda $$
1050 Alberni and Burrard
688-5050
A robata bar serves food grilled to order in front of the customers – the essential sushi bar experience for people who won't eat raw fish. Chiyoda was designed in Japan, right down to the shapely little beer glasses. The bar is a set of concentric circles: a wood counter, a band of ice with the day's offerings displayed in wicker baskets, an inner circle of grills, and then the chefs, who hand over your food on long paddles that look like pizza peels. Snapper, prawns, oysters, eggplant, mushrooms, onions, potatoes; there are about 30 choices to be grilled, seasoned with soy, lemon and ponzu sauce and served, looking pretty, of course. Chiyoda's bar can be hilariously convivial. Lunch Mon to Fri, dinner daily.

Ossu Japanese Restaurant $$
755 Burrard and Robson
681-6778
Ossu specializes in sukiyaki at dinner time, and some of the tables in this very modern, very black restaurant are equipped with burners for authentic, cook-your-own food. There's a sushi bar too, with a friendly chef, and an electronic sushi ordering machine, if you feel like playing with gadgets. The best time to go to Ossu is lunch, when you can choose from 15 noodle dishes, or have the generous *shokado bento*, lunch in stacking lacquer boxes. Dinner daily, lunch daily except Sunday.

JEWISH

Kaplan's Deli $$
5775 Oak and 41st
263-2625
Tucked into a mini-mall on the road that leads to Seattle and to the Victoria and Gulf Islands ferries, Kaplan's is the traveller's last chance for authentic Jewish deli food. Eat in at booths, or take your chopped liver, herring, lox, and home-made corned beef with you. The cinnamon buns are justly famous. Open breakfast, lunch and dinner daily, except Jewish holidays.

Cafe Mercaz $
Jewish Community Centre
950 W. 41st and Oak
266-9111
Food served at the JCC's cafeteria is prepared under rabbinical supervision and satisfies kasruth requirements for orthodox Jews. Two hot main dishes available every day – vegetarian pizza, spinach lasagne –

frozen takeout is also available. The latkes are splendid. Lunch, dinner, Mon to Thurs, no dinner Fri, closed Sat, no dinner Sun.

KOREAN

Seoul House $$
36 E. Broadway and Ontario
874-4131
Seoul House serves a full menu of Korean and Japanese food, but for best results stick to the Korean side of the menu. Decor here is generic Japanese, with tatami rooms around the perimeter of the main dining room. Seoul House is almost always busy. Make a reservation even if you want to eat dinner at six on a Tuesday. Lunch Mon to Sat, dinner daily.

MEXICAN

Topanga Cafe $
2904 W. 4th and Macdonald
733-3713
A Kitsilano institution, the Topanga has been serving heaping plates of Cal-Mex food at low prices for 12 years. Kids can color blank menu covers while waiting for food; adults can scan the hundreds of framed copies of the same drawing on the walls for inspiration. No reservations. There are only 40 seats, so arrive before 6:30 or after 8 if you don't want to wait in line. Lunch and dinner daily except Sun.

El Mariachi $$
735 Denman and Robson
683-4982
The most authentic Mexican food in the city can be found in this small, family-style restaurant, with its

Diego Rivera posters, and the odd pinata for atmosphere.

Husband-and-wife team Arcelia and Giovanni Vagge (she's Mexican, he's Italian) are especially good at seafood: try crab-stuffed puff-pastry tortillas, fillet of sole in a sauce of fresh coriander, or prawns cooked with smoky-tasting chipotle peppers. Excellent chicken with molé sauce – the 28-ingredient sauce is a subtle, nutty, spicy, bitterly chocolate concoction. On weekends, you need reservations. Dinner only, Tues to Sun.

PORTUGUESE

April in Portugal $$
3229 Kingsway and Joyce
438-0626
Kingsway and Joyce Road is not so far to drive if you end up in Portugal, or at least a reasonable facsimile thereof. April in Portugal, a pretty little restaurant hung with travel posters, is a dine and dance restaurant on the weekend, jammed with people hot-footing it between courses. During the week, it's a sleepy little restaurant with excellent food – and especially good fish – at very low prices.

Order grilled Portuguese sausage: it comes resting on the back of a terra-cotta pig, flames from burning *aguardente*, the Portuguese equivalent of grappa, licking it from below. Pork and clams and salt cod are Portuguese menu standards; try quails hunting style for something different. The wine list has plenty of choice under $20. Dinner Tues to Sun, lunch Tues to Fri.

SPANISH

La Bodega $$
1277 Howe near Davie
684-8815
The dark, cosy tapas bar under the Chateau Madrid fills every night. Endless plates of patatas bravas – potatoes fried and doused in a spicy tomato dressing – and mussels in vinaigrette, and *chorizo* sausage, are washed down with gallons of beer, tubs of wine and pitchers full of sangria.

Eat as little as you like, or as much, come in a big noisy party, or with your one best friend, have lunch, or stay till 1 AM – La Bodega is a kind of rolling Spanish theatre that lets you do precisely what you please. Want a bit of gritty reality, proof that La Bodega is gutsy enough, and Spanish enough to introduce the subject of death at the dinner table? Check out the young, rather thin and sad bull's head mounted on the wall. Olé! Lunch and dinner daily to 1 AM.

THAI

Malinee's Thai Food $$
2153 W. 4th near Yew
737-0097
If you'd like an introduction to Thai food, Malinee's is the best place in Vancouver to start. Chef Kem Clasby is from Bangkok, co-owners Stephen Bianchin and Ted Hamilton are Canadians who lived in Thailand for two years. Together, they make a team that can not only produce authentic and very good Thai food, but can tell you about it too.

Specials are worth ordering; once it was a steamed whole red snapper, marinated in oyster sauce, ginger, cilantro, red pepper and lime juice – superb. Steamed fish with ginger, pickled plums, and red chili sauce is on the regular menu. Dinner daily, lunch Mon to Fri.

Sawasdee Thai Restaurant $
4250 Main and 26th
876-4030
Lineups formed outside the door when this pleasant, skylit restaurant – the oldest Thai restaurant in Vancouver – first opened. Now Thai restaurants are popping up everywhere from New Westminster to Kitsilano, and the competition is fierce. Sawasdee on Main (the Granville Street Sawasdee just isn't as good) still offers some of the best Chinese-influenced Thai food in town. You won't find the subtleties of Malinee's here. There are more stir-fries, and food that tastes like what you'd find at a plain, home-cookin' restaurant in Thailand.

The tiny chilies the Thais call rat turds wait like landmines for the unwary – be careful when you eat the excellent stir-fried spinach. Red curry with slices of roast duck in a fruit sauce is hot but sweet. Home-made coconut ice cream is sometimes available. Service here is so gentle and friendly that you start to believe in the Land of Smiles as something more than just a travel agent's cliché. Dinner daily except Mon.

VIETNAMESE/ CAMBODIAN

Pho Hoang $
3610 Main and 20th
874-0810
Pho – a steaming bowl of beef soup – is the Vietnamese equivalent of a hamburger. Pho restaurants, serving up to 30 varieties of beef soup, have been popping up lately on Vancouver streets. Pho Hoang is the oldest and one of the most welcoming to those who don't know the routine: soup comes with fresh herbs, chilies, and lime on the side, add them to taste. Drink Vietnamese coffee, filter brewed at your table. No alcohol, no cards. Lunch and dinner daily except Wed.

Phnom-Penh $
244 East Georgia and Gore
682-5777
On a quiet back street on the fringe of Chinatown, the Phnom-Penh serves the best garlic and pepper whole prawns – head, shell and all – in the city. In this robust food, the Chinese part of Vietnam's culinary heritage is especially evident. Try the warm beef salad; the slices of beef are crusted with ground salt and pepper. It's a family restaurant with modest furnishings and a genuine feeling of hospitality. Lunch and dinner daily, except Tues.

Quilicum/Theodore Wan

George, the Native Indian chef at the Quilicum Restaurant.

WEST COAST

Raintree $$
1630 Alberni and Cardero
688-5570
The Raintree is the one essential place to eat if you want to put your finger on the pulse of regional food in Vancouver. The big, cool room has an elegant West Coast feeling to it, and the menu is tuned to what's fresh and local. Chef Rebecca Dawson makes superb, hearty soups, and has imaginative, if sometimes overly complicated ways with seafood. Smells from the in-house bakery waft down the stairs to greet you – an encouraging welcome at any time, but especially so when you're about to eat the Raintree's lavish weekend brunch. Don't miss dessert, particularly the sky-high apple pie. You can get wine from Raintree's resolutely local wine list in half-glass taster sizes.
The Raintree kitchen also cooks for Leon's, the casual bar downstairs on the building's main floor. As far as I know, this is the only place in

town you can buy an organic beef burger. Leon's stocks local beers and a respectable number of single malt scotches.
Lunch and dinner daily, brunch Sat and Sun.

Quilicum West Coast Native Indian Restaurant $$
1724 Davie and Denman
681-7044
Quilicum serves the original northwest coast cuisine in a basement "longhouse" that's actually more reminiscent of a clearing in a forest: a narrow path between raised concrete platforms, a dozen or so log columns, low tables and walls and columns hung with northwest coast art, most of it for sale.

Heavenly bannock bread, baked sweet potato with hazelnuts, alder-grilled salmon and, for the adventuresome, soap-berries for dessert – Quilicum is far more than just a novelty restaurant. Seafood dishes are safest here, the baked juniper duck and the caribou stew can be disappointing. Dinner daily, lunch Mon to Fri.

This chapter has been written by Eve Johnson, food critic at the Vancouver Sun.

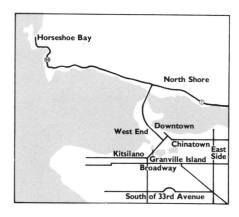

BY LOCATION

Broadway (between Main and Granville)
Caffe Barney, see Breakfast/Brunch
Kirin Seafood House, see Chinese, Dim Sum
Landmark Seafood House, see Chinese, Noodles
Passionate Pizza, see Pizza
Tojo's, see Japanese
Seoul House, see Korean

Chinatown
Hon's Wun Tun House, see Chinese, Noodles
Ming's, see Chinese, Dim Sum
Phnom Penh, see Vietnamese/Cambodian

Downtown
Bacchus, see Lunch
Il Barino, see Italian
La Bodega, see Spanish
Cafe Fleuri, see Breakfast/Brunch
Chartwell, see Lunch
Chiyoda, see Japanese
Le Crocodile, see French
Dynasty, see Chinese
Gallery Cafe, see Lunch
Kirin, see Chinese

Olympia Oyster and Fish Co., see
Seafood
Ossu, see Japanese
Piccolo Mondo, see Italian
Scanwich, see Breakfast/Brunch
Settebello, see Outdoors
Starbucks, see Espresso Bars
William Tell, see Continental

East Side
Accord, see Late Night
April in Portugal, see Portuguese
Arriva, see Italian
Cannery, see With a View
Japanese Deli House, see Lunch
Marineview Coffeeshop, see Seafood
Noor Mahal, see East Indian
Pink Pearl, see Chinese
Pho Hoang, see Vietnamese/
Cambodian
Rubina Tandoori, see East Indian
Sawasdee, see Thai
Szechuan Chongqing, see Chinese

Granville Island
Isadora's, see Breakfast/Brunch

Kitsilano
Bishop's, see Contemporary
Bridges Bakery and Bagels, see
Espresso Bars
Bread Garden, see Espresso Bars
Danann Mondial Cafe, see
Breakfast/Brunch
Flying Wedge, see Pizza

Malinee's, see Thai
Naam, see Vegetarian
Nyala, see Ethiopian
Santa Fe Cafe, see Contemporary
Shijo, see Japanese
Topanga Cafe, see Mexican
Vassilis Taverna, see Greek
Won More, see Chinese

North Shore
Capers, see Breakfast/Brunch
Chesa Seafood House, see Seafood
Dundarave Concession, see
Outdoors
Tomahawk, see Breakfast/Brunch

South of 33rd Avenue
Cafe Mercaz, see Jewish
Kaplan's, see Jewish
Seasons, see With a View

West End
Chez Thierry, see French
Delilah's, see Contemporary
English Bay Cafe, see With A View
Fresgo Inn, see Breakfast/Brunch
Le Gavroche, see French
El Mariachi, see Mexican
Quilicum, see West Coast
Raintree, see West Coast
Starbucks, see Espresso Bars
Steamers and Stews, see Seafood
Teahouse at Ferguson Point, see
Outdoors
Won More, see Chinese

GETTING AROUND

PUBLIC TRANSIT 68
City Buses, SeaBus, SkyTrain

COACH LINES 73

CARS 73
Car Rentals, Parking

TAXIS 74

TRAINS 74

FERRIES 75
Schedules, Fares, Travel Tips, Short Ferry Trips

VANCOUVER INTERNATIONAL AIRPORT 80
Getting There, Airport Parking, Airport Services

FLIGHTS TO VICTORIA AND SEATTLE 81
Downtown Victoria, Victoria Airport, Downtown Seattle

PUBLIC TRANSIT

CITY BUSES

B.C. Transit operates a system that
accepts exact coin fares, tickets and
passes. Coin fare is $1.25 adult and
$.65 concession. Concession fares
apply to senior citizens, children age
5 to 13, and high school students
with GoCards. Transfers, issued only
when the fare is paid, are valid for 90
minutes for two-way travel and are
good on buses, the SeaBus and the
SkyTrain.

Tickets and passes are sold by
retail outlets (look for a blue and red
"Faredealer" sign in the window),
not by transit operators. Tickets are
sold in books of ten for $11.25 adult,
$6.50 concession. Monthly passes
are $50 adult, $29 concession. These
are one-zone fares but are valid for
travel across zones (if you want to go
outside Vancouver city limits, for
example) as long as it's not rush
hour. To get to and from the suburbs
during rush hour, you pay more.

Day passes ($3.50 adult, $1.75
concession) are good for unlimited
travel after 9:30 AM weekdays, and
all day Sat, Sun or holidays. These
are sold by machines at SeaBus or
SkyTrain stations (but not before
9:30 AM weekdays), or at retail
outlets.

Transit information is available at
261-5100, seven days a week, 6:30
AM to 11:30 PM. Persevere and you

DOWNTOWN VANCOUVER

1 World Trade Centre
2 The Landing
3 Sinclair Centre
4 Harbour Centre
5 SFU Downtown Campus
6 Woodward's Dept. Store
7 Army & Navy Dept. Store
8 YWCA
9 Royal Centre Mall
10 Christ Church Cathedral (Anglican)
11 Hotel Vancouver
12 Pacific Centre Mall
13 The Bay Dept. Store
14 Vancouver Centre Mall
15 Holy Rosary Cathedral (Catholic)
16 Main Post Office
17 Queen Elizabeth Theatre/ Playhouse
18 Bus Depot
19 Vancouver Public Library
20 Travel Infocentre
21 Vancouver Art Gallery
22 Eaton's Dept. Store
23 Law Courts
24 Orpheum Theatre
25 YMCA
26 Pacific Cinémathèque Pacifique
▰▰▰ Buses/Taxis only
● SkyTrain Station
■ Hotel
⌐⌐⌐ Underground Shopping Centre
◄— Traffic Direction

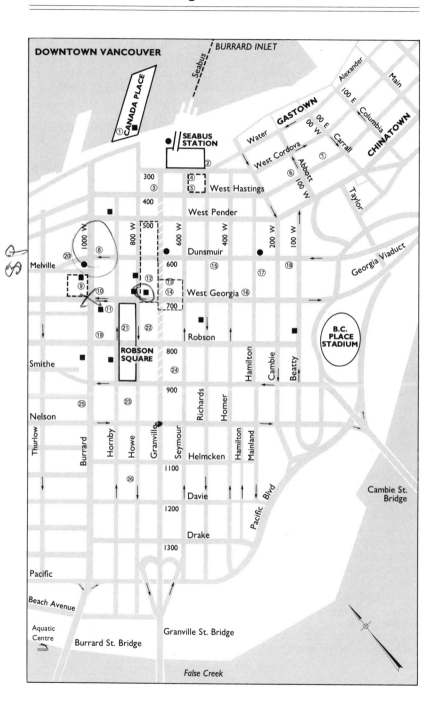

will eventually get through to this busy number.

Service on most routes ends about 1 AM. Then "Night Owl Service" (a bare-bones service on major streets) comes into effect until about 3 AM.

A *Transit Guide* that shows all the bus routes is published by B.C. Transit. The guide is reasonably priced and is available at newsstands. Bus shelters at major intersections often have route maps posted on them. Fare dealers have free guidebooks called *Discover Vancouver* describing transit routes to all Lower Mainland attractions.

On the North Shore

West Vancouver buses (which are blue) are on a different system. To travel to West Van – roughly anywhere west of the Lions Gate Bridge on the North Shore – call West Van transit information at 985-7777. Although the blue West Van buses are a separate system, transfers from B.C. Transit are valid.

In North Van – that is, east of the Lions Gate Bridge – buses are part of the B.C. Transit system.

The "Around the Park" Bus

From the end of Apr to Oct, a special bus (#52 Around the Park) goes around Stanley Park on Sat, Sun and holidays from 10–6. Catch it at the foot of Alberni St. by Lost Lagoon, or at stops on Denman St. or on Stanley Park Dr. Frequency, ranging from every 20 minutes to every hour, depends on the weather.

Airport Bus

See Vancouver International Airport later in this chapter for details.

Scenic Bus Routes

A few Vancouver bus routes are particularly scenic and are an easy, cheap way to see the city. Needless to say, avoid rush hour. Some suggestions are:

* **The #250 Horseshoe Bay** bus to West Van along Marine Dr. to Horseshoe Bay. Catch this blue West Van bus on downtown Georgia St. going westbound. This is about a 50-minute trip each way.

* **SeaBus** to North Vancouver (described below).

* **The #52 Around the Park** bus in Stanley Park (see above).

* **The #351 Crescent Beach** bus to White Rock and Crescent Beach south of Vancouver near the U.S. border. On this trip the destination is more scenic than the route. Catch the bus downtown at designated stops on Howe St. or at Broadway and Granville. The trip takes about an hour and a half each way.

* **Skytrain** to the New Westminster Public Market (described below).

SEABUS

Crossing Burrard Inlet every 15 minutes during the day since 1977, the SeaBus connects downtown to North Vancouver, reducing the rush hour snarl on the bridges. Two 400-passenger catamaran ferries, the *Burrard Otter* and the *Burrard Beaver*, make the 13-minute trip. Unfortunately, there is no deck, but the views are spectacular.

The SeaBus is part of the B.C. Transit system: the same fares apply and transfers can be used. It leaves from the old CPR Station on Cordova near Granville and goes to Lonsdale Quay, where there's a lively public

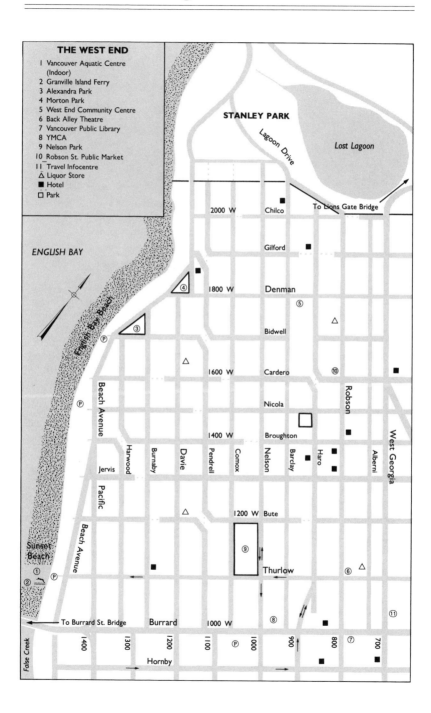

THE WEST END

1 Vancouver Aquatic Centre (Indoor)
2 Granville Island Ferry
3 Alexandra Park
4 Morton Park
5 West End Community Centre
6 Back Alley Theatre
7 Vancouver Public Library
8 YMCA
9 Nelson Park
10 Robson St. Public Market
11 Travel Infocentre
△ Liquor Store
■ Hotel
□ Park

STANLEY PARK

Lagoon Drive

Lost Lagoon

To Lions Gate Bridge

ENGLISH BAY

English Bay Beach

2000 W   Chilco

Gilford

1800 W   Denman

Bidwell

1600 W   Cardero

Nicola

1400 W   Broughton

Robson

West Georgia

Beach Avenue

Harwood
Burnaby
Davie
Pendrell
Comox
Nelson
Barclay
Haro
Alberni

Jervis

Pacific

1200 W Bute

Sunset Beach

Beach Avenue

Thurlow

1000 W

To Burrard St. Bridge   Burrard

False Creek

1400   1300   1200   1100   1000   900   800   700

Hornby

A renovated CP train station in Gastown is now the SeaBus terminal.

market. The market has everything from clothing boutiques and toy stores to vegetable stalls (food downstairs and shops up). A sunny plaza off the market has a spectacular view of Burrard Inlet and downtown. The restaurants, fast food outlets and pub will come in handy once you've finished exploring.

The SeaBus operates every 15 minutes Mon to Sat during the day and every 30 minutes on Sun and during the evening (till just after midnight). Avoid the downtown to North Van trip during afternoon rush hour.

Connections with SkyTrain can be made at the downtown SeaBus terminal.

Bicycles are allowed on the SeaBus only on weekends and holidays. Riders must pay another full fare for their bikes.

SKYTRAIN

The SkyTrain is Vancouver's rapid transit system. It runs 25 km (15 mi.) from Surrey and New Westminster to the Canada Place Pier (Waterfront Station) downtown. At the centre of the city the SkyTrain goes underground, but much of the line is elevated, somewhat like the Seattle monorail. So far it is a single line with 17 stations.

Trains with two to six cars arrive every three to five minutes and cruise at 80 km/h (50 mph). A trip from one end to the other takes 32 minutes. The trains have no drivers but are run by computers monitored at SkyTrain headquarters. Security and information officers ride the trains and are at stations.

Tickets are sold by machines at each station; exact change is not necessary.

If you're curious about SkyTrain, have a short ride to the Broadway Station where you can stop for lunch in Little Italy on Commercial Dr, north of the station. For a longer ride, the New Westminster Public Market is a fine destination. Take the train to the New Westminster Station and you'll find the market about half a block away on Front St., right at the edge of the Fraser River.

About 25 km (15 mi.) of elevated and underground track lead the SkyTrain from downtown to New Westminster and Surrey.

COACH LINES

Bus Depot
Dunsmuir at Hamilton
662-3222
This phone number is an information line for all coach lines coming into the bus depot but it is almost continually busy. Most companies have an office in town that you can call directly.

Airport Express
273-9023
Leaves Level 2 of the airport every 15 minutes from 6 AM-midnight. Passengers are collected from major downtown hotels and the bus depot every 30 minutes. The fare is $7.25.

Cascade Coach Lines
662-3222
1-795-7443 (Chilliwack)
Buses go up the Fraser Valley as far as Harrison Hot Springs.

Greyhound
(800) 661-8747
Goes across Canada and to Seattle.

Maverick Coach Lines
255-1171
Buses go north up the Sunshine Coast to Powell River, and up the mainland coast to Whistler, Blackcomb and Pemberton. Buses also go to Nanaimo on Vancouver Island.

Pacific Coach Lines
662-8074
Buses go to Victoria (See also Tours).

Quick Shuttle
591-3571
New quick bus service to Bellingham Airport, downtown Seattle and SeaTac Airport. The three-hour trip from downtown to downtown costs $25.

CARS

CAR RENTALS

Avis
757 Hornby near Georgia
682-1621

Budget
450 W. Georgia at Richards
685-0536

Hertz
1128 Seymour near Davie
688-2411

Tilden
1140 Alberni near Thurlow
685-6111

Rent-a-Wreck
1085 Kingsway near Fraser
876-7155
Cheap car rentals.

On the other hand for something more grand, a Porsche, Corvette convertible, Mercedes or Excalibur, call:

Budget
1705 Burrard at 1st
736-3388

Exotic Car Rentals
1820 Burrard at 2nd
644-9128

PARKING

The main parkades are the Pacific Centre (entrance on Howe at Dunsmuir), the Bay (entrance on Richards near Dunsmuir) and Robson Square (entrance on Smithe and Howe).

Parking meters are strictly enforced, and cars are towed (even if you have out-of-province plates) from rush hour "no parking" areas. Check the parking meter and signs for times. Parking in commercial alleys is illegal. See also Essential Information (Motor Vehicles).

TAXIS

Your chances of hailing a cab in Vancouver are slim unless you're downtown. Head to a large downtown hotel or call any of the following:

Black Top
731-1111
Request a Checker car with "collar-and-tie service" which is a black late model Olds, guaranteed spotless, along with a neatly dressed and friendly driver. All at no extra cost.

MacLures
731-9211

Vancouver Taxi
255-5111
Has oversized cabs for wheelchairs or other large items.

Yellow Cab
681-3311
Yellow or Black Top will take you for a personal tour of the city on their suggested routes. Prices are the regular meter rate.

TRAINS

VIA Rail
(800) 561-8630 toll free (Canada)
The two major railways in Canada amalgamated their transcontinental service into VIA Rail. The transcontinental train arrives and departs from the Canadian National Railway station at Main and Station St. three days a week. Call the above number for reservations and information. Call 669-3050 for arrivals and departures.

B.C. Railway
631-3500
Operates out of the train station at 1311 W. 1st St. in North Vancouver. If you have an inclination to see more of British Columbia — the Coast Mountains, forests and some small interior towns — take the B.C.

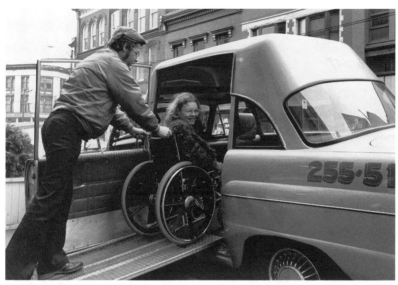

Special cars designed to carry wheelchairs are available from Vancouver Taxi.

Rail passenger train 253 km (157 mi.) northeast to Lillooet. You can get there and back in a day, with a two-hour stopover for lunch and exploration. The train leaves every day in summer at 7:30 AM and travels via Horseshoe Bay, Squamish and Whistler, arriving in Lillooet at 1 PM. (You could go on to 100 Mile House, Quesnel or Prince George, but it would be at least a two-day trip.) The train arrives back in North Vancouver at 8:35 PM. The return fare is $45 with discounts for seniors and children.

See also Sights (Royal Hudson/ M.V. *Britannia*).

FERRIES

B.C. Ferry Corp. has one of the largest and most modern ferry fleets in the world, transporting 19 million people and 7.5 million vehicles annually.

All of the boats except one were built in B.C., and some are extraordinary vessels. There are five "C" Class vessels, often called superferries because they are the largest of their type in the world: most carry 360 vehicles and 1500 passengers. These big boats, the *Queen of Cowichan, Coquitlam, Surrey and Oak Bay* have bridges, loading facilities, propellers and rudders at both ends, so they can sail in either direction.

B.C. Ferry Corp is responsible for some innovative remodelling to make boats even larger, to accommodate the increasing traffic between the mainland and Vancouver Island. The remodelling principle was to stretch and lift. The first renovation in 1968 was to suspend an additional car deck, like a mezzanine, from the ceiling of the existing car deck, increasing the capacity

from 110 to 150 cars. Then, a year later, B.C. Ferry started cutting some of its boats in half vertically, inserting a 25-m (84-foot) mid-section and welding the three sections together to increase capacity to 200 cars. A few years later it even cut four of the stretched boats in half horizontally! Another car deck was inserted, making these ferries both stretched and lifted. The *Queen of Esquimalt, Saanich, Vancouver and Victoria* have been converted so that they carry over 300 vehicles.

A restaurant, snack bar, newsstand and ship-to-shore telephone are on the larger boats. There is no smoking in the vessels. Pets must remain on the car deck.

SCHEDULES

For sailing times call 685-1021 for a 24-hour recorded announcement. Or pick up a schedule at the Vancouver Travel Infocentre at 1055 Dunsmuir

Zipping across Burrard Inlet, the SeaBus ferries commuters between downtown and North Vancouver.

near Burrard or at the major hotels. You can also turn the TV to channel 4 before 9 AM for a continuous broadcast of sailing times. Schedules are printed daily on the first page of the classifieds in the *Vancouver Sun*.

Vancouver has two ferry terminals. Tsawwassen is an hour's drive south from downtown. Sailings from this terminal go to Swartz Bay (a 30-minute drive from Victoria), Nanaimo and to the Gulf Islands. Horseshoe Bay, the other ferry terminal, is a 30-minute drive north from downtown. Sailings from here go to Nanaimo, Bowen Island and up the mainland coast.

The two busiest routes are from the mainland to Vancouver Island. Each of these crossings takes one and a half hours. From the Victoria Day weekend in late May to Labour Day, there are generally hourly sailings from each terminal from 7 AM-10 PM. There are exceptions to this – always double-check the schedule.

FARES

There are 25 routes with different fares, but here are one-way fares for the most popular routes, from the mainland to Vancouver Island:

Driver or passenger: $5.25
Child (5-11): $2.25
Cars $18.75
RVs: $24.50

B.C. seniors, but not their vehicles, travel free Mon to Thurs, except holidays.

Bus fare from downtown Vancouver to downtown Victoria, including ferry fare, is $17.50.

TRAVEL TIPS

The few problems involved with the ferries such as car line-ups and medi-ocre food can be overcome. The so-lution to the food is simple: pack a picnic lunch. The other problems require some planning.

Car Passengers

For reservations call 669-1211. Res-ervations for vehicles are accepted only on certain routes: the Inside Passage to Prince Rupert, Prince Rupert to the Queen Charlotte Islands, and Tsawwassen to the Gulf Islands. All other routes are first come, first served.

Reservations to the Gulf Islands must be accompanied by payment. Reserve by phone and use Visa, Mastercard or American Express.

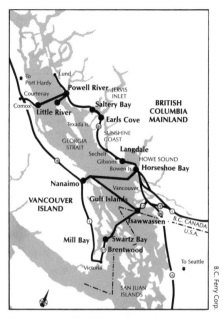

Summer and holiday reservations should be made as far in advance as possible. At any time during the summer it is wise to arrive early if you are taking your car.

Once on the ferry, don't lose you car – it the quickest way to be spotted as a tourist. Some boats have three car decks, so remember which one your car is on.

Avoid peak times, weekends and holidays, especially during the summer. The worst times are Fri afternoon and evening, Sat morning, Sun afternoon and evening and holiday weekends. Also, try to plan your trip before sunset. You'll miss the scenery if you're sailing in the dark.

Leave your car behind if possible, especially at busy times. But on holiday weekends don't count on leaving it at the Tsawwassen parking lot. Even though there is parking for

A B.C. Ferry boat in Horseshoe Bay.

1250 cars, the lot is frequently full, and parking continues for 3 km (2 mi.) down the causeway. Other possibilities are to travel as a foot or bus passenger.

Foot Passengers

Foot passengers can avoid car line-ups and walk right on board. It's too far to take a taxi to either ferry terminal. Public transportation to Tsawwassen is long, involved and not practical if you have luggage. Call B.C. Transit (261-5100) for bus information. The #250 Horseshoe Bay blue bus goes directly from downtown Georgia St. to within walking distance of the Horseshoe Bay terminal. Call 985-7777.

Foot passengers must purchase tickets at least 10 minutes before sailing time. If you board as a foot passenger but need bus transportation for the other side, you can buy a ticket from the bus driver on board

the ferry (the bus goes onto the ferry) during the first 30 minutes of the trip; listen for the announcement. You then board the bus before the ferry docks to go to downtown Victoria, Nanaimo or Powell River, depending on which ferry you're on. You can get off the bus at designated stops before downtown if you wish.

Foot passengers can check luggage at the ferry terminal where tickets are sold. Put on the appropriate luggage tag so your bag will end up at the right destination. You can carry your bags onto the ferry, but there are no lockers and space is often at a premium.

Bus Passengers

Buses are the first vehicles on and off the ferries. To get to Victoria, take a Pacific Coach Lines bus. It leaves from the bus depot in downtown Vancouver 70 minutes before almost every sailing. No reservations are necessary, and the fare ($17.50) includes the cost of the ferry. You can board the bus at the bus depot or at designated stops on the way. To arrange for the bus to stop and pick you up, you must phone Pacific Coach Lines (662-8074) at least an hour before the bus leaves.

If your destination is Nanaimo or the Sunshine Coast, catch a Maverick Coach Lines bus (255-1171). Buses to Nanaimo are generally every two hours, or three times daily for the Sunshine Coast. Maverick is the line to take for all departures from Horseshoe Bay.

SHORT FERRY TRIPS

Personally, I'm sold on the ferries. Nothing can beat the scenery, salt air and lounging on the deck on a sunny day. If the weather is good, take a jacket and binoculars out on deck to watch the marine traffic: fish boats, freighters, sailboats, yachts, tugs and other ferry boats. You may even catch sight of seals, otters or whales.

Some of the following short ferry trips are perfect if you want a little

ORCINUS ORCA, the Killer Whale

More killer whales are found off the coast of British Columbia than anywhere else in the world. Of the local population of 350 whales, 80 reside in southern waters — the Strait of Georgia, Juan de Fuca Strait and Puget Sound. On a B.C. Ferry trip you can occasionally see a group of dorsal fins 60 to 120 cm (2 to 4 ft.) long cruising Active Pass or the waters by Tsawwassen. The whales live and travel in pods of five to fifty.

The *Orcinus orca* is 7 to 9 m (21 to 27 ft.) long and can swim at 20 km/h (12 mph), leaping out of the water when it travels at top speed. Because it is a toothed whale and a successful predator, it has ended up with the unfortunate name of killer whale. Generally, it feeds on salmon but also preys on porpoises, seals, sea lions, birds and even other kinds of whales.

Whales

SURFACING AND BLOWING PREPARING TO DIVE

Blue

Finback

Sei

Humpback

Sperm

Killer

Male   Female

Marine Resources Branch

fresh air as well as a chance to see the coastal waterways. Save these trips for a sunny day; it makes a big difference.

Horseshoe Bay to Bowen Island

This is the shortest trip on B.C. ferries, about 20 minutes to go 5 km (3 mi.) one-way. It is possible to do this trip from Vancouver in an afternoon, even with a stopover on Bowen. Take the bus to Horseshoe Bay and travel as a foot passenger or take a car. Phone B.C. Ferry Corp. for times and prices.

Sunshine Coast

Another pleasant day trip. The mainland coast north of Vancouver is accessible by a road-and-ferry system for only about 160 km (100 mi.) because of the rugged fiord-cut terrain. This area is called the Sunshine Coast. Phone Maverick Coach Lines (255-1171) for times and fares to Gibsons, a village on the coast (also home of "The Beachcombers" television series). The ferry ride from Horseshoe Bay to Langdale is 40 minutes, and then there is a short bus ride along the craggy coast into Gibsons. Call B.C. Ferry Corp. for sailing times and fares if you are taking your car.

Gulf Islands

Sail to the peaceful Gulf Islands from Tsawwassen, perhaps to Galiano or Mayne, the two closest islands. Both are popular bicycling destinations – Mayne is the more compact and less hilly. If you are taking a car, make sure you have a ferry reservation, especially on summer or holiday weekends.

See also Excursions from Vancouver (The Gulf Islands).

VANCOUVER INTERNATIONAL AIRPORT

The airport is situated on an island at the mouth of the Fraser River, 13 km (8 mi.) from downtown. It is Canada's second-busiest airport with 325,000 takeoffs and landings handling 10 million passengers a year. The major airlines at the main terminal are: Air Canada, Canadian Airlines, Air BC, United, Delta, Continental, American, Horizon, British Airways, Lufthansa, Qantas, Air New Zealand, Cathay Pacific, Japan Airlines, Air China, Singapore, and Korean. The smaller South Terminal services regional airlines.

Transportation between the two terminals is not regular. Call the connecting airline and they will arrange transportation, or take a taxi.

GETTING THERE

Getting to the airport by cab costs about $20 from downtown. For one or two people it's cheaper to take the Airport Express bus (273-9023) since the fare is $7.25. It leaves every 30 minutes from the major downtown hotels. You can also flag it down at Broadway and Granville or at 41st and Granville.

Airlimo provides a flat rate, 24-hour limousine service between the airport and various locations ($26 to downtown). Phone 273-1331 to book.

Public transit buses to and from the airport unfortunately involve a transfer and so are not recommended if you have luggage. But if you want to go by bus from downtown, take a #20 Granville south to 70th and Granville, where you transfer to the #100 Airport that goes to the airport terminal. Going into town, take the #100 Port Coquitlam Centre/New Westminster Station and transfer at 70th to the #20 Victoria.

AIRPORT PARKING

A huge parking lot in front of the terminal holds 2500 cars, and an economy lot for overflow and long-term parking is on the right as you approach the terminal. A free yellow shuttle bus will transport you from these lots to the terminal; look for pickup spots in the parking lot. If you are staying for a short time and are lucky, you may get one of the parking meters in front of the terminal on each level. Valet parking is available on levels 2 and 3. Drop off rented cars in the main lot at the end closest to the terminal.

AIRPORT SERVICES

An airport concierge service is open from 6:30 AM-midnight on level 3. Tourist information booths are on levels 1 and 2. The airport has organized a helpful service of roving goodwill ambassadors called Green Coats that will help you with any problem. Look for green cardigans and badges saying "Information."

Hotel courtesy phone boards are on levels 1 and 2. A money exchange is on each level. Other services are: post office, bookstore, duty-free shops, gift shops, bank machines, video games room, barber shop, newsstand, flower shop, a B.C. specialty shop, an interfaith chapel and credit card fax machines.

FLIGHTS TO VICTORIA AND SEATTLE

DOWNTOWN VICTORIA

Air BC
278-3800
Harbour to harbour seaplane service. Depart from Vancouver harbour near the Bayshore Inn and land 35 minutes later in front of the Empress Hotel in Victoria's Inner Harbour. $184 return; weekend and excursions rates available.

Helijet Airways
273-1414
A 12-passenger Sikorsky helicopter will transport you from Vancouver harbour heliport to the Victoria heliport, a few minutes from the Parliament Buildings. A free shuttle service is provided to the downtown. $194 return with weekend and excursion rates.

VICTORIA AIRPORT

It is generally cheaper to fly from airport to airport, but it can be less convenient as it involves a 30-minute drive to and from the city at either end. Three airlines provide this service: Air BC (278-3800), Helijet Airways (273-1414) and Time Air (682-1411).

DOWNTOWN SEATTLE

Lake Union Air
(800) 826-1890
Floatplanes leave from the Air BC terminal beside the Bayshore and land at Lake Union an hour and 15 minutes later. A free shuttle takes you downtown in five minutes. All flights are weather permitting. $125 return.

SIGHTSEEING

THE SIGHTS 84

GRANVILLE ISLAND 84
What to See, Special Events, Places to Eat, For a Cool Drink,
Getting to the Island

THE ROYAL HUDSON/M.V. BRITANNIA EXCURSION 89

CHINATOWN 91

TOURING VANCOUVER 94
In the Air, On the Water, Bus Tours, Other Tours, Special Interest Tours

CALENDAR OF EVENTS 100

THE SIGHTS

Thanks to the sea, mountains, climate – and the history of the place – there are things in Vancouver that you can't do or see anywhere else. Many sights are described in this section and elsewhere in the book, but don't miss the top 10 listed below:

1. **Granville Island,** see below
2. **The Royal Hudson,** see below
3. **Robson Street,** see Shopping Areas
4. **Museum of Anthropology,** see Museums/Art Galleries
5. **A walk in the forest,** see Parks/Beaches/Gardens
6. **A ferry ride,** see Getting Around (B.C. Ferries)
7. **Chinatown,** see below
8. **Stanley Park seawall,** see Parks/Beaches/Gardens
9. **Dr. Sun Yat-sen Classical Chinese Garden,** see Parks/Beaches/Gardens
10. **Jericho Beach to Spanish Banks,** see Parks/ Beaches/Gardens

Approaching the official entrance to Granville Island.

GRANVILLE ISLAND

Granville Island was dredged out of the mud flats of False Creek in 1913. It was totally industrial and remained unnoticed until 1973 when the federal government decided to rescue the island. Most of the industries were persuaded to leave, but the buildings were kept and given a facelift. The public market opened in 1979 and became a raging success. Now, Granville Island is a desirable place, and the federal government regulates the businesses, gearing most to food, marine activities and arts and crafts.

The island looks peculiar, easygoing and friendly. The exteriors of the industrial buildings have been jazzed up with bright colours. They were never architectural wonders – in fact some were not much more than sheds – but the idea was to blend the old and the new, and it works.

Granville Island especially works as a people-place. It is not too trendy or touristy, and there is far more to do than just shop. Even though the Public Market is the star attraction, there are many other sights and activities on the island.

WHAT TO SEE

Granville Island Information Centre
666-5784

In addition to maps, brochures and helpful information officers, a continuous 12-minute slide presentation will give you an overview of the history of Granville Island.

Granville Island Public Market

Nothing can beat the market for one-stop food shopping. Where else can you get boneless chicken breasts, a quart of fish stock, fresh basil, salmon roe, Callebaut baking chocolate, cheese-and-onion buns and serrano chilies, all under one roof? If you're fixing a picnic (perhaps to take to Kits Beach a few blocks away), here is everything you need.

A fruit grower's day stall at Granville Island Public Market.

On a dull day, the market building is dry, warm and full of bright colours, lively people and wonderful things to taste. In hot weather, some of the huge glass doors lift up so that you are right out on the shore of False Creek, where you can sit, sample your purchases and watch tugs and sailboats go by.

The market is open 9-6 every day in the summer (May to Sept), and is closed Mon in the winter. See also Shopping.

Sea Village

The only residents of the island, and one of the few houseboat communities in Vancouver.

Emily Carr College of Art and Design

Its two galleries are open every day.

Boat rentals

Kayak rentals from Ecomarine Ocean Kayak Centre, power boats from the Granville Island Boat Rentals and canoes from Adventure Fitness. See Sports/Recreation for more details.

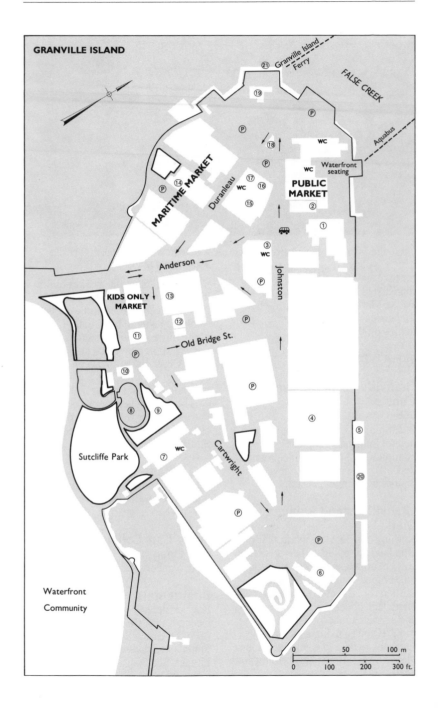

1 Arts Club Theatre
2 Arts Club Revue Theatre
3 Granville Island Info Centre
4 Emily Carr College of Art
5 Jonathan's Restaurant
6 Granville Island Hotel
7 False Creek Community Centre
8 Water Park
9 Adventure Playground
10 Isadora's Restaurant
11 Waterfront Theatre
12 Cartwright Gallery
13 Granville Island Brewery
14 The Lobster Man
15 Net Loft
16 Circle Craft Market
17 Blackberry Books
18 La Baguette et L'Échalotte
19 Bridges Restaurant
20 Sea Village floating homes
21 Boat Rentals
🚌 Bus Stop
wc Washroom
Ⓟ Parking
☐ Park

Sea Village on Granville Island is one of the few floating home communities in Greater Vancouver.

Galleries

The best galleries are the Cartwright (1411 Cartwright) for crafts, the Grace Gallery (1406 Old Bridge) for contemporary painters and sculptors and Granville Island Graphics and Paperworks (both at 1650 Johnston) for prints.

Many craftspeople welcome you into their studios and others invite you to peer through the windows. Some are weaver Diana Sanderson (#15-1551 Johnston), the tapestry makers at Fibre Art Studio (1610 Johnston), gold- and silversmiths (1334 Cartwright), Joel Berman, maker of contemporary glass (1244 Cartwright), Kakali Handmade Papers (1249 Cartwright), the glassblowers at New-small and Sterling (1440 Old Bridge), quiltmaker Pat Cairns (1420 Old Bridge) and the apprentices to Haida Indian carver Bill Reid (the Duranleau St. side of the Net Loft building).

Water Park

One of the most imaginative playgrounds in the city, located beside Isadora's Restaurant. The wading pool has stationary fire hoses for dousing intruders.

Tennis

Courts are beside the False Creek Community Centre. They are open to the public and are free.

Theatres

Three theatres are on the island: the Arts Club, the Arts Club Revue and the Waterfront. See Entertainment/Culture.

Blackberry Books

One of the best bookstores in town.

Tour the Granville Island Brewery

Island Lager is the best brew in British Columbia. For more details, see Special Interest Tours later in this chapter.

The Granville Island Ferry sails from the West End to Granville Island or the Maritime Museum in Vanier Park – a refreshing way to travel.

Kids Only Market

See With the Kids (Day Trips).

SPECIAL EVENTS

Granville Island is a popular location for festivals such as bluegrass, comedy, jazz, wooden boats, writers and crafts. Free events happen at the front and the back of the market building. Check with the Information Centre to see if anything is on when you're there.

PLACES TO EAT

There are many take-out stands in the market, and you can get gourmet take-out food from La Baguette. Create a picnic and sit outside by the water behind the market, or eat at one of the island's restaurants.

Isadora's
Casual place with the best food on the island. See Restaurants (Breakfast/Brunch).

Jonathan's
Seafood with a view at medium prices.

The Keg
A steakhouse.

Bridges
Pub food in the pub, light meals in the bistro and elegance upstairs. Their wonderful outdoor deck makes you feel as though you're in Marseilles.

Granville Island Hotel
Bistro, dining room and outdoor café.

FOR A COOL DRINK

Arts Club Theatre Lounge
A small lounge with a great view.

Bridges Neighbourhood Pub
A lively pub atmosphere.

Pelican Bay
At the Granville Island Hotel.

GETTING TO THE ISLAND

By Boat
Granville Island Ferries (684-7781) runs continuously from the south foot of Thurlow St. behind the Vancouver Aquatic Centre to Granville Island for $1.25 adult, $.50 child. Service is daily from 7:30 AM-10 PM in the summer, and 7:30-8 in the winter. The ferry also goes to Vanier Park, daily 10-5 in the summer, weekends only in the winter.

By Bus
Catch a #51 Granville Island bus at Broadway and Granville. It runs until 6:30 PM.

By Car
If you're not a patient driver, go by boat or bus. There is much less traffic if you go weekdays, and the earlier in the day, the better. On weekends, park on 2nd or 3rd Avenue east of Burrard, a 10-minute walk from the market. Line-ups and parking on the island can be horrendous. Before 7 PM parking is limited to three hours – stay longer and you'll be quickly towed away. Covered pay parking is available.

THE ROYAL HUDSON/ M.V. BRITANNIA EXCURSION

This is the best day trip from Vancouver, combining a train and boat ride up and down the spectacular B.C. coast.

The Royal Hudson is a regal steam locomotive that runs up the coast to the logging town of Squamish 64 km (40 mi.) north of Vancouver. The train steams out of the B.C. Rail train station in North Vancouver at 10:30 AM and chugs through picturesque West Vancouver (beach cottages and lavish waterfront mansions perched on cliffs and surrounded by mammoth Douglas-firs). But suddenly you are in the wilds of the Coast Mountains and the train tracks are hanging onto a cliff with the ocean 30 m (100 ft.) below. Waterfalls plummet beside you and hawks circle above.

Province of British Columbia

Sit at the back of the train so you can see the engine as you round curves and be sure to sit on the left side for the journey up or you'll be looking into the cliff.

The trip to Squamish takes about two hours, and you have an hour and a half to explore or have lunch before the return trip. Unless you're from a small B.C. town and have seen it all before, use the time to wander around and have the barbecued salmon buffet later on the boat.

The M.V. *Britannia* is a step or two above B.C. Ferry boats. There are two seating levels with huge windows and a sundeck on top. The boat returns by the same route, but the view from the water is entirely different. (Bring binoculars, the West Van houses look even more sumptuous from the water.) You cruise through Howe Sound, Burrard Inlet, English Bay and Vancouver Harbour, sailing past Stanley Park and downtown, then dock at

The last operational steam locomotive in Canada, the Royal Hudson, goes on day trips up the coast to Squamish.

Coal Harbour by the Bayshore Inn at 4:30 PM. A free shuttle bus will take you to the train station in North Vancouver to retrieve your car, or you can walk downtown in 10 minutes.

The pacing of the train and boat excursion is perfect – you are never bored, left waiting or feel rushed. You return relaxed even after a full day.

I recommend taking the train up and the boat back because the boat can be cool in the morning, but you could reverse this. The train and boat trip is $42 with discounts for children and seniors.

It is also possible to take the Royal Hudson both to and from Squamish ($24 adult, return fare), but the boat is definitely worth the extra money.

The boat/train day trip is oper-

Shoppers in Chinatown.

CHINATOWN

ated by Harbour Ferries (688-7246). Tickets must be purchased 48 hours before departure; this can be done over the phone with Visa, Mastercard, or American Express. You can also purchase tickets from their dock at Coal Harbour beside the Bayshore Inn, at the B.C. Rail Station in North Van (1311 W. 1st St.) or from the Vancouver Travel Infocentre at 1055 Dunsmuir (683-2000). The train runs Wed to Sun from late May to late Sept, and daily in July and Aug. Reserve well in advance for weekends.

Try to avoid driving to the B.C. Rail station, even though parking is free. You will be returned there at the height of rush hour and will have to inch back across the Lions Gate Bridge. Instead, in the morning, take the #740 Royal Hudson special transit bus that goes from downtown, to the station and back. Hotel pick-up is also possible. Get more bus information when you buy your tickets.

Walking into Chinatown is like stepping into a movie set, being in another time and place with all the sights, smells, sounds and tastes of another culture. Street life is one of the reasons Chinatown is such a distinctive neighbourhood; the sidewalks are bustling, noisy and often jammed with curious foodstuffs spilling out from the stores.

The heart of the Chinese community is Pender St. from Carrall to Gore, and Keefer St. from Main to Gore. The best time to visit Chinatown is at lunch hour or on Sunday when it is liveliest. Parking is difficult, and if you do find a spot you'll want to stay longer than the meter allows. Park in a lot or leave your car at home. Chinatown is only a 20-minute walk from Georgia and Granville.

The Chinese are Vancouver's oldest and largest ethnic group. They first came in 1858 to join the Fraser Valley gold rush and were later

CHINATOWN/GASTOWN/JAPANTO

imported in large numbers to construct the Canadian Pacific Railway. Today Vancouver has the second largest Chinese community in North America after San Francisco. There are about 100,000 Chinese people; few live in Chinatown, but many shop there. The adjacent residential community east of Gore St. is largely Chinese; you may notice the bilingual street signs.

Although all of Chinatown has been declared a historic site and is protected, the two blocks of Pender west of Main form the real historic area. Here are the best examples of the distinctive style of Chinese architecture found only in Vancouver's Chinatown; recessed balconies, ornamental roof lines and curved roof tiles. These buildings were constructed at the turn of the century by Chinese clan associations or societies, which often provided for the welfare of new immigrants or needy families since the Chinese were not allowed citizenship and had no rights until 1947. Today the Chinese community is active and respected in all aspects of city life.

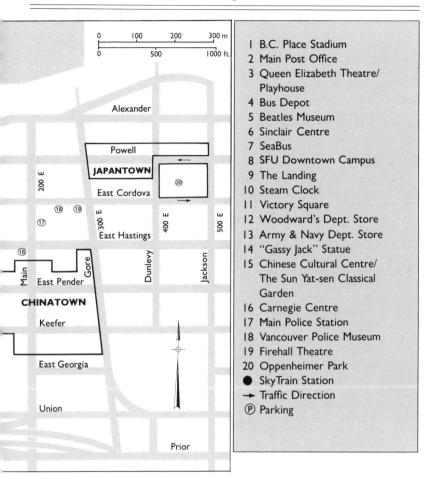

0 100 200 300 m
0 500 1000 ft.

Alexander

Powell

JAPANTOWN

East Cordova

200 E

300 E

400 E

500 E

East Hastings

East Pender

Main

Gore

Dunlevy

Jackson

CHINATOWN

Keefer

East Georgia

Union

Prior

1 B.C. Place Stadium
2 Main Post Office
3 Queen Elizabeth Theatre/ Playhouse
4 Bus Depot
5 Beatles Museum
6 Sinclair Centre
7 SeaBus
8 SFU Downtown Campus
9 The Landing
10 Steam Clock
11 Victory Square
12 Woodward's Dept. Store
13 Army & Navy Dept. Store
14 "Gassy Jack" Statue
15 Chinese Cultural Centre/ The Sun Yat-sen Classical Garden
16 Carnegie Centre
17 Main Police Station
18 Vancouver Police Museum
19 Firehall Theatre
20 Oppenheimer Park
● SkyTrain Station
→ Traffic Direction
Ⓟ Parking

At 50 E. Pender is the **Chinese Cultural Centre,** which holds classes in English and Chinese, Chinese arts and crafts, and tai-chi. The building is the entrance to **Dr. Sun Yat-sen Park.** This 1-ha (2.5-acre) park includes a garden designed in the People's Republic and built with the help of $6 million worth of labour and materials donated by the people of China. This Ming Dynasty-style garden is the only classical Chinese garden outside of China. The entire park is walled to preserve the sanctuarylike feeling of this type of garden. See also Parks/Beaches/Gardens.

Along Pender towards Main St. are stores selling rattan, porcelain and silk garments, the best spot to find inexpensive gifts. Stop in at **Ming Wo** at 23 E. Pender, one of the best cookware stores in town, crammed with every imaginable kitchen utensil. Just a couple of doors away is **China West** at 41 E. Pender, a treasure chest of cheap toys, novelties, calligraphy equipment, and Chinese jackets and slippers.

Once you cross Main St. you are in the thick of the food markets. Prices in Chinatown are cheaper than anywhere else, especially for produce, fish, poultry and meat. Stop at one of the bigger markets (try **Yuen Fong** at 242 E. Pender) and you'll find dozens of cans, bottles and packages of things you've never seen before. Watch butchers skillfully wield their cleavers to chop up barbecued pork or duck in the windows of the meat markets.

Turn right at Gore, walk past more markets, then turn right at Keefer St. This is bakery row. The one closest to Main, the **Keefer Chinese Bakery,** is my favourite. Try a barbecued pork baked bun (slightly sweet dough with barbecued pork inside), a coconut or custard tart, or a coconut-filled bun.

On Keefer near Main is the **Van-China Trade Centre,** selling goods made in the People's Republic: clothing, cushion covers with pictures of Marx and Mao, and toiletries like sandalwood soap. A few doors down, at the corner of Keefer and Main, is the **Ten Ren Tea and Ginseng Co.** selling an enormous variety of Chinese teas that promise everything from simple refreshment to the curing of all sorts of ailments. Drop by for a complimentary cup of hot tea after a sticky treat from the nearby bakeries.

Most of the restaurants in Chinatown are Cantonese, the style of Chinese cooking that most Westerners are familiar with. It is generally subtly flavoured dishes of stir-fried vegetables with fish, poultry or pork. But now is your chance to experiment with Cantonese-style lunch, dim sum. See Restaurants (Chinese) for a description of Chinese cooking, including dim sum.

TOURING VANCOUVER

In Vancouver you can see the sights by bus, boat, steam locomotive, helicopter, Rolls-Royce, float plane, hot-air balloon or paddle wheeler.

IN THE AIR

Harbour Air
688-1277
Seven tours are available, ranging from a 20-minute tour of the city ($55 per person) to an all-day outing that combines a return flight to the Gulf Islands with a day of sailing (and fishing, if you like) aboard a 13.8-m (46-ft.) catamaran, and includes a gourmet picnic lunch or dinner ($190 per person with discounts for groups of 5 or more).

In the spring and summer there are daily commuter flights to the Gulf Islands from Vancouver Harbour.

Vancouver Helicopters
683-4354
Tours leave from either the Vancouver harbour heliport or from Grouse Mountain. City and mountain tours from Grouse Mountain start at $25 per person for a 5-minute tour; a coastal mountain tour with a stop on a glacier costs $275 per person.

Westwind Balloon Tours
530-1633
These hot-air balloon tours depend on good weather, and wind direction determines the destination. A 60- to 90-minute trip with a professional pilot costs $165 per person, maximum five people. Following the French tradition, champagne is served at the end of the flight.

ON THE WATER

Granville Island Boat Rentals
682-6287 (seasonal)
Guided tours of False Creek and Burrard Inlet can be arranged for one to four people. The captain/tour guide will inform you on all points of interest from False Creek all the way up Indian Arm; cost is $50/hour, and you must book in advance. Tours are conducted in a 5-m (17-ft.) outboard, so dress accordingly.

Harbour Ferries
687-9558
Tour the city in a paddle wheeler! Harbour Ferries offer a 90-minute tour of Burrard Inlet. You'll see Lions Gate Bridge, Stanley Park, the city skyline and the workings of a busy port. Cost is $18 adult, with discounts for seniors and children.

S.S. Beaver Steamship
682-7284
This modern replica of a 19th-century paddle wheeler will take you on a daytime cruise up rugged Indian Arm, or for an evening cruise in the harbour. The four-hour Indian Arm cruise costs $34 adult, with discounts for seniors and children. Both cruises include a mesquite-grilled salmon barbecue. All tours run June to Sept only.

River Tours
250-3458
Three-and-a-half-hour cruises on the busy Fraser River where you'll see tugs, log booms, freighters — a fascinating look at a working river. $19 for adults with discounts for seniors and children. Relaxing and scenic 6-hour cruises on the Pitt River cost $37.

Also for private charters, see Sports/Recreation (Cruising). For short scenic ferry trips, see Getting Around (Ferries).

BUS TOURS

City and Nature Sightseeing
683-2112
A 3½ hour mini-bus tour includes the downtown area and Stanley Park, Queen Elizabeth Park, a stop at the Vancouver Museum and Planetarium, and time to shop at Granville Island. Cost is $25 adult, $20 child (12 and under).

Gray Line Bus Tours
681-8687
Tours include a 3½-hour city tour in a large coach, an evening tour with dinner at a restaurant specializing in Northwest cuisine and a boat cruise in English Bay with a stop at Granville Island. Another tour explores the North Shore (with the option of a skyride up Grouse Mountain).

LandSea Tours
687-5640
Stanley Park, downtown Vancouver, Granville Island, Gastown and Chinatown are included in this 18-passenger coach tour. The tour lasts 3½ hours; cost is $24 adult.

Pacific Coach Lines
662-7575
Tours of Vancouver range from a 90-minute tour ($16 adult) that covers the downtown highlights and Stanley Park to an all-day tour of downtown and the North Shore that includes a ride on the SeaBus and the Grouse Mountain Skyride ($46 adult). Children are half-fare on all tours.

Vance Tours

222-1966

A mini-bus takes you through downtown, Stanley Park, Shaughnessy, Queen Elizabeth Park, out to UBC and stops for a visit to the Granville Island Public Market. Tours lasts 3½ hours, cost is $24 adult with discounts for seniors, teens and children. A shorter tour is also available.

Also see Getting Around (City Buses).

OTHER TOURS

Historical Walking Tours of Gastown

683-5650

Gastown's namesake, raison d'être and first inhabitant was a saloon-owner named Gassy Jack Deighton back in 1867. After the big fire that destroyed Vancouver in 1886, the area was rebuilt with warehouses and hotels. Once the Depression hit, it became a skid row and remained derelict until the late 1960s when it was declared a historic site. Gastown underwent a beautification program: trees were planted, antique lamp standards and cobblestone streets were installed, and overhead wires were buried.

The new Gastown never materialized into a dynamic and essential part of the city, but the area is attractive and the architecture significant. The buildings are the city's oldest and most predate 1900. It is a pleasant place to stroll and shop on a sunny afternoon. Water St. from Richards to Columbia is where you want to be.

At the corner of Water and Cambie is an odd contraption, the world's first steam clock. It is powered by an underground steam system used to heat the neighbouring buildings. Every quarter-hour the whistle blows, and on the hour steam spews from its works. A statue of the loquacious Gassy Jack stands in Maple Tree Square at the other end of Water St.

Street parking is scarce. Use the Woodward's Parkade, entrance on Water St. Most stores in Gastown are open Sundays.

Popular walking tours of Gastown are conducted daily during the summer. The four different tours are free and take 40 minutes. They leave from the steam clock and the Gassy Jack statue. Call for schedule.

Horse Drawn Carriage Tours

681-5115

A 50-minute narrated tour of Stanley Park leaves every half hour from the zoo's lower parking lot in a 26-passenger carriage. $10 adult. Private tours in a 2- to 6-person carriage can also be reserved. $100/hr.

Fridge's Early Motion Tours

687-5088

See the city in a Model A Ford convertible. A one-hour downtown tour costs a minimum of $45, or $18 per person for more than two people. Follow the suggested route or devise your own.

Vancouver Vintage

683-6464

A 1930s Ford sedan will take you on a 2½-hour tour of the city; cost is $150 for the car, which holds up to four passengers. If a shorter tour appeals to you, there is also a one-hour tour for $60.

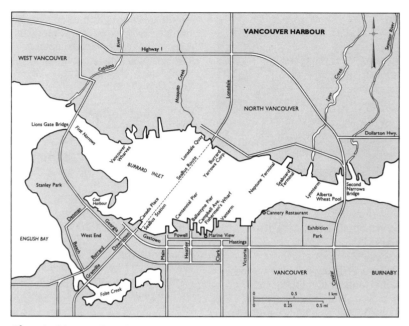

Classic Limousine Service
669-5466
Dream up your own route, or sit back in your "ultrastretch" Cadillac and leave the rest up to the driver. Prices run from $50 to $75 per hour according to make (Lincoln, Cadillac, Mercedes) and whether or not you want "ultra," "super" or just plain "stretch."

Star Limousine
983-5577
Tour Vancouver in a chauffeur-driven Rolls-Royce with narration by the driver, who will stop wherever you like. Standard routes take one to three hours, and range from $65 to $100 per hour, depending on what make of limo you prefer.

SPECIAL INTEREST TOURS

Port of Vancouver
666-6129
At the Vanterm container facility at the north foot of Clark Dr. is a public viewing area, open year-round Tues to Fri, 9-noon, and 1-4. In the summer they are open Sun from 12:30-4:30 and there are one-hour tours.

Granville Island Brewery
1441 Cartwright, Granville Island
688-9927
Tour this small hi-tech brewery run by a German brewmaster. Tasting room and retail sales. Half-hour tours are offered seven days a week at 2 PM Mon to Fri, and 1 and 3 on Sat and Sun.

Granville Island Brewing

Seymour Demonstration Forest
432-6286
Go for a 1½-hour walk with a professional forester identifying local vegetation and discussing forest management techniques. The demonstration forest is a new park just opened to the public. This is a family-oriented outing on an easy trail. Tours are at noon and 2 on Sundays during the summer. Take the Lillooet Rd. exit from the Upper Levels Hwy. A guide-yourself brochure is also available at the park.

University of British Columbia
Free drop-in walking tours Mon to Fri at 10 and 1 during the summer, call 228-3777.

Separate tours of the UBC dairy farm on campus, summer only. Milking begins at 2:30 PM; to book a tour call 228-4593.

Discover the many uses of subatomic particles at TRIUMF, the world's largest cyclotron. Free 90-minute tours are given twice daily in summer, twice weekly in winter. No reservations necessary except for large groups. Located at 4004 Wesbrook Mall south of 16th Ave., call 222-1047.

B.C. Sugar Refinery
123 Rogers off Powell
253-1131
See the sugar museum, an 18-minute film and tour part of the refinery, 9:30-3:30, Mon to Fri.

Alberta Wheat Pool
South end of Second Narrows Bridge
684-5161
A one-hour tour of the wheat-loading facility at the Port of Vancouver, Tues to Thurs at 10 and 2. Must be over 16 years old. Phone for reservation.

Simon Fraser University
Free tours of the campus are conducted by students every hour from 10:30-3:30, July 1 to Labour Day. Call 291-3210.

Canada Place
999 Canada Place,
north foot of Howe
688-8687
Find out what's under the teflon-coated white sails: visit the Vancouver Trade and Convention Centre, see the World Trade Centre, observe the operations of the cruise ship terminal, and enjoy a stroll through the luxurious Pan Pacific Hotel and along the scenic outdoor promenade. Free guided tours are given daily but schedule varies; phone for times and reservations.

THE SEA FESTIVAL

The Sea Fest is a week-long outdoor festival in July and is centred around English Bay in the West End. Besides outdoor concerts, volley-ball tournaments on the beach, a carnival, pancake breakfast, parade along Beach Ave., salmon barbecues and open house on visiting naval ships, the two big events are the fireworks and the infamous Nanaimo – Vancouver Bathtub Race. Check the newspapers or the *West Ender* for events.

Each year the fireworks are bigger, splashier and more expensive, attracting 400,000 spectators! They are set off in the middle of English Bay and can be seen from Kitsilano, the West End and West Vancouver. Traffic is horrendous in the West End that evening; park downtown and walk or watch from Kitsilano or West Vancouver.

THE PACIFIC NATIONAL EXHIBITION

The PNE, classified as an agricultural fair, has been held every August since 1910. It opens mid-August and ends on Labour Day. A parade from downtown to the PNE grounds starts the fun.

This fair is one of the largest in North America. You'll see horse shows, prize livestock, horticulture and craft shows. There are logger sports, the Miss PNE Pageant, a petting zoo, an international food pavilion and entertainment stages. You can wander through educational and cultural exhibits or eat Tom Thumb doughnuts and corn dogs on the midway after a 95 km/h (60 mph) roller coaster ride.

Baby-sitting is provided by St. John's Ambulance staff at a nominal rate. Phone B.C. Transit regarding special PNE buses. The schedule of events is in the newspaper or phone 253-2311.

Gates open daily from 10:30-10:30 and the grounds until midnight. Admission is charged, but there are free days for seniors and children.

See also With the Kids (Playland).

CALENDAR OF EVENTS

January 1 Polar Bear Swim Club dips into English Bay, 665-3424.

Late January to mid-February Chinese New Year is celebrated with the traditional Dragon Parade in Chinatown on a Sunday afternoon. Chinese Cultural Centre, 687-0729.

March-April Vancouver Wine Festival, 872-6622.

April 1-7 Festival of Fools at Granville Island, 666-5784.

Mid-April Peace March, 736-2366.

Easter Antique Car Easter Parade to Queens Park in New Westminster, 522-6894.

May Vancouver International Marathon, 685-5616. Vancouver Children's Festival, 687-7697. Annual Pacific Rim Kite Festival at Vanier Park, 669-5677. Port Day, open house featuring free harbour cruises sponsored by the Port of Vancouver, 666-6129.

Late May New Westminster Hyack Festival celebrates Queen Victoria's birthday, 522-6894.

Late June Canadian International Dragon Boat Festival on False Creek, Chinese Cultural Centre, 683-4448

Late June – Early July Du Maurier International Jazz Festival, Jazz Hotline, 682-0706.

July 1 Canada Day Celebrations, Canada Place, 666-7200. Gastown Grand Prix bicycle race, 435-2593. Steveston Salmon Festival, 277-6812.

Mid-July Vancouver Folk Music Festival, 879-2931. The Seafest and the Nanaimo-Vancouver Bathtub Race, 684-3378.

July – August Free entertainment at Robson Square, lunch hours and evenings, 660-2830.

Late July – Early August Early Music Festival, UBC School of Music, 732-1610. Vancouver Chamber Music Festival, St. George's School, 736-6034.

Early August Vancouver International Comedy Festival, Granville Island, 683-0883. Powell Street Japanese Festival at Oppenheimer Park. Squamish Days (logger sports), 892-9244. Vancouver International Triathlon, 737-2453.

Mid-August Abbotsford International Airshow, 852-8511.

Late August Pacific National Exhibition, 253-2311.

September The Fringe Festival (theatre and performance art), 873-3646. Indy Vancouver car race, 661-7223.

September – October Vancouver International Film Festival, 685-0260.

Late October Vancouver Writers Festival, 681-6330.

Early November Hadassah Bazaar, Hadassah-Wizo of Vancouver, 263-2778.

Mid-November Hycroft Christmas Fair, 731-4661. Christmas Craft Market, Granville Island, Circle Craft Co-op, 669-8021.

Early December Carol ships in English Bay and Burrard Inlet, 682-2007. Sinter Klaas arrives by steamboat in New Westminster, 522-6894.

Mid-December Children's Winterfest, 687-7697.

December 31 First Night, outdoors New Year's celebration at Robson Square, 669-9894.

PARKS/BEACHES/GARDENS

AMBLESIDE PARK/CENTENNIAL SEAWALK 102

CAPILANO RIVER REGIONAL PARK 102

DR. SUN YAT-SEN CLASSICAL CHINESE GARDEN 103

GROUSE MOUNTAIN 105

JERICHO BEACH TO SPANISH BANKS 106

LIGHTHOUSE PARK 106

LYNN CANYON PARK 107

MOUNT SEYMOUR PROVINCIAL PARK 107

NITOBE MEMORIAL GARDEN/UBC BOTANICAL GARDEN 109

QUEEN ELIZABETH PARK/BLOEDEL CONSERVATORY 109

REIFEL MIGRATORY BIRD SANCTUARY 110

SEYMOUR DEMONSTRATION FOREST 111

STANLEY PARK 111
On Foot in Stanley Park, Getting Around the Park,
Vancouver Aquarium

PACIFIC SPIRIT PARK (University Endowment Lands) 120

VanDUSEN BOTANICAL GARDENS 124

AMBLESIDE PARK/ CENTENNIAL SEAWALK

Ambleside is a shoreline park at the north foot of the Lions Gate Bridge. Except for the extreme east end where the bird sanctuary is, this is a manicured city park, good for a family picnic if you don't mind crowds.

There are tennis courts, pitch and putt golf, a refreshment stand, boat launch, playground, fitness circuit and duck pond. The best part of Ambleside Park is the 1.2-km (3/4-mi.) sandy beach facing the entrance to the harbour. Right before you as you sunbathe on the beach are the comings and goings of a busy port. Freighters, tugboats, cruise ships, pleasure craft and windsurfers all pass by.

The Royal Hudson, Canada's only regularly running steam locomotive, chugs through the park on its way to and from Squamish. The rumbling locomotive, billowing steam and blasting its whistle, always causes a commotion and everyone stops and waves. In the summer from Wed to Sun it rolls by at 10:45 AM and in the late afternoon.

You can stroll along the water another 1.6 km (1 mi.) to Dundarave Pier at the foot of 25th St. You must detour once or twice to the road behind the beach, but mostly you walk on the beach or the seawalk that runs from 18th to 24th St. It's an easy walk with the ocean on one side and beachside residences on the other. (Dogs are not allowed on the seawalk but have their own path alongside separated by a chain-link fence.) At the end, at 24th St., go two blocks north to Dundarave for lunch. **Capers** at 2496 Marine Dr. is an ex-

cellent casual restaurant serving healthy food. Return to Ambleside the way you came, rather than along the road.

From downtown, take any blue West Van bus, except #254 British Properties or #257 Horseshoe Bay Express, to the park.

CAPILANO RIVER REGIONAL PARK

This North Shore park is on a strip of land along the Capilano River, from Grouse Mountain to Burrard Inlet. The park is wide at the top and very narrow from the middle down. The river is tempestuous (it is used for whitewater kayaking) and has gouged a deep canyon along its course. Although park trails are well kept, the surroundings are dramatically wild: rapids, plunging cliffs and huge timber, all in a misty rain forest setting.

At the very top of the park is the Cleveland Dam, separating Capilano Lake from the river and regulating the city's water supply. Park your car at the dam. There is a view in either direction from the top of the dam. Maps of the trails are available here.

A salmon hatchery is a 10-minute hike down the path on the east side. It hatches about two million salmon eggs a year, and the outdoor displays and fish tanks are open at any time. The hatchery is interesting but is often packed since it's a popular spot on the bus tour route.

Hike the trails above Dog's Leg Pool (marked by a signpost) on either side of the river. Go down one side of the river, cross the footbridge after Dog's Leg Pool and take another path back up to the dam. Or you can hike all the way to the

Suspension bridges span canyons on the North Shore.

mouth of the river, about 7 km (4.5 mi.), but the width of the park is sometimes not much more than the width of the trail, which occasionally goes through residential neighbourhoods.

The Capilano Suspension Bridge, a well-publicized attraction, is a swinging wood and cable bridge hanging 69 m (230 ft.) over the canyon. Unfortunately, $5 is charged to walk across. While the bridge is spectacular and a good walk for people who don't want to negotiate the paths, the views from Capilano

River Park are free. If you must walk across a swinging bridge, there's no charge for the one at Lynn Canyon Park. See With the Kids (Day Trips).

From downtown, take the blue West Van bus #246 Lonsdale Quay/Highland. At Edgemont and Ridgewood, transfer to the #232 Grouse Mountain.

DR. SUN YAT-SEN CLASSICAL CHINESE GARDEN

This beautiful walled garden at 578 Carrall near Pender in Chinatown is the result of a co-operative effort by the people and governments of China and Canada, and it is a significant local treasure. The Ming Dynasty-style garden is the first classical Chinese garden to be built outside of China. In 1985, 52 artisans from China spent 13 months creating the garden, using only traditional methods and materials. Most of the materials came directly from China (donated by the Chinese government, as was the labour), and no power tools, nails or screws were used in the construction.

You leave the hustle and bustle of Chinatown when you enter this enclosed garden sanctuary. The emphasis here is very different from that of Western gardens — don't expect flashy displays of brightly coloured flowers. The garden is tiny, only 1300 m² (one-third of an acre), yet as you stroll through pavilions and over bridges and pebble-mosaic pavements, you'll feel a spaciousness

Dr. Sun Yat-sen Classical Chinese Garden

created by the careful arrangement of rocks, plants, water and architecture. The garden is characterized by both harmony and contrast: craggy evergreens and contorted limestone rocks suggest a miniature landscape contained within architecture boasting white-washed walls, curving tiled roofs, and shiny lacquered beams. Splashes of colour are provided by seasonal flowers and schools of goldfish in the pond.

To understand the symbolism of particular plants or architectural elements, join one of the guided tours that are offered several times a day.

The Dr. Sun Yat-sen Garden is the only classical Chinese garden outside of China.

Art exhibitions are usually on display in the main pavilion; a gift shop is located near the exit.

Hours are 10-8, May to Sept; winter hours are 10-6. Admission is $3.50 with discounts for children, seniors and families. Call 689-7133 for tour and cultural event information.

Beside the classical garden is Dr. Sun Yat-sen Park, which is a free public park. While somewhat less elegant than its neighbour, the park is also a walled enclosure that is a very pleasant place to stroll or rest. It features a Chinese pavilion, the Pavilion of Gratitude, set in a large pond, and walkways through local and Asian shrubbery. The park also has an entrance on Columbia at Keefer. Hours are the same as the classical garden.

GROUSE MOUNTAIN

This 1200-m (4000-ft.) mountain has one of the best views of the city and is a fun family outing or a quick escape from the city — nothing too strenuous and lots to keep the kids amused. Go on a clear day.

Capilano Rd. ends at the base of a tramway that takes you most of the way up Grouse Mountain. Grouse is in the centre of the row of mountains lining the North Shore. You can easily distinguish it at night because of the brilliant arc lights along the ski runs.

A 50-passenger gondola glides you up the steep mountainside, skirting tree-tops, with miles and miles of wilderness surrounding you. But over your shoulder is civilization – Vancouver and all of the Lower Mainland are laid out in miniature down below. In eight minutes you're 1100 m (3700 ft.) above sea level and near the top of Grouse Mountain. The skyride on the tram is $11 with discounts for seniors and children.

In winters when there is enough snow (artificial or otherwise), Grouse is a popular learn-to-ski spot. Don't be surprised to see ski runs and a complex of services when you get off the tram. Although the area immediately around the tram is civilized, there is plenty of wilderness. If you're after the wilds, take the Peak Chairlift ($3) up another 120 m (400 ft.).

On Grouse there are picnic tables and lawns where you can find a quiet place to sun-bathe or read. If you're feeling more energetic, hike the well-marked trail around Blue Grouse Lake in less than an hour. Guided three-hour hikes ($15) leave daily from the Peak Chairlift. Phone 984-0661 to reserve.

Helicopter tours of the mountains and lakes in back of Grouse Mountain leave from the lift at the top of the mountain. Costs range from $25 to $75 per person, depending on the length of the tour. Phone 683-4354.

Off to one side of the lift is an adventure playground made of logs and ropes with a kid-size suspension bridge and a hand rope-tow. Tiny ponies give rides around a corral.

The outdoor beer garden, right beside the Peak Chairlift, is the most pleasant place to eat or sit in the sun with a cold drink. As you might expect, the main restaurant has a knockout view. It's open for dinner only and is expensive, but dinner includes the cost of the tram.

Phone 986-6262 for more information and see also Sports (Skiing).

From downtown, take the SeaBus to North Vancouver and transfer to any bus going up Lonsdale, then transfer to a #232 Grouse Mountain which goes to the base of the tram. In the summer #236 also leaves from the SeaBus terminal on the North Shore for Grouse Mountain. Another way to get there from downtown by public transit is to catch the blue West Van bus #246 Lonsdale Quay/ Highland, which goes over Lions Gate Bridge. At Edgemont and Ridgewood, transfer to the #232 Grouse Mountain.

Heritage West, E. David McIntyre

JERICHO BEACH TO SPANISH BANKS

This chain of beaches is active with windsurfers, swimmers, sailors, picnickers and sunbathers but is over 3.2 km (2 mi.) long so is never congested.

Start your walk at the foot of Alma St. at Point Grey Rd., where there is a small wooden structure, the Hastings Sawmill Store Museum. Built in 1865, it is the oldest existing structure in Vancouver, one of a handful of buildings to survive the great fire that destroyed the city in 1886. Cross the small park and go past the Royal Vancouver Yacht Club, the Jericho Tennis Club and Brock House (a restaurant and senior citizen's centre). Jericho Beach Park is straight ahead. There are paths through the park and around a duck pond, or you can walk along the beach. The Department of National Defence once owned this land and built the huge concrete wharves where you can see the foundations of airplane hangars that were here until the mid-1970s. The Vancouver Hostel, the large white building set back from the beach, is a former RCAF barracks.

Jericho Sailing Centre is next, and then Locarno Beach and Spanish Banks. Directly across Burrard Inlet are the Point Atkinson Lighthouse and Bowen Island. Keep going around the farthest point, Point Grey, if you want to sun-bathe nude at Wreck Beach.

There are concession stands and washrooms en route.

From downtown take the #4 Fourth Ave. bus or the #7 Dunbar. Get off at Fourth and Alma, and walk four blocks north to the water.

LIGHTHOUSE PARK

Point Atkinson Lighthouse, built in 1912, sits at the tip of a wilderness area not far from the city centre. Park trails take you by mammoth Douglas-firs, rocky cliffs and smoothly sloping granite rocks that line the shore (a perfect sun-bathing and picnicking area). The water is not as warm as at the city beaches, but after you lie in the sun on hot granite rocks for two hours, it feels just right.

In the parking area is a map that shows the two main trails to the lighthouse. Follow one path down and the other back for a round trip of about 5 km (3 mi.) that takes less than an hour. At the point, you can see Point Grey and the University of British Columbia campus directly across Burrard Inlet; to the south-west across the Strait of Georgia, the mountain tops of Vancouver Island are visible on clear days.

Watch for bald eagles and their large ragged nests in the forks of tall trees. The largest Douglas-fir trees here, 61 m (200 ft.) tall and 500 years old, are the best example of virgin forest in the Lower Mainland. An

unusual tree, the arbutus, recognizable by its smooth, peeling, orange-red bark, is the only broadleaf evergreen in Canada.

You can hike in Lighthouse Park all year, even on wet days, but it is popular and can be crowded on summer weekends. Point Atkinson Lighthouse is a functioning lighthouse and is open to the public for tours on the hour, every hour, Wed to Sun, 11-5 during the summer.

To drive to the park, go west on Marine Dr. 10 km (6 mi.) past Park Royal Shopping Centre. On your left at Beacon Lane is a small wooden sign directing you a short distance south to Lighthouse Park.

From downtown, take the blue West Van bus #250 Horseshoe Bay.

LYNN CANYON PARK

See With the Kids (Day Trips).

Point Atkinson Lighthouse in Lighthouse Park, a good hiking and swimming spot with one of the last stands of virgin timber in the Lower Mainland.

MOUNT SEYMOUR PROVINCIAL PARK

Mount Seymour is convenient for your first taste of hiking in the mountains because it's close to the city and a road goes part of the way up the mountain. Even if you don't feel like hiking, drive up the 13-km (8-mi.) parkway for the magnificent views and a picnic. The best views are on the way down.

Most of the trails start at the top parking lot, which is at the end of the road. A chairlift, also at the top parking lot, takes you to the 1200-m (3950-ft.) level. It operates weekends in dry weather in summer and fall and every day during the ski season. The fee is $3 adult and $1.50 child.

A signboard at this parking lot shows the paths and their distances. Trail maps are available at the signboard and the park office. The main trails are well marked and

Nitobe Garden, a peaceful touch of Japan.

maintained but can get wet, so wear sturdy shoes for walking and hiking boots for the more rigorous trails. Snow is often around until June at this altitude, so the best time to hike is from July until November.

Remember that you are in very different climatic conditions than in the city. Clouds can move in quickly and reduce visibility dramatically. Pack a rain jacket, wear warmer clothes than you would down below and keep to the trails.

The Goldie Lake Trail is the shortest and easiest. A half-hour walk will take you around the lake, through a hemlock and cedar forest with some Douglas-firs. The largest trees in the area are 250 years old, and lower down on the slopes some of the Douglas-firs are 800 years old. Two other recommended trails are Dog Mountain and Mystery Lake; each takes about three hours for a fairly easy round trip.

On your way back down the mountain parkway, stop at the Vancouver lookout. A city map will help you to identify Lions Gate Bridge, Stanley Park, Simon Fraser University, the oil refineries of Ioco and Port Moody, etc.

On clear days distant points are visible. To the southeast, the state of Washington's Mount Baker rises majestic and alone out of the clouds. The range of mountains due south are the Olympics, also in Washington. (Another perfect view of these mountains is from Dallas Rd. in Victoria.) Towards the west are the American San Juan Islands, the Gulf Islands and Vancouver Island.

Please remember that you are not allowed to remove anything from a provincial park and that pets must be leashed at all times.

Winter facilities are downhill, cross-country, snowshoe trails, cafeteria, day lodge, ski and snow-shoe rentals, tobogganing and ski lessons. See also Sports (Skiing).

Access by car only, via the Second Narrows Bridge, Keith Rd. and Mt. Seymour Parkway.

Enter a sweet-smelling tropical world at the Bloedel Conservatory in Queen Elizabeth Park.

NITOBE MEMORIAL GARDEN/UBC BOTANICAL GARDEN

Nitobe Garden is a gem: Japanese landscaping objectives of harmony, balance and tranquillity are clearly met by the blend of indigenous fir and cedar with classical arrangements of shrubbery, waterfalls and small bridges over gurgling streams. The garden was started 25 years ago and has an established and serene feeling. There are no lawns and you must stay on the paths, but there are benches on which to pass a quiet moment.

The garden is a five-minute walk west along Marine Dr. from the Museum of Anthropology, so go to both; they are fine examples of Pacific Rim cultures. From mid-October until mid-March, Nitobe is open weekdays 10-3 and during the summer, daily from 10-6. There is a small admission fee.

The parking lot and entrance to the main botanical garden (228-4208) is about 1.6 km (1 mi.) down Marine Dr. beside Thunderbird Stadium. There are several parts to the botanical garden. The Asian Garden is on this side of Marine Drive and a pathway under the road leads you to the Food, Physick, Winter, Alpine and B.C. Native gardens. The Asian Garden is in a cedar forest where all the underbrush has been replanted with 400 varieties of rhododendrons, giant lilies, magnolias and other Asian plants. The Food Garden has a spectacular display of espaliered fruit trees. The Physick is a formal sixteenth century herb garden. In the Native Garden you can walk from a coastal rain forest into the semiarid environment of the interior of the province, all in 3 ha (8 acres).

From downtown, take the #10 or #4 UBC bus. When you get off the bus, check the campus map for exact directions. In the summer the #42 Spanish Banks/Chancellor takes you right to the garden from 10th Ave. and Alma.

QUEEN ELIZABETH PARK/BLOEDEL CONSERVATORY

Queen Elizabeth Park is off Cambie St., between 29th and 37th Ave. It is a spacious, beautifully landscaped park with ornamental flowerbeds, shrubs, trees and lots of grass. The park is on "Little Mountain," the highest spot in the city. At the top are two abandoned quarries that have been transformed into huge sunken rock gardens, full of blossoms, shrubbery, ponds and waterfalls at every level. It's a fabulous display of landscaping.

The park facilities include a restaurant with a smashing view, 20 tennis courts, pitch and putt, lawn bowling and picnic spots.

The big attraction at Queen E. Park is the Bloedel Conservatory at the top of the mountain. The building is a plexiglass dome, 42 m (140 ft.) in diameter, covering a small jungle and desert. It is a multisensory experience: you feel the heat and humidity, see and smell the lush tropical growths, watch a hundred brightly coloured tropical birds flying freely, and hear parrots squawking and a stream rippling beside you. A path takes you on a short circular walk and ends up in a desert. Guaranteed to cheer you up on a rainy day.

The conservatory is open every day but Christmas, 10-9 in summer and 10-5 in winter. Admission is $2.40 adult with discounts for seniors, children and families. Phone 872-5513 for more information.

From downtown, take the #15 Cambie bus.

REIFEL MIGRATORY BIRD SANCTUARY

The bird sanctuary is located on tidal marshes at the mouth of the south arm of the Fraser River, a 45-minute drive from downtown Vancouver. At the entrance you can buy a bag of

Canadian Wildlife Service, Environment Canada

seed and get a map of the 3.2 km (2 mi.) of paths, but then you are on your own. There are no guides or tours to tell what's what. Bring a bird book, binoculars and a warm jacket. Remember it is a refuge, not a tourist attraction, so the amenities are for the birds. Take the path on the dike to see the marshy flatlands of the delta – it's extraordinary country. A four-storey observation tower and several blinds (wooden shelters with viewing slats) give you views of birds you won't get anywhere else. The refuge is heavily inhabited in fall, winter and spring.

Reifel is not accessible by public transit. To get there, drive south on Highway 99. After the George Massey Tunnel take the first exit west to Ladner via River Road. Past Ladner, there is a turnoff to Westham Island where the Reifel Sanctuary is located.

Open daily 9-4 (and later according to the season). Admission $3 adult, $1 child or senior. For information call 946-6980.

SEYMOUR DEMONSTRATION FOREST

See Sightseeing (Special Interest Tours).

STANLEY PARK

City parks usually bring to mind lawns, picnic tables, civic memorials and a few stately old trees. These you'll find at Stanley Park, but it's the size, the wildness and the ocean that make this park one of a kind. Stanley Park is HUGE, and though the edges tend to be manicured, the dense forest in the centre is a natural area with only a few paths and a road cutting through. The ocean almost encircles the park, and along the shore are sandy beaches and a seawalk with spectacular views.

The aquarium and the zoo are the biggest attractions, but there are dozens of other activities for exercise, fun or a lazy time in the sun.

Stanley Park is one of the largest inner city parks on the continent and a mere 15-minute walk from downtown. Originally its 400 ha (1000 acres) were swamp and rain forest. The forest was a dense growth of Douglas-fir, cedar and hemlock; the swamp that filled the low-lying area is now Lost Lagoon. Several small Indian villages were once on the land, and Indian trails have become park paths.

The area was logged in the 1860s and later became a military reserve. With great foresight (considering the population of the city was then about 1000), one of the first city council resolutions in 1886 was to petition the federal government to turn the military reserve into park-

land. The park was opened in 1888, and an official ceremony with Governor General Lord Stanley took place a year later.

Getting there: The #19 Stanley Park bus starts from the East End and goes through downtown to the park entrance at the foot of Alberni St. The bottom of Alberni or Beach Ave. are the best entrances if you're on foot.

Stanley Park is a very popular spot. My advice is not to take your car into the park at all on summer weekends unless the weather is bad. If you do drive around the park, remember that vehicle traffic is one way, counterclockwise, so you must use the Georgia St. entrance. Park attractions are well marked.

ON FOOT IN STANLEY PARK

The park is a peninsula rimmed by a seawall and walkway all along the water. The walk introduces you to the ocean, the harbour and the forest, as well as spectacular views of the mountains and the city. All this in only the two hours that it takes to walk the 10.5 km (6.5 mi.).

If there is one thing you do in Vancouver, walk around the seawall. It gives you the best idea of what living in this city is like. Go on Sunday if you want to be part of the parade of joggers, cyclists, dogs (which must be leashed), anglers and the hundreds of people out strolling. Go on a weekday morning if you prefer quiet. The seawall path is clearly divided: one side for pedestrians and the other side for cyclists – but look out anyway.

Start at either English Bay or the park entrance at the foot of Georgia St. Walking east from the Georgia St.

entrance, you pass by the Vancouver Rowing Club and the Royal Vancouver Yacht Club. A causeway leads to the naval reserve training base called the HMCS *Discovery* (the last of the original military base), on Deadman's Island, a former Indian burial ground. Hallelujah Point is next, where Salvation Army revival meetings were once held.

On the water side of the path is a large metal box enclosing a cannon, the Nine O'Clock Gun. Beginning in 1890, the gun was sounded as a curfew to fishermen, ending weekend fishing. Now it is a time signal electronically fired at 9 PM.

At Brockton Point, once a pioneer cemetery where there is now a small lighthouse, you can see the Lions Gate Bridge ahead. The totem poles on your left were carved on the north coast of B.C. by the Kwakiutl and Haida in the late nineteenth cen-

Sandy beaches and a seawalk encircle Stanley Park.

tury. They are the initial stage of an Indian village reconstruction that was never completed. Two Indian canoes, each dug from a single cedar log, are under cover near the totems. Some dugout canoes have measured as long as 18 m (60 ft.).

Directly west of the totems is a grassy area used for cricket, field hockey and rugby.

Next is Brockton Oval, a cinder jogging track. Rugby and soccer games are held in the oval's centre, and there is a pavilion with washrooms, hot showers and a refreshment stand.

The seawall path passes the *Girl in a Wetsuit* statue sitting on a rock off the shore. You'll notice a similarity between it and the famous mermaid statue in Copenhagen Harbour. The sculptor who made

Activities of all sorts surface at Stanley Park in good weather.

this piece was inspired by the Danish work, but transformed it to show a more modern, adventurous and down-to-earth figure.

Next is a replica of the figurehead of the *Empress of Japan*, a deluxe steamship that once sailed to and from the Orient. At Mile 2, a children's water playground is on your right. On your left is Lumbermen's Arch, made of rough Douglas-fir and erected in 1952 to honour workers in the logging industry. This was the site of one of the original Indian villages.

Lions Gate Bridge marks the halfway point of the walk around the park. Slightly beyond is Prospect Point, named for the stunning viewpoint 60 m (200 ft.) above. The S.S. *Beaver*, a Hudson's Bay Company vessel and the first steamship on this coast, was wrecked in 1888 on the rocks here. Just past the point are cormorants nesting on the rock-faced cliff above the seawall.

The seawall turns to the southwest, and the view is of English Bay, Vanier Park with the conical-roofed planetarium and Kitsilano. Along this part of the seawall you will pass Siwash Rock, and you may run into anglers fishing for bottomfish. The first beach you encounter is called Third Beach.

The story of Siwash Rock is Vancouver's best-known Indian legend. Long ago, a young Indian was about to become a father. He decided to swim the waters of English Bay until he was utterly spotless so that his new-born could start life free from the father's sins. The gods were so impressed that they made him immortal in the form of Siwash Rock. Two smaller rocks, representing his

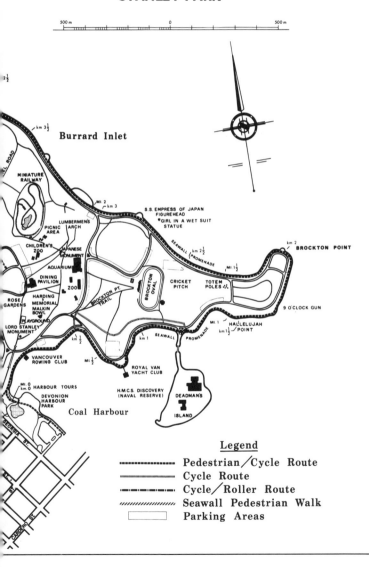

STANLEY PARK

Narrows

Burrard Inlet

MINIATURE RAILWAY

LUMBERMENS ARCH

PICNIC AREA

CHILDREN'S ZOO

JAPANESE MONUMENT

AQUARIUM

DINING PAVILION

ZOO

HARDING MEMORIAL MALKIN BOWL

ROSE GARDENS

PLAYGROUND

LORD STANLEY MONUMENT

BROCKTON PT TRAIL

BROCKTON OVAL

CRICKET PITCH

TOTEM POLES

S.S. EMPRESS OF JAPAN FIGUREHEAD

GIRL IN A WET SUIT STATUE

SEAWALL PROMENADE

BROCKTON POINT

9 O'CLOCK GUN

HALLELUJAH POINT

SEAWALL PROMENADE

VANCOUVER ROWING CLUB

ROYAL VAN YACHT CLUB

HARBOUR TOURS

DEVONION HARBOUR PARK

H.M.C.S. DISCOVERY (NAVAL RESERVE)

DEADMAN'S ISLAND

Coal Harbour

GEORGIA ST

CARDERO ST

Legend

- ⋯⋯⋯⋯ Pedestrian/Cycle Route
- ⋯⋯⋯⋯ Cycle Route
- ⋅—⋅—⋅— Cycle/Roller Route
- ⫽⫽⫽⫽⫽ Seawall Pedestrian Walk
- ☐ Parking Areas

THE STANLEY PARK FOREST

The forest is made up of western red cedar, spruce, hemlock and giant Douglas-fir, the largest tree native to Canada. The biggest Douglas-firs in the park were logged in the 1860s, and the trees that look so huge today were actually culls. The enormous stumps in the pitch and putt course give an indication of their size, about 60 m (200 ft.) high, equal to a 16-storey building! These trees are thought to be about 800 years old. On Cathedral Trail, which goes north from the west side of Lost Lagoon, are the Seven Sisters, huge first-growth cedars that are perfect examples of trees used by the Northwest Coast Indians for totem poles.

Bigleaf maple   Red alder   White birch   Lodgepole pine   Black cottonwood   Grand fir   Western hemlock   Douglas-fir   Western red cedar

Canadian Forestry Service

wife and son, are up in woods overlooking Siwash Rock.

If you're hungry and prefer Eggs Benedict to fish and chips, walk up to the lovely Teahouse Restaurant at Ferguson Point for lunch. About 800 m (½ mi.) past the point is the swimming pool at Second Beach, used for roller skating in the winter.

If you've had enough walking and want to return to your starting point, cross the road behind the pool and head back to Lost Lagoon. Waterbirds on the lagoon include Canada Geese, trumpeter swans, mallards, wood ducks and coots. Pictures on a signboard on the west side of the lagoon help identify them. Lost Lagoon, originally a tidal inlet, was so named by Indian poet Pauline Johnson because the water often disappeared at low tide. The main road through the park is actually a causeway that acts as a dike to keep the lagoon at a constant level.

If you want to continue along the water, the seawall extends for about 1.6 km (1 mi.) outside Stanley Park. Or you can take advantage of the sports facilities between Second Beach and the lagoon. There is an inviting pitch and putt course and putting greens where you can rent equipment. (This is one of the best spots to see the remains of the ancient fir trees that were logged in the 1870s; you can clearly see the springboard holes in the stumps.) The Lawn Bowling Club is open to visitors, and there are tennis courts and shuffleboard. The excellent Beach House Restaurant by the

PAULINE JOHNSON (1862 – 1913)

This legendary Indian "princess" was born in Ontario, the daughter of a Mohawk chief and an Englishwoman. She gained acclaim for her poems of Indian life and spent much time touring North America and England giving poetry readings. She settled in Vancouver and from Chief Capilano learned local Indian legends, which she retold in a collection entitled *Legends of Vancouver.*

She often went canoeing at Lost Lagoon in Stanley Park, and her ashes are buried near Ferguson Point where there is a memorial to her. She is best known for her poem "The Song My Paddle Sings" and a collection of poems entitled *Flint and Feather.*

tennis courts has both casual and more elegant dining rooms plus outdoor decks for lunch and dinner.

In this same area, between the road and seawall, is a playground with an old fire engine for children to scramble over. The tarmac by the playground is used for ethnic dancing or square-dancing on summer evenings, and everyone is welcome to join in. On weekday afternoons in July and August (weather permitting), the Vancouver police run a Kid's Traffic School here for children five to eight years old. Children drive pedal cars through "streets" and learn about intersections, crosswalks, traffic lights, other cars, etc. It starts at 2 PM; show up early because it's first come, first served.

Another hub of activity is by the zoo, which is modest but nevertheless the most visited attraction in the park. There is no admission, so stroll through to see the frisky otters, seals and penguins, the crowd favourites.

The Children's Zoo, slightly west, is heaven for small children. Most of the animals are in a large open area and are free to move around to-gether and with the children. All the usual barnyard animals are there, eager to be petted.

Beside the Children's Zoo are pony rides and a miniature steam locomotive that takes children and adults on a ride through the forest. Because it's the hit of the park, there are often line-ups, so try early in the day. The train runs every day in the summer and on dry weekends in the winter. Adults pay $1.70 and children and seniors 85¢. The pony rides operate in the summer only and cost $1.

Directly south of the children's zoo is a cafeteria-style Dining Pavilion with a view of 275 varieties of roses and an outdoor theatre, Malkin Bowl.

GETTING AROUND THE PARK

Take advantage of the #52 Around the Park bus that runs around Park Dr. on Sat, Sun and holidays during the summer. Ask for a transfer (good for 90 minutes) when you board the bus, so you can get on and off as often as you like for one fare.

Nothing beats walking in the park, but one stupendous sight, the view from Prospect Point, is hard to get to on foot. The lookout there is perched on the top of the cliff, and the view of the North Shore is unforgettable. The mountain directly in line with Lions Gate Bridge is Grouse Mountain, recognizable by the ski runs. The two scraggy peaks just west of Grouse are called The Lions. (They do look more like lions from an easterly perspective.) These peaks were named by Pauline Johnson since they reminded her of the lions in Trafalgar Square. Because The Lions are crouched at the narrow entrance of the harbour, the expression "Lions Gate" came to be. The grassy area at the foot of the far side of the bridge is the Capilano Indian Reserve. (The Capilano Indians also own the land on which Park Royal Shopping Centre is built.)

A very sleek restaurant at Pros-

Children love the old fire engine at Ceperley Playground in Stanley Park.

pect Point has a huge sundeck and glass-walled dining area looking over the harbour and the North Shore mountains.

VANCOUVER AQUARIUM

The Vancouver Aquarium, Canada's largest, has over 6000 marine species.

Near the entrance is a marine life exhibit called the B.C. Hall of Fishes. Tanks depict specific coastal regions, such as Vancouver shores, the west coast of Vancouver Island and the rocky bottom of the Strait of Georgia. The Rufe Gibbs Hall displays fish and plant life from the lakes and rivers of B.C. There is also a fascinating display about salmon, showing their life stages and spawning habits.

The MacMillan Gallery presents tropical marine life around the world:

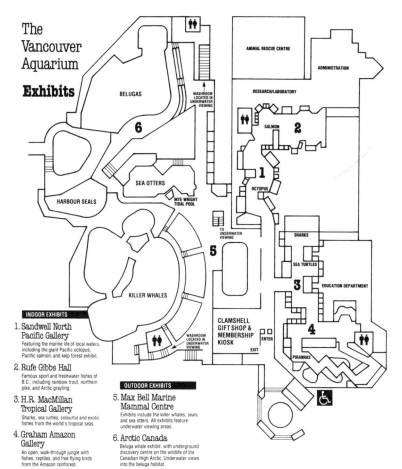

The Vancouver Aquarium

Exhibits

BELUGAS

ANIMAL RESCUE CENTRE

ADMINISTRATION

WASHROOM LOCATED IN UNDERWATER VIEWING

RESEARCH/LABORATORY

6

SALMON 2

1

OCTOPUS

SEA OTTERS

MYE WRIGHT TIDAL POOL

HARBOUR SEALS

TO UNDERWATER VIEWING

SHARKS

5

SEA TURTLES

3

EDUCATION DEPARTMENT

KILLER WHALES

CLAMSHELL GIFT SHOP & MEMBERSHIP KIOSK

ENTER

4

WASHROOM LOCATED IN UNDERWATER VIEWING

EXIT

PIRANHAS

INDOOR EXHIBITS

1. Sandwell North Pacific Gallery
Featuring the marine life of local waters, including the giant Pacific octopus, Pacific salmon, and kelp forest exhibit.

2. Rufe Gibbs Hall
Famous sport and freshwater fishes of B.C., including rainbow trout, northern pike, and Arctic grayling.

3. H.R. MacMillan Tropical Gallery
Sharks, sea turtles, colourful and exotic fishes from the world's tropical seas.

4. Graham Amazon Gallery
An open, walk-through jungle with fishes, reptiles, and free flying birds from the Amazon rainforest.

OUTDOOR EXHIBITS

5. Max Bell Marine Mammal Centre
Exhibits include the killer whales, seals and sea otters. All exhibits feature underwater viewing areas.

6. Arctic Canada
Beluga whale exhibit: with underground discovery centre on the wildlife of the Canadian High Arctic. Underwater views into the beluga habitat.

Vancouver Aquarium

sharks, sawfish, giant turtles and magnificently coloured tropical fish. From here you enter the Amazon River exhibit and are surrounded by nature as it is on the banks of the Amazon. Tropical birds fly freely, jungle plants grow around crocodile pools, and tropical bugs (such as giant cockroaches, scorpions and praying mantises) crawl around behind glass. You'll see boa constrictors, poisonous frogs and tanks of

piranhas. It's a short but gripping walk.

The aquarium has outdoor pools for the beluga and killer whales, with underwater viewing windows. Smaller tanks hold playful seals and otters.

Feeding times and show times for the whales are posted at the door. The whale shows focus on learning about these magnificent creatures — you won't see beach balls bounced

Vancouver Aquarium/Finn larsen

off noses. Tours start at 1:15. Everything is included in the price of admission. (Everything, that is, but a stop at the Clamshell Gift Shop, the best spot in town for souvenirs.)

The Vancouver Aquarium (682-1118) is a nonprofit society. It receives no public funding and so admission rates are a little steep: $7 but with discounts for seniors and children. However, the new beluga and harbour seal pools were designed so they are visible from outside the aquarium. Open daily year-round. Hours from mid-June to early Sept are 9:30-9; mid-Oct to mid-March, 10-5 and the rest of the year till 6. Call for hours and show times.

PACIFIC SPIRIT PARK
(University Endowment Lands)

The University Endowment Lands (UEL) were originally a 1200-ha (3000-acre) parcel of land given to the University of British Columbia in 1923 to be sold as the university needed revenue. Because of the

The whale shows at the Vancouver Aquarium are not just a show, but an education too.

Depression and small wartime demand, most of the land remained intact except for logging operations done before the turn of the century. The existing forest is 100 years old, but narrow strips of the original 500-year-old forest can be seen at the very tip of Point Grey and on the southern cliffs over the Fraser River.

The Endowment Lands now consist of 1000 ha (2500 acres), of which almost 800 ha (2000 acres) is Pacific Spirit Park. This is considerably larger than Stanley Park, but by comparison is used by a miniscule number of people. Even though the 58 km (33 mi.) of trails are perfect for hiking, jogging and horseback riding, you can meander through the forest and not encounter a soul. No need to worry about getting lost; the park is cut by three major roads that provide landmarks.

The wildlife is varied but elusive.

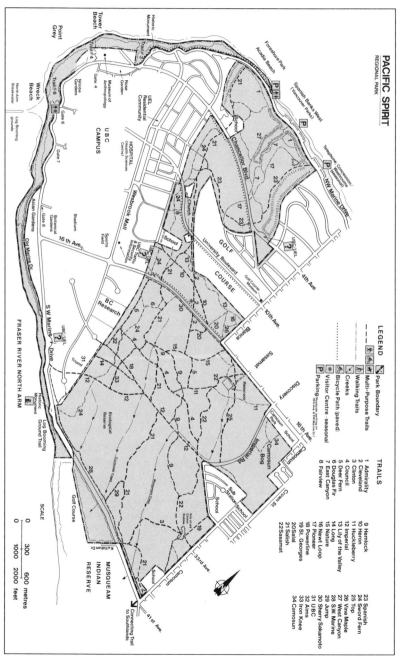

A WALK IN THE FOREST

Although remnants of original forest, in the form of stumps, are in many of parks, there is virtually no old growth in the Lower Mainland. You may see a solitary tree left because it was not choice material or because it grew on too steep a slope. While second growth is not as dramatic, some trees are now 130 years old and are quite impressive.

Because 90 per cent of B.C. is covered in trees, you must have a walk in the forest to experience the real west coast. Here are suggestions for accessible trails that are easy family walks unless otherwise noted:

1. **Pacific Spirit Park, Swordfern Trail.** The trailhead is across S.W. Marine Drive from the viewpoint and historic monument. Less than an hour for the return trip. See Pacific Spirit Park.

2. **UBC Botanical Garden, B.C. Native Garden.** This is a pretty tame walk but it gives you the idea. Half an hour for the return trip. Small admission charge for the garden. See UBC Botanical Garden.

3. **Cypress Falls Municipal Park**, West Vancouver. Most locals have never heard of this park or confuse it with Cypress Provincial Park. West Vancouver is protective about this gem – no sign even indicates you've arrived. Find Woodgreen Place on a map; the park is at its end. Take the trail heading uphill at the back of the playing field. It's an easy 10-minute walk to the lower falls and the foot bridge. Then the path climbs for about 15 minutes to a logging road. Turn left on the logging road, cross McCrady Bridge and take the first marked trail to the left. Take the next trail branching off to the left and it will soon lead to a spectacular view of the upper falls in extremely lush moss-covered forest. Other trails go off to the right but keep the creek

close by on your left and you will end up back at the lower falls. Some seniors and small children would find the trail above the lower falls a bit ambitious. An hour and a half for the return trip.

4. **Capilano River Regional Park.** Start at the top and hike down on the west side of the river to Marine Drive. You can leave your car at the top and take a bus back up Capilano Road. Two hours one way. See Capilano River Regional Park.

5. **Lighthouse Park.** The Valley Trail is parallel to the road from the parking lot to the lighthouse on the east side. One hour return. See Lighthouse Park.

6. **Buntzen Lake**. It's almost an hour's drive to the lake from downtown but this small lake in the midst of the forest and mountains is beautiful. From the picnic area take the interpretative loop trail on a half-hour walk. The park is very busy on weekends, go midweek. Take Hastings St. to the Barnet Hwy., and go through Port Moody to loco. Watch for signs to Anmore and Buntzen Lake.

7. **Stanley Park, Merilees Trail.** The trail starts on the water side of Park Drive just past Prospect Point and parallels the shoreline on the cliff above the seawall. You'll come across the mammoth 500-year-old cedar that was featured in *National Geographic*. (See map in Stanley Park section.) Less than an hour return.

8. **Lynn Headwaters, Lynn Loop Trail.** As in all Greater Vancouver Regional District Parks, trails are very well maintained and marked and maps are available at the park entrance. Walk the loop trail in a counter-clockwise direction so you are going downhill at the steep section. Don't miss the short detour to the viewpoint (it's marked) at the top of the loop. Some sections may be a bit steep for seniors and small children. Two hours return.

Squirrels, chipmunks, voles, moles, bats, weasels, mink, raccoons, otters, foxes, skunks, coyotes and snow-shoe hares all live in the park, but you will only see them if you are a keen observer. Bald eagles are easy to spot soaring overhead or perched on tree tops.

A visitors' information centre and nature house is on 16th Ave. midway through the park. Naturalists often lead walks through the forest; phone 224-5739 for the schedule.

If you are striking out on your own, you will find Pacific Spirit to be a welcoming place with fairly easy trails. Trail #24, Swordfern, in the southwest corner of the park is recommended as being a typical B.C. coastal forest with cedar and fir trees. The trail starts from S.W. Marine Dr. opposite the viewpoint and historical monument (marking Simon Fraser's 1808 trip down the Fraser River). On the same side of the street as the monument, another trail, a steep trail, descends to the Fraser and the largest log booms grounds in Canada. Here you will pass a remnant of old-growth forest .

Another section of the park recommended for hiking is the north section above Spanish Banks. The East and West Canyon trails, #7 and #27, form a convenient loop. These trails are through alder and broad-leaf maple and have a gentle grade down to the water making the return walk a little strenuous. Start from Chancellor Blvd.

In the northeast corner is the Camosun Bog, the oldest bog in the Lower Mainland. Because of its special nature the parks people are focussing on this area, adding a boardwalk and interpretative signs.

Pacific Spirit Park is simply a refreshing walk in the forest, a chance to get away from the city, just 20 minutes by car from downtown traffic at Georgia and Granville.

From downtown, take the #10 or #4 UBC bus.

VanDUSEN BOTANICAL GARDENS

Originally a 22-ha (55-acre) golf course, VanDusen (at Oak and 37th) is now the largest botanical garden in the city. Tranquillity envelopes you as you wander around the ponds, lawns and hundreds of varieties of trees, shrubs and flowers. The rhododendron walk, with one of the best collections in Canada, is overwhelming in its prime in May. All of the plants are well labelled and are arranged by species and place of origin for those interested in horticulture; for the rest of us, it's an enjoyable stroll.

The hedge maze at the far end of the park is baffling and fun. (Don't worry about the kids, it will only keep them guessing for a few minutes; and it's shoulder height so you can see out even if you can't get out.) There is a restaurant with an open-air deck at the entrance.

Summer hours are 10-9 and winter hours are 10-4, seven days a week. Phone 266-7194. Guided tours are offered every day at 2, June through Aug, weather permitting. Admission $4 with discounts for seniors, children and families.

From downtown, take the #17 Oak bus to the park.

MUSEUMS/ART GALLERIES

MAJOR MUSEUMS 126
Museum of Anthropology, Vanier Park Museum Complex
(Vancouver Museum, H.R. MacMillan Planetarium, Maritime Museum,
Gordon Southam Observatory, City of Vancouver Archives), Science World,
Vancouver Aquarium

OTHER MUSEUMS 132

PUBLIC ART GALLERIES 134
Vancouver Art Gallery, Other Public Galleries

PRIVATE GALLERIES 137
Major Galleries, Artist-Run Galleries, Photo Galleries,
Indian or Inuit (Eskimo) Galleries, Print Galleries, Craft Galleries

Museum of Anthropology

Totem poles in the Great Hall of the Museum of Anthropology.

MAJOR MUSEUMS

Museum of Anthropology
6393 N.W. Marine,
University of British Columbia
228-3825

If you visit only one museum in Vancouver, make it the Museum of Anthropology. It is stunning. The museum houses artifacts from all over the world but focusses on the arts of the Indians of the Pacific Northwest. The award-winning building, designed by Arthur Erickson, was inspired by Northwest Coast Indian cedar houses. Apart from what it contains, the building is an architectural stroke of brilliance.

Once you walk through the carved front doors and into the Great Hall, you will be awestruck by the monumental totem poles and carvings. You can almost feel the power of the carved spirits depicted on the poles in the form of ravens, bears, frogs and humans. At the back of the Great Hall is a 13.5-m (45-ft.) glass wall that looks out on the unspoiled cliffs of Point Grey, boasting more totem poles, traditional Haida houses, Burrard Inlet and a backdrop of mountains.

Other Northwest Coast Indian works on display include exquisite gold and silver jewellery, intricate argillite sculptures (argillite is a jet-black slate found in British Columbia's Queen Charlotte Islands), bone carvings, baskets and a collection of amazing ceremonial masks.

Also featured is contemporary Indian art such as the massive sculpture *The Raven and the First Men,* designed and carved by Bill Reid. Finished in 1980, it was created from a block of 106 laminated yellow cedar beams and took five people more than three years to complete. The carving is an enormous, menacing, smirking raven perched on a partially open clamshell. Teeming inside the shell are human figures struggling either to emerge or retreat. These humans are unsure, terrified and awed; it is the Haida legend of the beginning of man.

The Museum of Anthropology's permanent collection is not locked away as in other museums, but is totally accessible. Visitors are encouraged to pull out the glass-topped storage drawers.

Join a guided walk introducing the collection (phone 228-5087 for times) or use the excellent booklet called *Guide to the UBC Museum of Anthropology.* You should walk to the Great Hall and experience the totem poles for a few minutes before doing anything else.

An impressive new ceramics wing has just opened. It features over 600 pieces, mainly European ceramics from the 15th to 19th century.

A variety of special events takes place throughout the year, often on Sunday afternoons. There are also special changing exhibits, so the museum definitely warrants return visits.

The museum is on the University of British Columbia campus. To drive there, go west on Fourth Ave. until the road forks at N.W. Marine

The Raven and the First Men, a carving by Bill Reid in the Museum of Anthropology, depicts the Haida legend of the beginning of man.

Dr. Take the right and follow it until you are on the campus; then look out for the museum, which is on the north side of the road. Or take the #4 or #10 UBC bus, which will let you off in the middle of the university campus; the museum is a 10-minute walk northward (check the map at the bus stop when you get off). Admission $4 with discounts for children, seniors and families. Closed Mon, free on Tues. Hours are Tues, 11-9; Wed to Sun, 11-5.

VANIER PARK/KITSILANO BEACH

1 Kitsilano Showboat
2 Kitsilano Pool (Outdoor)
3 Maritime Museum
4 Granville Island Ferry
5 Vancouver Museum/
   H. R. MacMillan Planetarium
6 Vancouver City Archives
7 Southam Observatory
8 Academy of Music
9 Coast Guard Station
Ⓟ Parking
--- Path

0 ———— 500 m
0 ———— 1500 ft.

ENGLISH BAY

Granville Island Ferry

Hadden Park

Public Dock

VANIER PARK

FALSE CREEK

Seaforth Park

To Granville Island

Ogden
McNicoll 1000
Whyte
Creelman 1200
Greer 1400
1600
1800
2000

Point Grey Road
Park
Cornwall
Kitsilano Park
York
West First
West Second
West Third
West Fourth
West Fifth

Macdonald
Stephens
Trafalgar
Larch
Balsam
Vine
Yew
Arbutus
Maple
Cypress
Burrard
Pine
Chestnut
Fir

Seawall

Shopping Area

West Fourth Ave. Shopping Area

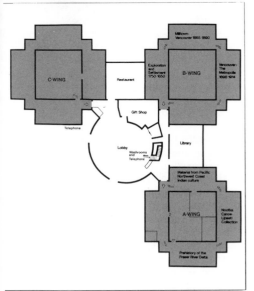

Vancouver Museum and Planetarium Association

VANIER PARK MUSEUM COMPLEX

Vanier Park is on the waterfront by the Kitsilano end of the Burrard St. Bridge and is the home of the Vancouver Museum, along with the H.R. MacMillan Planetarium, the Gordon Southam Observatory, the Maritime Museum and the City of Vancouver Archives.

The museum and planetarium are in the same building, a distinctive landmark because of its conical roof. The roof shape is patterned after the conical, woven cedar bark hats worn by the Northwest Coast Indians, a reminder that the land surrounding the museum was once the site of an Indian village. Outside the building is a huge, stainless steel sculpture of a crab, which, according to Indian legend, guards the entrance of the harbour.

Vancouver Museum
736-7736
A visit to the Vancouver Museum (formerly the Centennial Museum) is an easy way to learn about Vancouver's past. Exhibits vividly depict the city's story from the time of exploration to the beginning of the First World War. Among other things, you will see a full-size trading post, the steerage section of an immigrant ship, a car from the first CPR passenger train to arrive in 1887 and a good selection of Pacific Northwest Indian artifacts.

The temporary exhibits tend to be small but delightful; two recent shows were on the art of Japanese packaging and Royal commemoratives.

The museum is open seven days a week in July and Aug, closed Mon the rest of the year except holidays; hours are 10-9 in the summer and 10-5 in the winter. Admission to the Vancouver Museum *only* is $6 with

The Vancouver Museum and Planetarium building, with its distinctive conical roof, in Vanier Park.

discounts for children, seniors and families. Admission to both Vancouver and Maritime museums is $7 with discounts for the same groups.

H.R. MacMillan Planetarium
736-3656
The planetarium explores the universe with shows each afternoon and evening. Evening shows are not recommended for children under eight.

A rock music light show is featured every evening. Arrive before showtime for any performance, as no latecomers are admitted.

Closed Mon in winter. Admission to the astronomy show is $4.25 with discounts for children, seniors and families. Admission to the rock music show is $5.50 with no discounts.

The deck of the *St. Roch*, the first ship to travel the Northwest Passage from west to east. A National Historic Site, the ship is housed in the Maritime Museum.

forms, photographs, models, engines and navigating equipment.

Many special events take place at the Maritime Museum, particularly in the summer. Restored heritage vessels are moored at the museum wharf, called Heritage Harbour.

Granville Island Ferries runs between the Aquatic Centre and the Maritime Museum wharf daily in summer, and on weekends the rest of the year; call 684-7781.

Open daily from 10-5 except Wed night when the museum is open til 9 PM and is free. Admission $3 with discounts for children, seniors and families. See Vancouver Museum for special rates for both Vancouver and Maritime museums.

Maritime Museum
737-2211

The Maritime Museum, located behind the Vancouver Museum, is easy to spot because of the tall Kwakiutl totem pole that stands before it.

The highlight of the museum is the completely restored *St. Roch,* a two-masted schooner that was the first ship to sail the treacherous Northwest Passage from west to east. (It took the captain and eight crew members over two years to complete the voyage.) The *St. Roch* was also the first ship to circumnavigate North America. It is now an official National Historic Site, and there are guided tours throughout the day.

Other exhibits tell the story of Vancouver as a port and of sea-based activities in this part of the world. Galleries display naval uni-

Gordon Southam Observatory
738-2855

The observatory is the small domed building beside the museum-planetarium complex and is open for public star-gazing. An astronomer explains how the new 50-cm (19.5-in.) reflector telescope works and how to use it. If you have a 35-mm SLR camera, phone for details on their "shoot the moon" program – you can take your own pictures of the moon on clear, full moon evenings.

Open every evening during the summer. During the winter, open Fri, Sat and Sun evenings when the sky is clear. Call ahead to check. Admission is free.

City of Vancouver Archives
736-8561

Behind the Southam Observatory is a building that looks like a concrete bunker. It is the City of Vancouver Archives. Walking into this building is like entering another world. The atmosphere is positively serene – it must be the most tranquil government office in the city. If you're fed up with traffic and crowds, it's the place to spend a few hours poring over local history.

In the main foyer is a changing exhibit, usually of wonderful old Vancouver photographs, and an automated slide show presents recent photo acquisitions. The archives house public records from

Science World is housed in a sparkling geodesic dome.

City Hall, private papers of historical value, maps, newspaper clippings, books, and most interesting of all, historical photographs. Everything is indexed if you're looking for something specific, but the photographs are displayed in binders that you can leaf through for hours.

Open Mon to Fri, 9:30-5:30.

Science World
1455 Quebec,
near Terminal and Main
687-7832

This is a fun, hands-on museum inside a geodesic dome. Many "please

The blacksmith's shop at Burnaby Village Museum, a reconstruction of a small B.C. town at the turn of the century.

touch" exhibits are intended to help both kids and adults understand science while having a whole lot of fun. Demonstrations and films on gravity, bubbles, lasers, etc., take place each day. In the Search Gallery which is devoted to natural history, you can crawl into a beaver lodge, watch a functioning beehive and see tree roots suspended from the ceiling. The Omnimax Theatre, the world's largest domed screen, may be showing a film on the Earth from space, seasons, or wings. The gift shop is sensational.

Admission to just the museum is $7 for adults with discounts for seniors and children; admission to the museum and Omnimax is $10 for adults. Located across from the Main Street SkyTrain Station. Summer hours are daily 10-6 and Fri and Sat until 9. Winter hours are 10-5 and Sat until 9. The museum can get very busy – if you can't take crowds, avoid Sat and Sun afternoons.

Vancouver Aquarium
See Parks/Beaches/Gardens (Stanley Park).

OTHER MUSEUMS

Burnaby Village Museum
6501 Deer Lake, Burnaby
293-6501
This museum is a 2-ha (5-acre) display of a typical, turn-of-the century community. The reconstructed village consists of a barber shop, church, dentist's office, pharmacy, Chinese herbalist, general

store, schoolhouse, log cabin, photographer, the oldest steam engine in B.C. and so on. The print shop, sawmill, blacksmith shop and ice cream parlour are operational; throughout the village, guides in period costume explain the various goings-on. A miniature train, the Burnaby Central Railway, takes children for a ride around the village. Old-time crafts and baking are demonstrated throughout the year, and the village puts on special seasonal activities.

In the summer a vaudeville show is staged every Sunday afternoon. Statutory holidays are usually special event days featuring a variety of family entertainment and activities. You are welcome to bring along a packed lunch in the summertime, as picnic facilities are available. Christmas is one of the best times, with strolling carollers and musicians, haywagon rides, and traditional decorations and crafts.

Getting there: From downtown, it is a 20-minute drive. Take the Trans-Canada Highway #1 or #401 eastbound and exit at Kensington.

Open 11-4:30, seven days a week from mid-March to mid-Oct, and mid-Nov to mid-Dec. From mid-Oct to mid-Nov it is open Sun only. Closed throughout Jan and Feb. Admission $4 adult with discounts for children, seniors and families.

B.C. Sports Hall of Fame and Museum
BC Place Stadium
687-5520
The history and development of 68 sports are displayed at the Sports Hall of Fame. There are photos, Olympic medals, trophies, personal mementoes and equipment from all the big-name athletes and events in B.C. A permanent exhibit called "B.C. at the Olympics" features B.C. athletes who have won Olympic medals from 1912 to the present.

The museum will reopen late 1991 inside the stadium.

Hastings Sawmill Store Museum
Jericho Park, 4th and Alma
228-1213
The museum is like a country town museum with lots of artifacts – photos, Indian baskets, early clothing and furniture, all jumbled together. Worth a stop if you're in Jericho Park. Open seven days a week from June to mid-Sept, 10-4; winter hours are Sat and Sun afternoons only, from 1-4. Admission by donation.

B.C. Transportation Museum
17790 No. 10 Highway, Cloverdale
574-4191
The largest transportation collection in the Pacific Northwest has over 100 cars and trucks (including John Lennon's famous Rolls-Royce), as well as railway artifacts and a few airplanes, all housed in 5400 m² (60,000 sq. ft.) of covered exhibition space.

Open 10-5 seven days a week from mid-May to Labour Day; closed Mon the rest of the year. Admission is $3 with discounts for children, seniors and families.

Beatles Museum
Collector's RPM Record Store
456 Seymour near Pender
685-8841
The Beatles Museum is a memory lane, full of every record, poster and

marketing gimmick ever associated with the Beatles. It's amazing how much stuff you recognize (the pink plastic Beatles wallet I had forgotten I once owned is now a museum piece). Admission is free.

Open Mon to Wed and Sat, 10-6; Thurs and Fri till 9, and Sun noon-5.

Vancouver Police Museum
240 E. Cordova and Main
665-3346
The history of the Vancouver Police Department is told through displays of gambling, weapons, counterfeit money and notorious Vancouver crooks. Open seven days a week from 11:30 - 4:30; admission is free (donations appreciated).

Buddhist Temple
9160 Steveston Highway, Richmond
274-2822
An impressive example of Chinese architecture that houses an active Buddhist temple. Leave your shoes outside to enjoy the traditional artwork in the heavily incensed interior. Open daily from 10-5; no admission charge.

Canadian Museum of Flight and Transportation
13527 Crescent Rd., Surrey
535-1115
A collection of vintage aircraft including a Tiger Moth, a CF-100 Canuck and a Flying Banana helicopter, plus a technical library and gift shop. The aircraft are on display from mid-May to late Oct, 9-4 seven days a week; the library and gift shop are open all year. Admission is $2 with discounts for children and seniors. An annual open house (free admission) is held the third weekend of June.

PUBLIC ART GALLERIES

Information on current shows at both public and private galleries is in *Vancouver Magazine,* the *West Ender,* and the What's On column of Thursday's *Vancouver Sun* and Friday's *Province.*

Vancouver Art Gallery
750 Hornby, Robson Square
682-5621
Vancouver's old courthouse, built in 1911, was transformed into the new Vancouver Art Gallery in 1983, completing the Robson Square complex. The architect of the courthouse, Francis Rattenbury, also designed the Empress Hotel and the Legislative Buildings in Victoria.

The former elegance of the courthouse remains: ornate plaster work and a glass-topped dome over a majestic rotunda that showers the centre of all four floors with natural light. The neoclassical style was popular for administrative buildings because of the weight and authority lent to them by Greek and Roman architectural features in the form of imposing columns, domes and entries guarded by lions. The main entrance has been moved to Robson St., but do look at the stately old entrance and square on the Georgia St. side.

Off the main lobby is the gift shop, the children's gallery and access to the restaurant upstairs. Past the children's gallery is a stairway up to the gallery library in the former law library. You can feel the tranquil atmosphere of the old law chambers here in the annex, with its quiet marble halls and heavy wooden doors. The former Supreme Court Chamber is largely intact as the gallery boardroom. The refer-

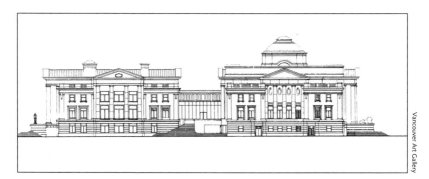

Vancouver Art Gallery

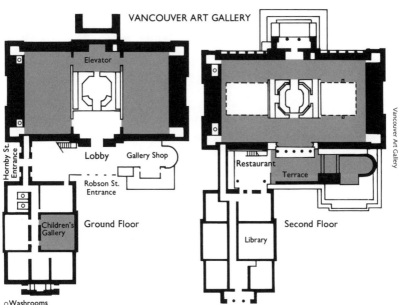

VANCOUVER ART GALLERY

Vancouver Art Gallery

o Washrooms
Third and Fourth Floors Not Shown

ence-only library is well stocked with art books, over a hundred different art magazines, files on contemporary Canadian artists and gallery catalogues from all over the world.

Be sure to see the permanent gallery showing the work of Emily Carr, British Columbia's best-known artist. Her paintings from the early part of this century depict the power and mystery of nature in the form of looming forests, skies, totem poles and Indian villages.

When you reach the fourth and top floor of the gallery, take a look at the details on the walls and ceiling. In the original courthouse there was no fourth floor; it was introduced in a high-ceiling area to provide an intimate space for smaller art pieces.

The Vancouver Art Gallery has imposing appearance because it was once the courthouse.

The effect is somewhat bizarre, as you can now see architectural details close up rather than from the intended vantage point of the floor below.

The gallery is closed on Tues, but the restaurant and gift shop stay open. The gallery is open 10-5 on Mon, Wed, Fri, Sat; 10-9 on Thurs; noon-5 on Sun. Docent tours of exhibitions are given twice daily on weekdays. Admission $3.50 with discounts for children and seniors. Free on Thurs after 5 PM. The Gallery Cafe has the best outdoor seating downtown.

Burnaby Art Gallery
6344 Deer Lake Ave., Burnaby
291-9441

Charles H. Scott Gallery
Emily Carr College of Art
and Design
1399 Johnston, Granville Island
687-2345

Simon Fraser University
Art Gallery
Burnaby Mountain, Burnaby
291-4266

Surrey Art Gallery
13750 – 88th Ave., Surrey
596-7461

University of British Columbia
Fine Arts Gallery

Main Library, UBC
228-2759

MAJOR PRIVATE GALLERIES

Bau-Xi Gallery
3045 Granville and 14th
733-7011

Buschlen/Mowatt
111 – 1445 W. Georgia near Nicola
682-1234

Crown Gallery
562 Beatty near Dunsmuir
684-5407

Diane Farris Gallery
1565 W. 7th near Granville
737-2629

Equinox Gallery
2321 Granville and 7th
736-2405

Heffel Gallery
2247 Granville and 6th
732-6505

ARTIST-RUN GALLERIES

Contemporary Art Gallery
555 Hamilton near Dunsmuir
681-2700

Or Gallery
314 W. Hastings near Hamilton
683-7395

Pitt International Galleries (PIG)
36 Powell and Carrall
681-6740

Students' Concourse Gallery
Emily Carr College of Art
and Design
1399 Johnston, Granville Island
687-2345

Western Front
303 E. 8th near Kingsway
876-9343
Art exhibitions at the Front Gallery;
a small theatre hosts performance
art, poetry readings, jazz and new
music events.

Women in Focus
849 Beatty near Smithe
682-5848

PHOTO GALLERIES

Presentation House
333 Chesterfield, North Van
986-1351

INDIAN OR INUIT (ESKIMO) GALLERIES

Images for a Canadian Heritage
779 Burrard and Robson
685-7046

Inuit Gallery
345 Water near Richards
688-7323

Knot-La-Cha
270 Whonoak off Marine Dr.
beside the Capilano Indian Reserve
987-3339

Leona Lattimer Gallery
1590 W. 2nd and Fir
732-4556

Marion Scott Gallery
671 Howe and Georgia
685-1934

Wickaninnish Gallery
1666 Johnston St. (in the Net Loft)
Granville Island
681-1057

PRINT GALLERIES

Granville Island Graphics
1650 Johnston, Granville Island
687-8914

Paperworks Gallery
1650 Johston, Granville Island
687-8914

CRAFT GALLERIES

Circle Craft
1666 Johnston, Granville Island
669-8021

Cartwright Street Gallery
1411 Cartwright, Granville Island
687-8266

Crafthouse Gallery
1386 Cartwright, Granville Island
687-7270

Gallery of B.C. Ceramics
1359 Cartwright, Granville Island
669-5645

ENTERTAINMENT/ CULTURE

AT THE MOVIES 140
First-Run, Rerun, Alternative Cinema

THEATRE 141

CLASSICAL MUSIC 143

DANCE 145

The Arts Hotline (684-ARTS) provides information on events in music, dance, theatre, visual arts and museums. Hotline hours are 9-5:30, Mon to Sat. Or visit their office at 884 Granville near Smithe (in the Granville entrance of the Orpheum Theatre), which is also a Ticketmaster outlet.

Tickets for most major events are sold through Ticketmaster outlets and can be purchased over the phone with Mastercard, Visa or American Express. Call 280-4444.

AT THE MOVIES

FIRST-RUN

All the downtown movie theatres (except Cineplex) are along Theatre Row, two blocks of Granville St. from Robson to Nelson. Cineplex is a complex of 10 small theatres in the lower level of the Royal Centre at Georgia and Burrard.

There are two old time theatres that show first-run films that the big theatres avoid. These are usually Canadian films, art films or foreign films. Both have special rates on Tuesdays and for seniors, the disabled and kids.

Ridge Theatre
3131 Arbutus and 16th
738-6311

Park Theatre
3440 Cambie at 18th
876-2747

RERUN

Vancouver has a number of rerun theatres worth hunting out. These theatres feature double bills that cost less than a single first-run film. Their ads are in the newspapers, and films change about two or three times a week.

Hollywood
3123 W. Broadway near Trutch
738-3211

Starlight Cinema
935 Denman at Barclay
689-0096

ALTERNATIVE CINEMA

Pacific Cinémathèque
1131 Howe near Helmcken
688-FILM
This is a "non-profit educational society devoted to the appreciation and study of the film medium," which means art and experimental films rather than mainstream movies. Their program is organized into series or themes such as Postwar Italian Cinema, Luis Bunuel or samurai films. Phone the Cinémathèque or get detailed schedules from Duthie's Bookstore (Robson and Hornby) or the Vancouver Public Library.

You must purchase a $5 annual membership, which is unfortunate for visitors, but because of the low admission price it is still not much more expensive than regular cinemas. The programming will not suit everyone, but serious film-goers will see rarely shown films.

THEATRE

Check the entertainment section of the daily newspapers, the *West Ender* or *Vancouver Magazine*.

Arts Club Theatre

1585 Johnston, Granville Island
The most active theatre in town, the Arts Club, has two stages on Granville Island that operate year round (and profitably at that).

Formerly a chain and forge warehouse overlooking False Creek, the building was turned into a spacious, modern theatre. Attached to the theatre is a bar overlooking the water.

The Arts Club Revue Theatre is next door. It's a cabaret or revue-style theatre with tables and chairs on tiers, perfect for late-night theatre, small productions, musicals and concerts. Drinks are served.

A new Arts Club stage is opening in 1992 at Alberni and Bute. Phone for information.

For reservations and tickets for any Arts Club production, call the box office at 687-1644, Mon to Sat, 9:30-5. If improvisation interests you, ask about late-night weekend shows at the Revue Theatre; they're often hilarious.

Back Alley Theatre

751 Thurlow near Robson
688-7013
Besides some quality productions, one quirky and bizarre theatrical event has filled the theatre to capacity every weekend for years. The concept is called Theatresports, improvisational theatre in a sports context: generally two teams of five actors, a referee who makes calls ("Two minutes for obscenity!"), three judges, points and cheering

fans. Themes are set (Hamlet was a big hit) but there are no scripts. Theatresports has become a cult in Vancouver, so reserve tickets. Other improv comedy takes place during the week. Phone for the schedule.

Bard on the Beach

Vanier Park
It looks like Vancouver is finally ready to support outdoor Shakespeare. Productions are in an airy festival-sized tent behind the museum during the summer. Phone the Arts Hotline (684-2787) for schedule. You might want to bring a cushion.

Firehall Arts Centre

280 E. Cordova and Gore
689-0926
Until 1975, 280 E. Cordova was the original No. 1 Firehall. It's now a 125-seat theatre housing three companies: Touchstone Theatre, Axis Mime and the Firehall Theatre Co. Dance events and concerts are also staged here.

Orpheum Theatre

Smithe between Granville and Seymour
665-3050
The Orpheum Theatre is the home of the Vancouver Symphony Orchestra. It was built in 1927 for the Orpheum vaudeville circuit based in Chicago. When vaudeville died out, the theatre was converted into a movie house and then deteriorated over the years. In the 1970s, its owner wanted to turn it into a movie theatre complex but was prevented by a "Save the Orpheum" campaign, which ended with the city purchasing the building. The Orpheum

Glen Erickson

The Orpheum, home of the Vancouver Symphony Orchestra, is a mid-sized theatre with excellent acoustics.

Queen Elizabeth Theatre and Playhouse
Georgia and Hamilton
665-3050
The Q.E. complex houses the huge 2800-seat Queen E. Theatre and the smaller Vancouver Playhouse, a 650-seat theatre used by the resident Vancouver Playhouse Company. Usually six major Vancouver Playhouse productions run from fall to spring. Opera, dance and touring theatrical productions frequently hit the stage of the Q.E. Theatre. Tickets are available at Ticketmaster (280-4444).

became the home of the VSO after being restored to its 1920s style. Many other musical events are held there.

The theatre is dramatically ornate, with huge 1000-bulb crystal chandeliers, gilt ornamental plasterwork, a painted domed ceiling and the original Wurlitzer organ. In 1983 a new entrance and foyer were added, which unfortunately do not match the grandeur of the old theatre.

You may be able to persuade the man at the stage door (on Seymour St.) to let you have a look around if you can't make it to a concert. Tours of the building are given twice a week; call the Arts Hotline (684-2787) for information.

Presentation House
333 Chesterfield and 4th St., North Vancouver
986-1351
A dynamic community arts centre combining a recital hall, theatre, museum, archives and a gallery specializing in photography.

Theatre under the Stars (TUTS)
687-0174 (seasonal)
It does seem odd that one of Canada's rainiest cities has a tradition of outdoor theatre. Malkin Bowl, the theatre in Stanley Park, was built in 1934 as a bandshell and has been at the mercy of the elements ever since. The TUTS productions are often popular musicals such as *My Fair Lady* or *The King and I,* using professionals and amateurs. Shows are nightly except Sun, weather permitting, July and Aug. Pick a dry night, pack a blanket and perhaps a thermos of sherry, and take in some outdoor theatre. Curtain time is 8:30. Adults $14, seniors and children $8.

Vancouver East Cultural Centre
1895 Venables and Victoria
254-9578
Perhaps it's a sign of the times that a turn-of-the-century East End church

The Vancouver East Cultural Centre was once a church.

ver East Cultural Centre certainly has a neighbourly feel to it, but it would be unfair to leave the description at that. The VECC is one of the liveliest multipurpose performance spaces in the country, staging high-calibre theatre, music, dance and weekend shows for children.

Phone seven days a week for reservations and information. All seats are rush.

Waterfront Theatre
Cartwright St. and Old Bridge St.
Granville Island
685-6217
Family entertainment by Carousel Theatre and original works by B.C. playwrights sponsored by the New Play Centre are performed at the Waterfront Theatre. Other independent productions are also staged here.

CLASSICAL MUSIC

New music, early music, choral music, symphony, opera, chamber groups, string quartets – the choice is yours. Information on current concerts is in the What's On columns in Thursday's *Sun* and Friday's

Don't miss any opportunity to hear the Purcell String Quartet.

Province, Vancouver Magazine, the *West Ender* and at the two classical record stores in town, Sikora's and The Magic Flute (see Shopping, Records).

Festival Concert Society
736-3737

Sunday morning is an awkward time for visitors in any city. Except for indulging in a three-hour brunch, there isn't much to do. The Festival Concert Society has an alternative; a Coffee Concert Series every Sunday morning from Sept through June at the Queen Elizabeth Playhouse, 630 Hamilton near Georgia.

The concert may be jazz, folk, classical music, dance, theatre or opera. Not only does it fill that Sunday morning gap, but it costs only $4 and inexpensive baby-sitting

is available. Buy tickets at the door the day of the concert; the box office opens at 10 AM and the show starts at 11 AM.

If you still want brunch after the concert, your best bet in the neighbourhood is the William Tell at 765 Beatty or a short walk to Chinatown for dim sum (see Restaurants, Chinese).

Purcell String Quartet

This popular ensemble constantly receives rave reviews for its performances, held everywhere from Carnegie Hall to remote B.C. communities. Its varied repertoire ranges from baroque and classical to contemporary works, including many Canadian compositions that the quartet commissions. A demanding touring and recording schedule means that an opportunity to see the Purcell String Quartet should not be missed.

Vancouver Bach Choir
921-8012

The Vancouver Bach Choir performs three major concerts in its regular season, including a Handel's *Messiah* sing-along each Christmas. The 150-voice choir, considered to be the most significant nonprofessional choir in the city, tours extensively and frequently wins international competitions. The Bach Choir performs at the Orpheum Theatre.

Vancouver Chamber Choir
738-6822

Western Canada's only professional choral ensemble has an extensive international touring schedule and records regularly. Vancouver concert series include a series of choral masterpieces at the Orpheum,

a chamber music series at Ryerson
United Church at 45th and Yew and
Sun afternoon concerts in the Hotel
Vancouver ballroom.

Vancouver New Music Society
874-6200

The New Music Society promotes
twentieth-century music such as
concerts by the Philip Glass Ensemble and interdisciplinary performances incorporating dance or
film. Emphasis is on contemporary
composers. Most of the seven annual
concerts are held at the Vancouver
East Cultural Centre.

Vancouver Opera Association
682-2871

The VOA has been staging operas
since 1960 and performs four major
works a year, often with international
stars. The season runs from October
to May at the Queen Elizabeth
Theatre. Popular works such as *La
Traviata, Carmen* or *Madama
Butterfly* are balanced by more
esoteric operas.

Vancouver Recital Society
736-6034

Two of the most successful concert
series in Vancouver are offered by
the Recital Society. The summertime
Chamber Music Festival is held St.
George's School, a private school
with park-like grounds. An optional
dinner is served outdoors or you are
welcome to bring a picnic. Tickets
are hard to come by but a few are
often available at the door. If not, you
could at least attend the half-hour-
long pre-concert. Phone for information.

The main series (Sept to Apr)
showcases upcoming international

performers. The society has built
quite a reputation for finding the
best of these performers. The
Playhouse is the perfect venue for
these intimate concerts.

Early Music Vancouver
732-1610

EMV is the most active musical
society in the city. The aim of the
society is to promote medieval,
renaissance and baroque music,
using the instruments of the time.
Concerts are held at venues all over
the city. Tickets are usually available
at the door. The society also organizes one of the most important
summer festivals of early music in
North America, held at UBC every
July and August.

Vancouver Symphony Orchestra
684-9100

New conductor Sergiu Comissiona
has just taken over the podium of the
VSO. Most concerts are at the
Orpheum except in summer when
the VSO performs several free
outdoor concerts.

DANCE

Check *Vancouver Magazine,* the
West Ender or the What's On column
in Thursday's *Sun* or Friday's
Province for current dance listings.
The Dance Centre is a nonprofit organization that provides information
on dance activities in the city; call
872-0432.

New and upcoming companies to
watch for are Kokoro Dance,
Jumpstart, Dancecorps, Mascall
Dance and Kinesis Dance.

David Cooper

Anna Wyman Dance Theatre
662-8846

This is the best known of Vancouver's dance companies. It was the first modern dance company to perform in China and sold out the entire tour. The company is flashy, professional, aggressive and exuberant. The performances are spectacles, with colourful costumes, dazzling props and bold lighting. Accessibility is vital to this group, so don't expect the vanguard of experimentalism; the dancers would rather reach out and amuse you with a combination of music, drama and humour.

Ballet British Columbia
669-5954

Since its premiere in 1986, it has staged many well-received performances at the Queen Elizabeth Theatre (its regular venue) and throughout Canada. The repertoire ranges from established classical ballet to contemporary commissions.

Three dancers from Ballet British Columbia in *Return to the Strange Land*.

EDAM
876-9559

Experimental Dance and Music is a collective devoted to postmodern dance using a variety of techniques: ballet, modern dance and improvisation. They also perform for children, teach dance and composition, and go on national tours.

Karen Jamieson Dance Company
872-5658

The award-winning choreography of Karen Jamieson is bold, energetic and contemporary. The company makes a point of featuring Canadian composers, designers and artists.

NIGHT LIFE

JAZZ **148**

RHYTHM 'N' BLUES **148**

COMEDY **148**

A NICE QUIET BAR **148**

LIVELY PUBS AND BARS **149**

NEIGHBOURHOOD PUBS **150**

SUPPER CLUBS **150**

DISCOS **150**

ROCK CLUBS **151**

GAY CLUBS **152**

Complete entertainment listings are in the *West Ender,* the *Georgia Straight,* Thursday's *Sun* and Friday's *Province.*

JAZZ

Call the Jazz Hotline at 682-0706 for current and upcoming jazz events.

Alma Street Cafe
2505 Alma at Broadway
222-2244
Good mainstream jazz in a restaurant with good food.

Grunt Gallery
209 E. 6th at Main
875-9516
Adventurous underground jazz on Wed night, unlicensed. Schedule varies, phone to check.

Cafe Django
1184 Denman at Davie, upstairs
689-1184
Live jazz Thurs to Sat, blues on Mon.

Carnegie's
1619 W. Broadway and Fir
733-4141
Good mainstream jazz Mon to Sat. Six dollar minimum charge.

Hot Jazz Society
2120 Main and 5th
873-4131
Dixieland, New Orleans and swing. Dance floor.

Cafe Bergman
52 Powell near Carrall
688-9668
Jazz and blues Tues to Sat. Tends to be more mainstream on weekends.

RHYTHM 'N' BLUES

Yale Hotel
1300 Granville and Drake
681-9253
One of the seedier neighbourhoods in town, but worth braving for the live R&B seven nights a week.

COMEDY

Punchlines Comedy Theatre
15 Water and Carrall
684-3015
Stand-up comedy at 9:30. Also 11:30 show on Fri and Sat (club is cleared in between shows). Amateur night on Mon; closed Sun.

Yuk Yuks
750 Pacific Blvd. at foot of Robson
687-5233
Stand-up comedy with full dinner menu available. Open Wed to Sat only. Thurs to Sat shows at 9 and 11; Wed is amateur night.

See also Entertainment and Culture (Back Alley Theatre).

A NICE QUIET BAR

Arts Club
1585 Johnston, Granville Island
687-1354
The Backstage Lounge has a waterfront view and books a variety of talent for after the Fri and Sat shows, smoky blues piano or hot jazz. Phone ahead if you want to know what's up.

Bacchus Lounge
Wedgewood Hotel
845 Hornby near Robson
689-7777
A bright and airy lounge with a view of the street. Full of glamorous people after work, but later becomes a nice quiet bar.

The Gallery
Hyatt Regency
655 Burrard at Melville
687-6543
An elegant private club atmosphere.

Garden Lounge
Four Seasons Hotel
791 W. Georgia and Howe
689-9333
Deluxe, expensive, with lots of greenery and deep lounge chairs.

Gérard Lounge
Le Meridien
845 Burrard near Robson
682-5511
An elegant but comfortable gentlemen's club-type atmosphere, with an unobtrusive grand piano to accompany conversation.

The Pub, Park Royal Hotel
540 Clyde, West Van
926-5511
The Tudor-style pub is really more of a quiet lounge with a fireplace and background music.

Sylvia Hotel
1154 Gilford west of Denman
681-9321
Spectacular view of English Bay from this nondescript but popular waterfront lounge.

LIVELY PUBS AND BARS

La Bodega
1277 Howe near Davie
684-8815
Spanish tapas bar with a very European atmosphere except for the clientele, who range from the new wave fashion crowd to flamenco guitarists. Very crowded on weekends, come before 8 PM. The food is good too.

Bridges
1696 Duranleau, Granville Island
687-4400
A lively pub with a marine theme, very casual.

Elephant and Castle
700 Dunsmuir and Granville,
Pacific Centre Mall
685-4545
Line-ups at lunch and after 5 PM with business people; a fun British-pub-style stand-up bar.

English Bay Café
1795 Beach and Denman
669-2225
A good spot to catch the sunset on English Bay. Technically, this is not a bar, and the liquor laws demand that you eat a little something.

George V
Hotel Georgia
801 W. Georgia and Howe
682-5566
Tudor-style pub, popular after work. Pub-style entertainment Thurs to Sat.

Night Court Lounge
Hotel Georgia
801 W. Georgia and Howe
682-5566
Like your rich uncle's den – dark
wood and wing-back chairs. Get a
table by the window at 5 PM, relax
and watch the world walk by. Video
trivia games in the evenings.

Unicorn Pub
770 Pacific Blvd. S., foot of Robson
683-4436
Live entertainment (Irish Rovers'
style), British pub food and a large
selection of ale create a lively, sing-
along atmosphere. The large
outdoor patio is popular in the summer.

NEIGHBOURHOOD PUBS

Not quite "the local," but they sure
beat beer parlours. Neighbourhood
pubs tend to be small, have decent
food, and serve liquor as well as beer
and wine. Usually open from 11 AM
to midnight or 1 AM. The central
pubs are:

Bimini
2010 W. 4th and Maple
738-2714

Darby D. Dawes
2001 Macdonald and 4th
731-0617

Dover Arms
961 Denman and Nelson
683-1929

Jeremiah's
3681 W. 4th and Alma
734-1205

Elephant Walk Pub
1445 E. 41st and Knight
324-1400

Stamp's Landing
610 Stamp's Landing, False Creek
879-0821

SUPPER CLUBS

Saturno
1320 Richards near Pacific
684-1320
Snazzy supper club with local and
international acts.

DISCOS

Most discos are open Mon to Sat to 2
AM, Sun to midnight.

Eclipse
1369 Richards near Pacific
688-7806
Teen club on Fri, after hours dance
club on Fri and Sat, 1-5 AM.

Graceland
1250 Richards (alley entrance)
688-2648
Splashy disco for the art and fashion
scene. Loud dance music, local art
on the walls and occasional live
bands. Current theme nights are
Afro/Carribean, Acid and Bad Boys.

Pelican Bay
Granville Island Hotel
683-7373
Sophisticated crowd at this disco
Thurs to Sat.

Madison's
398 Richards and Hastings
687-5007
Hi-tech nightclub for serious
dancers. Impressive light show and
sound system. Top 40 and AOR.
Open to 2 AM. Closed Sun.

The Warehouse
871 Beatty and Smithe
684-1313
Funk Thurs to Sat.

Nightclub Tour
Avoid line-ups and make an entrance
by driving up in a white limo. Star
Limousine Service (983-5577) has
nightclub tours of the in-spots
(Richard's, the Soft Rock, Madison's,
Club Soda and more).

ROCK CLUBS

Most are open to 2 AM Mon to Sat,
and to midnight on Sun.

Club Soda
1055 Homer and Nelson
681-8202
Large club with a good setup to
watch big-name local talent and not-
so-big touring talent.

Commodore Ballroom
870 Granville and Smithe
681-7838
The Commodore is probably the
best mid-sized venue in town. It
holds about 1200 people and generally stages rock concerts. The building was built in 1929 and has a
unique sprung dance floor. (The
bounce comes from the railway car
springs, rubber tires and horse hair
that support the wooden floor.) Once
you start dancing there's just no
stopping.

86 Street Music Hall
750 Pacific Blvd. S., foot of Robson
683-8687
Features big-name local and imported rock/pop bands. Usually
open Wed to Sun only.

Railway Club
579 Dunsmuir and Seymour,
upstairs
681-1625
One of the best clubs – a pleasant
place just for a drink but also books
the best bands in town. Jazz on Sat,
3-7 PM. Good lunches available on
weekdays. On weekends, arrive
before 10 or you won't get in; the
place is tiny and packed.

Richard's on Richards
1036 Richards and Nelson
687-6794
Still the most popular club in town.
The club spot for rising young
singles. Lavish interior, valet parking. Live and taped Top 40 music.
Proper dress Thurs to Sat.

Soft Rock Café
1925 W. 4th and Cypress
736-8480
Live music, dancing and full meals.
Closed on Mon, open the rest of the
week till 1 AM; line-ups are common
on weekends.

Town Pump
66 Water and Abbott
683-6695
Features original local and touring
bands seven nights a week; music
ranges from country and folk to
underground and funk.

GAY CLUBS

Celebrities Night Club
1022 Davie and Burrard
689-3180
A large disco for men and women;
open seven nights.

Denman Station
860 Denman off Robson
669-3448
The neighbourhood bar.

Heritage House Hotel
(formerly the Lotus)
455 Abbott and Pender
685-7777
Lounge and pub on main floor for
men and women open every night.
Downstairs lesbian bar is open Tues
to Sat and is for women only on Fri
and Sat.

Ms T's Cabaret
339 W. Pender near Richards
685-4077
Open Mon to Sat, for men and
women. Occasional live music.

Numbers Cabaret
1042 Davie and Burrard
685-4077
A disco for men only upstairs, men
and women downstairs. Pool tables.
Open seven nights.

The Odyssey
1251 Howe near Davie
689-5256
Live entertainment every Tues and
Wed, with a DJ the rest of the week.
Fri is men only.

Shaggy Horse
818 Richards and Robson
688-2923
For the older generation.

SPORTS/RECREATION

AUTO RACING 154
Indy Vancouver

BICYCLING 154
Routes, Rentals/Gear

CAMPING 158
Equipment Rental

CANOEING/KAYAKING/ROWING 158
Routes, Rentals

CRUISING 160
Instruction, Routes, Rentals

FISHING 162
Chartered Trips, Tackle Shops/Licences/Information, Where to Fish

FITNESS (Aerobics/Weights/Jogging) 165
Classes/Facilities, Exercise Gear, Jogging Routes

GOLF 167
Public Courses, Private Clubs, Pitch and Putt

HIKING/MOUNTAINEERING 169

HORSEBACK RIDING 169

HORSE RACING 170

PROFESSIONAL SPORTS 171
Hockey, Football, Baseball, Tickets

RIVER-RAFTING 171

SAILING 172
Cruise and Learn, Day Cruises, Charters

SCUBA DIVING 174
Where to Dive, Rentals

SKATING 175

SKIING 175
Downhill, Cross-Country, Rentals

SWIMMING 180
At the Beach, Outdoor Pools, Indoor Pools

TENNIS 183
Outdoor Courts, Night Tennis, Indoor Courts, Rentals

WINDSURFING 184

Without question, Vancouver is a sports-minded town. The city is a perfect example of how geography and climate can shape people's lives. Is it any wonder that people are enticed outdoors by the balmy climate, ocean and mountains? Is it any wonder that people in eastern Canada — as they try to keep their minds off the freezing weather for six months of the year — think primarily of work? Vancouverites have other things on their minds.

Sport B.C. is an umbrella organization that can put you in touch with any sports association or give you up-to-the-minute information on any sport in British Columbia. It is located at 1367 W. Broadway and Hemlock. Call 737-3000 during office hours.

Sports and recreational activities are listed here in alphabetical order.

AUTO RACING

INDY VANCOUVER
Normally Pacific Boulevard is a 50-km/h (30-mph) zone but during the Labour Day weekend you'll see maniacs whizzing by at 300 km/h (190 mph).

In 1990 Vancouver became one of the 16 events on the Indy circuit. The track around B.C. Place Stadium is 2.8 km (1.7 mi.) long and cars do 103 laps. The final race, on Sunday afternoon, only takes two hours but practices and time trials are held for two days before. Odds are grandstand tickets will be sold out but standing room tickets may be available. Phone 661-7223.

BICYCLING

The Bicycling Association of British Columbia operates an information hotline (731-7433) which lists all the current and upcoming bicycling events in the area and provides phone numbers for information on joining a group to cycle in the city or the country. The Vancouver Bicycle Club, for example, meets Sunday mornings at 10 AM at Broadway and Granville for a half-day trip in the city. Beginners and serious cyclists are welcome, but for safety's sake, no small children. The club also organizes overnight trips and will help you get the necessary gear if you are from out-of-town. The club's phone number is available from the association office at 737-3034.

Rental places are listed at the end of the Bicycling section. The "Vancouver Bicycle Map," available at cycle shops, is a detailed street map highlighting trouble spots for cyclists (bad intersections, high volume of traffic, steep hills, etc.), to help you select a route.

A few words of advice about cycling in Vancouver. Vancouver has few bike paths and riding on the sidewalks is illegal. Police do not hesitate to ticket cyclists for traffic violations. Bicycles are allowed on the SeaBus, the commuter ferry to the North Shore, but only on Sat, Sun and holidays, and the rider is charged double fare (exact change only). Cyclists are not allowed in the George Massey Tunnel under the Fraser River on Highway 99 south of the city, but from June through September a shuttle service will take you and your bike through the tunnel at designated times. Call 271-0337.

The main cycling event of the year is the annual Gastown Grand Prix held on July 1. Several streets are cordoned off to make a 900-m (1,000-yard) circuit. Racing starts in the morning with all categories of bicycles and cyclist, but at 2 PM the big race begins and is not over until 65 laps, for a total of 60 km (37 mi.), are completed at breakneck speed.

ROUTES

If you would rather cycle on your own, here are a few routes:

Stanley Park
The seawall, a 9-km (5.6-mi.) paved path along the shore of Stanley Park, is a wonderful ride because of the spectacular views. The seawall is not a complete circle, but connects with paths and roads. It is clearly divided in two: one side is for cyclists, the other for pedestrians. Cyclists must ride counterclockwise around the

Experience the variety and vastness of Stanley Park the easy way – by bicycle.

path and must dismount at a few designated busy spots. Start at the foot of Alberni or Georgia.

The seawall is a flat, easy ride that takes about an hour. If you must ride weekends when the park is very busy, be patient and careful.

There is also a perimeter road around the park which is more challenging because of the hills. The one formidable hill, underneath the Lions Gate Bridge, can be avoided by riding down to the seawall just after Pipeline Rd. The road is one-way going counterclockwise, so enter via Georgia and veer right. Except for this one hill, any road or bicycle path in the park is good for cycling. (See Stanley Park map.)

Port of Vancouver
You will ride past Bute Marina, Canada Place Pier, fish-packing

plants, cargo docks, grain elevators, etc. Start at the north end of Cardero, just east of the Bayshore Inn, where an unnamed asphalt service road runs close to the water. Ride east, picking your route carefully to stay close to the water; it is possible to ride almost to the Second Narrows Bridge.

The return trip is 15 km (9.3 mi.). The view is superb and the terrain flat, but watch for oblique railway tracks. Note that this road can be used only outside of work hours.

Shaughnessy

An exclusive old neighbourhood with elegant mansions along quiet tree-lined streets, this is a perfect area for meandering through on a bicycle. From downtown, take the Cambie St. Bridge south to 16th Ave., then turn right and go along 16th until you reach Tecumseh. Pick up picnic supplies at Max's Deli at Oak and 15th, and stop for a picnic at Crescent Park. Osler, Angus and the Crescent are the choice streets in Shaughnessy, but travel up the side streets as well. The Hycroft mansion at 1489 McCrae has been restored to its 1912 style and is sometimes open to the public. The other half of the neighbourhood is west of Granville.

To return downtown, use the Burrard St. Bridge; it's an easier ride and not as busy as the Granville St. Bridge. Return trip is 13 km (8 mi.).

False Creek – Granville Island – Vanier Park

This route is part of the city's 15-km (9-mi.) Seaside Bicycle Route that runs from Stanley Park along the north and south shores of False Creek to Pacific Spirit Park near the university. Much of the route is on

bicycle/pedestrian paths but occasionally it swings onto roads. You will find a map board about every kilometre (.6 mi.) along the route.

The shortened route that is suggested here takes you into the innovative waterfront community of False Creek, bustling Granville Island with its Public Market, and Vanier Park. Start at Reckless Rider Cyclery at Fir and 2nd where you can rent bicycles. Ride east on 2nd just onto the Granville Island causeway where you will see a Seaside Bicycle Route map board. Turn right into the False Creek area and ride until you are in front of a marina at Leg-in-Boot Square. You could stop here for a cappuccino at the Riviera Café or a beer at Stamp's Landing, a local pub.

Cycle back along this seawall to Granville Island, where you could eat lunch or spend the afternoon exploring. (See Sightseeing, Granville Island.) Or cross the island causeway and continue, keeping the water on your right, all the way to the Vancouver Museum, the planetarium and the Maritime Museum at Vanier Park. Snacks are available at the museum restaurant.

The return trip is about 6 km (3.7 mi.) and takes about two hours with stops.

Kitsilano Beaches

From downtown, cross the Burrard St. Bridge and keep right onto Cornwall Ave. Ahead a few blocks is lively Kits Beach, with a huge, outdoor salt-water pool. Farther down Cornwall (it becomes Point Grey Rd.) is Jericho Beach Park, which is quieter, Locarno Beach and then Spanish Banks. Follow a beach path through Jericho Park or cycle along N.W. Marine Dr. There are refreshment stands and washrooms at the beaches. The few hills on this route are not steep. Avoid rush hour.

The trip to Spanish Banks and back is 17 km (10.5 mi.).

University of British Columbia (UBC)

The campus is separated from the city by Pacific Spirit Park. Paved cycling paths run through it alongside University Blvd., Chancellor Blvd. and 15th Ave. There is a very steep hill as you approach UBC, so use 8th Ave., which is the least arduous and has one of the best views of the city (at 8th and Discovery). Tenth Ave. would be a good return route.

Round trip from downtown with a short stop would take about three hours. If you want a shorter trip or are riding at rush hour, take the Dunbar bus from downtown and rent bicycles at Dunbar Cycles (see Rentals/Gear at the end of Bicycling).

Southlands

This wonderful, oasislike spot (in the south end of the city beside the Point Grey Golf Course) resembles the English countryside. Southlands is the equestrian centre for the city, and you will encounter horses and riders on the bridle paths along the road. A good spot to stop for a picnic lunch is at the foot of Carrington St. Go right along the trail for a view of the Fraser River. Southlands is a gem of a place, great for a picnic, but there are no stores so pack a lunch.

There are hills on the route from downtown, 21 km (13 mi.) return, but Southlands is as flat as can be. Taking the bus to Dunbar Cycles

and renting bikes there would make the bike trip shorter, 7 km (4.3 mi.) return.

RENTALS/GEAR

Robson Cycles
1463 Robson near Broughton
687-2777

Stanley Park Rentals
676 Chilco and Alberni
681-5581
They also rent bicycles built for two.

Bayshore Bicycles
745 Denman at Robson
688-2453

Dunbar Cycles
4219 Dunbar near 26th
224-2116

Reckless Rider Cyclery
1840 Fir and 2nd
736-7325

Recreation Rentals
2560 Arbutus and Broadway
733-1605

Sports Rent
1192 Marine and Pemberton,
North Van
986-1605

If you are a cycling enthusiast, check out these stores for cycling gear:

West Point Cycles
3771 W. 10th and Alma
224-3536

Bikes on Broadway
620 E. Broadway at Fraser
874-8611

Bicycle Sports Pacific
756 Davie at Howe
682-4537

CAMPING

EQUIPMENT RENTAL

Two sporting goods stores rent camping equipment, one in Kitsilano and one on the North Shore. Phone in advance to reserve for summer weekends and be prepared to leave a deposit.

For information on renting camper vans and motor homes, check *The Yellow Pages* under Recreational Vehicles, Renting & Leasing. The vehicles can come equipped with linen, cooking and eating utensils, etc. Minimum rental period is usually a long weekend or one week.

Recreation Rentals
2560 Arbutus and W. Broadway
733-1605

Sports Rent
1192 Marine and Pemberton,
North Van
986-1605
Rents equipment for camping, hiking, mountaineering and more (although no cooking utensils).

CANOEING/KAYAKING/ ROWING

ROUTES

False Creek
Set off from Vanier Park, Sunset Beach or Granville Island and make a circular trip up False Creek. From Sunset Beach, go under the Burrard, Granville and Cambie bridges, past the old Expo site and B.C. Place Stadium to the end of False Creek.

On the return trip, go along the south shore to pass by the waterfront community of False Creek. You could stop at the Riviera Café by the False Creek Marina to quench your thirst. Next is Granville Island and the Public Market, then the commercial fishing docks between the Granville and Burrard bridges.

Now you are back where you started, having gone about 10 km (6 mi.) in about three hours. This trip is for the urban adventurer and care must be used because of the heavy marine traffic in False Creek.

English Bay
The shores of English Bay, towards Stanley Park or by Kits Beach and Spanish Banks, are good paddling territory. WARNING: Do not attempt to paddle under Lions Gate Bridge as currents there are fierce.

Deer Lake
Deer Lake is mostly a pastoral urban park, but 5 km (3 mi.) of wooded shoreline and wilderness surround the lake. Burnaby Art Gallery and Burnaby Village Museum, a reconstructed pioneer village, are within a short walk, and you can swim at the east end of the lake. A great picnic place to take the children or to go for a relaxing afternoon on the water.

Whitewater kayaking on the Capilano River on the North Shore.

Indian Arm

Indian Arm is a dramatically rugged inlet about 1.6 km (1 mi.) wide and 30.5 km (19 mi.) long, surrounded by 1200-m (4,000-ft.) mountains. Rent a boat at Deep Cove and paddle across Indian Arm to Jug Island, Combe Park or Belcarra Park. Or paddle south to Cates Park at the mouth of Indian Arm. A third alternative is to paddle all the way to the end of Indian Arm (four hours one-way) for a good look at coastal wilderness.

East of Vancouver

If you'd rather paddle on a lake (and have a car and a day to spare), head east to Alouette or Pitt Lake. WARN-ING: Strong winds can start up on both these lakes, so keep to the shore.

RENTALS

Ecomarine Ocean Kayak

1668 Duranleau, Granville Island
689-7575
Double and single kayaks by the hour or day. A friendly crew will give you pointers if you're just beginning.

Adventure Fitness

1528 Duranleau, Granville Island
687-1528
Canoes and power boats for rent. Handy to False Creek and English Bay.

Deer Lake Boat Rentals

Deer Lake
255-0081
On the east side of Deer Lake in Burnaby. Kayaks, canoes, rowboats, pedal boats and sailboats for rent by

the hour. Open June, July and Aug. This small lake is very busy on weekends, so go midweek if possible.

Deep Cove Canoe and Kayak Rentals
2156 Banbury
Deep Cove
929-2268
Deep Cove is near the mouth of Indian Arm, a spectacular wilderness fiord in North Vancouver. Deep Cove Canoe Rentals is just south of the government wharf at the end of Gallant St. Canoes, kayaks and rowboats for rent by the hour or day.

Recreation Rentals
2560 Arbutus at Broadway
733-1605

Sports Rent
1192 Marine Dr. at Pemberton, North Van
986-1605
Canoes, kayaks, rubber rafts and inflatables; many boating accessories may also be rented, from roof racks to snorkel sets. Minimum one-day rental.

CRUISING

INSTRUCTION

Boardwalk Yacht Club
1650 Duranleau, Granville Island
681-3474
Courses range from Basic Power Boating to Decorative Nautical Knotwork. They also offer a six-day cruise-and-learn vacation in the Gulf Islands that will earn you a Basic Power Boating and a Coastal Navigation Certificate. A 10-m (32-foot) cruiser takes up to four

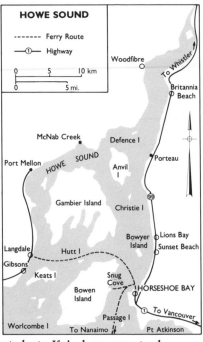

students. If six days seems too long, there is also an intensive Weekend Basic Power Boating that begins Fri evening and ends Sun evening during spring and fall.

ROUTES

For a taped Marine Forecast, call 270-7411.

Howe Sound/Strait of Georgia
Howe Sound and the Strait of Georgia have some of the best cruising waters in the world and are the only protected salt-water cruising areas north of San Francisco. In addition, there are 28 marine parks between Vancouver Island and the mainland.

Howe Sound has many islands to explore, so bring a picnic lunch and

The M.V. *Britannia* sails Howe Sound as part of the Royal Hudson/M.V. *Britannia* steam train and boat excursion.

find a secluded beach. Or cruise to Gibsons, where the CBC television series "The Beachcombers" was filmed.

If you want to meet other boaters, a lively spot is Snug Cove on the east side of Bowen Island, a short distance from Horseshoe Bay. There is a sandy beach at Deep Bay, the next bay north of Snug Cove. Chinook salmon fishing is good here all year.

Regular bus service takes you from downtown Vancouver to Horseshoe Bay, where you can rent a boat. Supplies are available within easy walking distance.

Burrard Inlet

For a marine view of the city, cruise up Burrard Inlet into the beautiful natural setting of Vancouver Harbour. You'll see freighters, float planes and cruise ships from all over the world, engaged in the varied activities of the continent's second-largest port. Then there is a quick transition into a wilderness area, with good fishing at the east end of the inlet.

RENTALS

Sewell's Landing Marina
6695 Nelson, Horseshoe Bay
921-7461
Motorboats by the hour, half-day or day; maps, fishing gear and licences also available here.

Granville Island Boat Rentals
By Bridges Restaurant, Granville Island
682-6287 (seasonal)
Power boats by the hour; weekday rates are the best deal. Fishing gear, maps and licences available.

Recreation Rentals
2560 Arbutus at Broadway
733-1605

Sports Rent
1192 Marine Dr. at Pemberton, North Van
986-1605
Aluminum boats and inflatables with motors; roof rack, fishing gear, life jackets, etc. all available for rent. Fishing licences available at North Van location only. Minimum one-day rental on all items.

FISHING

CHARTER TRIPS

You've come to B.C. and you want to catch a salmon, right? The sure way is to join a chartered fishing trip. The charter company looks after the details while you sit back and wait for the fish to bite. Charters are available by the half-day, day or week. Call any of these companies for more details:

Barbary Coast Yacht Basin
554 Cardero, north foot of Bute
669-0088

Bayshore Yacht Charters
1601 W. Georgia at Cardero
682-3377

Boardwalk Charters
216-1650 Duranleau
Granville Island
681-3474

Coho Fishing Adventures
104 E. 49th
324-8214

Sewell's Landing Marina
6695 Nelson, Horseshoe Bay
921-7461
Reasonably priced four-hour group charters (skippered), with a reduced "sightseeing" rate for those who would rather enjoy the scenery than fish. The sightseeing rate is a real bargain at $14.50 for the trip.

Tradewinds Yacht Charters
North foot of Jervis
683-1686

TACKLE SHOPS/LICENCES/ INFORMATION

If you'd rather go fishing on your own, you must find out about the local fishing restrictions. The tackle shops listed below are your best source of information. They will give you a current issue of the federal government's "B.C. Tidal Waters Sport Fishing Guide" and the provincial government's "B.C. Sport Fishing Regulations Synopsis for Non-Tidal Waters." Any of these shops will sell you a salt-water or fresh-water fishing licence and tell you where they're biting.

Downtown department stores also sell fishing licences. The two with the best selection of gear are Woodward's and Army and Navy. Army and Navy is particularly helpful and has the lowest prices in town.

The Department of Fisheries has a 24-hour toll-free information line in spring, summer and fall. Call (800) 663-9333 or 666-2268 in Vancouver for recorded information on restrictions, where and when to fish, which lures to use and the biggest fish caught that week.

For more detailed information call the Department of Fisheries at 666-0383 during office hours. The *B.C. Fishing Directory and Atlas,* available at most sporting goods stores, provides complete information on fishing locations.

Army and Navy
27 W. Hastings and Carrall
682-6644

West Coast Fishing Tackle
2147 E. Hastings near Victoria
254-6832

Fishing off the pier at Jericho Beach.

Hunter's Sporting Goods
2140 Kingsway near Victoria
430-3036

Three Vets
2200 Yukon and 6th
872-5475

Compleat Angler Tackle
4257 Fraser and 27th (rear)
879-8033

Ruddicks Fly Shop
3726 Canada Way, Burnaby
434-2420

WHERE TO FISH

Burrard Inlet
The Burrard Inlet is open all year. From July to Oct fish for coho along the north shore. Fish for chinook from Nov to Mar.

Howe Sound/Horseshoe Bay
The Horseshoe Bay/Howe Sound area offers the best chance of catching chinook or coho. There are chinook all year in Howe Sound, peaking in November and December. Coho are available in summer and fall. This is one of the most popular fishing spots on the Pacific coast, and there are marinas all along the coast at Fisherman's Cove, Whytecliff, Horseshoe Bay, Sunset Beach and Lions Bay. Free boat launches in the area are at Fisherman's Cove and Porteau Beach.

Some of the best fishing spots in

THE CATCH

Salmon

Chinook: 1.5 to 14 kg (3 to 30 lbs.)
Coho: the largest and most prized sportsfish in B.C.: 2 to 3 kg (4 to 7 lbs.)
Chum: 3.5 to 4.5 kg (8 to 10 lbs.)
Pink: 2 kg (5 lbs.)
Sockeye: 2 to 3 kg (5 to 7 lbs.)

Bottomfish

These are abundant and easily caught. The delicacies are sole, flounder, red snapper, rockcod, lingcod, halibut and perch. Look for these white-fleshed fish around pilings, reefs or rocky areas. Use tiny shore crabs or mussels as bait.

Freshwater Fish

Steelhead trout: 2 to 11 kg (5 to 25 lbs.)

Cutthroat: 2 to 9 kg (4 to 20 lbs.)
Kokanee: 0.5 kg (1 lb.) (Kokanee, landlocked salmon with deep red flesh, is considered the best eating fish in B.C.)

Shellfish

Crabs, shrimp, prawns, and bivalve molluscs such as clams, mussels, oysters and scallops, all thrive on the Pacific coast. However, bivalves found near populated areas are undoubtedly contaminated. Check with the Dept. of Fisheries for safe locations. WARNING: There is a natural phenomenon called "red tide," which is a bloom of reddish plankton in the ocean. Shellfish retain this plankton in their systems, where it does them no harm – but eating these shellfish can be deadly to humans.

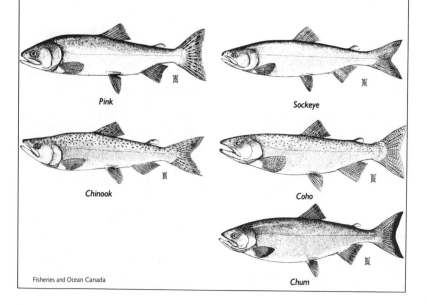

Pink

Sockeye

Chinook

Coho

Chum

Fisheries and Ocean Canada

Howe Sound are: Hole-in-Wall (on the mainland coast just north of the Horseshoe Bay Ferry Terminal), Queen Charlotte Passage (between Bowen Island and the mainland), Bowyer Island (off Sunset Beach), Grebe Islets (near Fisherman's Cove), Bowen Island (south end), Gambier Island (south end).

Sunshine Coast
Another hot spot for salmon fishing, especially from Secret Cove to Edgemont. It is a three-hour trip from Horseshoe Bay to the Sunshine Coast, including a ferry ride from Horseshoe Bay to Langdale. Boat rentals and charters are available at Secret Cove, Pender Harbour and Edgemont.

The Fraser River
A salt-water licence is needed below the town of Mission; above the town you must have a fresh-water licence. Information on access points to the many Fraser River sandbars is in the B.C. fishing guides mentioned earlier. Fish the mouth of the Fraser for sockeye during late summer; pink salmon are available in odd years.

Lakes and Rivers
For fresh-water angling, try the Squamish – Cheakamus River system, the lakes near the Sunshine Coast, or Pitt, Stave, Cultus and Harrison lakes east of Vancouver. The Vedder – Chilliwack River is prolific for steelhead and coho. There is good fishing all year at Buntzen Lake, a popular canoeing lake where no power boats are allowed.

The Skagit River system, 160 km (100 mi.) southeast of Vancouver, is the best for trout, especially fly-fishing.

On Vancouver's North Shore you can fish the Seymour River, the Capilano River and Lynn Creek, primarily for coho in late summer and early fall.

FITNESS
(Aerobics/Weights/Jogging)

CLASSES/FACILITIES

YMCA
955 Burrard and Barclay
681-0221
Open to men and women. A $6 day pass for nonmembers gives you access to drop-in fitness classes, weight room, pool, sauna, whirlpool, racquetball, squash and handball courts, and the rooftop track.

YWCA
580 Burrard and Dunsmuir
683-2531
Women only. A $6.75 day pass gives you fitness classes at all levels, plus access to pool, weight room and sauna. Membership not necessary.

Sweat Co. Fitness
808 Richards and Robson
683-7938
Drop-in fee available for co-ed workout, stretch, low-impact, dance and weight classes. Handy downtown location.

Vancouver Aquatic Centre
1050 Beach near Thurlow
665-3424
Moderate-level keep-fit classes morning and evening include land and water exercises. Also seniors keep-fit classes. Class fee includes

use of the pool. The Aquatic Centre also has a weight room, exercise bicycles and some baby-sitting facilities. Open seven days a week.

West End Community Centre
870 Denman near Nelson
689-0571
Reasonably priced drop-in exercise classes, weight room, tennis, racquetball and squash courts. Open seven days a week in winter; closed Sun in summer.

Ron Zalko Fitness
2660 W. 4th near Stephens
736-0341
Fitness classes at all levels, showers, and a complete weight room with computerized bikes. All facilities are available on a drop-in basis. North Van location also has tennis, swimming pool, jacuzzi, and steam bath. For visitors, they have reciprocal arrangements with other health clubs across the country.

The Fitness Group
3507 W. 4th and Collingwood
738-3488
A full program of drop-in exercise classes every day of the week. Weight room and exercise equipment.

EXERCISE GEAR

Forerunners
3504 W. 4th and Collingwood
732-4535

Racquets and Runners
3880 Oak and 23rd
733-9211

Running Room
1519 Robson and Cardero
684-9771
1834 W. 4th off Burrard
737-0684
3832 Oak and 22nd
731-9445

The Sports Medicine Shop
3708 Oak and 21st
734-0224
Specialists in modifying and resoling athletic shoes.

Fitness Solutions
1931 W. 4th near Cypress
732-0264

JOGGING ROUTES

Seawall, Stanley Park
The flat asphalt path along the seawall has stunning scenery to keep you going for the 10 km (6 mi.).

Lost Lagoon, Stanley Park
The circular path around the lagoon is accessible from the foot of Alberni St. It is a level, gravel pathway, about 1.5 km (1 mi.) long, excellent for an easy run.

Seawall, False Creek
The seawall starts at Fisherman's Wharf by the Burrard St. Bridge and runs past Granville Island and the community of False Creek to the Cambie Bridge. Return trip 5 km (3 mi.). If you need sustenance, stop at Isadora's (see Restaurants, Breakfast) on the edge of Granville Island near the seawall.

English Bay
A level pathway starts behind the Vancouver Aquatic Centre and follows the water's edge to Stanley Park, 2 km (1.2 mi.) one way.

Kits Beach/Vanier Park
A series of asphalt and dirt paths start at Vanier Park on the Kitsilano side of the Burrard St. Bridge. The paths follow the water around Kits Point, past the Vancouver Museum, planetarium, Maritime Museum, Kits Beach and the Kitsilano Yacht Club. The return trip is about 5 km (3 mi.) and is fairly flat.

Ambleside Seawall to Centennial Seawalk
The paths in Ambleside Park start at the east side and follow the water for the length of the park. You then have to pick your way along the beach and the road for a short distance until the beginning of the Centennial Seawalk. This 1.5-km (1 mi.) path is asphalt and completely flat. The views are wonderful – the city, Lions Gate Bridge, Stanley Park and the marine traffic.

GOLF

Golf is a popular year-round sport in Vancouver. If you enjoy watching golf, the big tournament is the B.C. Open, held every year in June. Call the B.C. Golf Association (294-1818) for details.

PUBLIC COURSES
(In the City)

Several courses are close to the centre of the city. They are listed here in order of popularity and playability:

Fraserview Golf Course
61st and Wales
327-3717
This most scenic of the municipal courses overlooks the Fraser River. Driving range, clubs and power carts for rent, cafeteria, bar. Fraserview is said to be the busiest course in the country. Par 71, 6165 yds.

University Golf Club
5185 University Boulevard
224-1818
This popular public course is scenic, well kept and the closest to the city centre. It is challenging but not punishing. There is a dining room and bar in the clubhouse; clubs and pull and power carts can be rented. Par 72, 6147 yds.

McCleery Golf Course
7170 Macdonald
261-4522
A relatively easy, wide-open municipal course adjacent to the Fraser River. Easy to walk. Clubs and pull carts for rent; the clubhouse has a coffee shop and bar. Par 72, 6168 yds.

Langara Golf Course
290 W. 49th near Cambie
327-4423
A well-treed municipal course; licensed dining room. Par 71, 6103 yds.

PUBLIC COURSES
(Near Vancouver)

There are about 20 other public courses in the outlying areas. Some particularly good ones are:

Gleneagles Golf Course

6190 Marine, West Van
921-7353
Nine holes. Near Horseshoe Bay.
Par 35 on the front, 2800 yds.

Greenacres Golf Course

5040 No. 6 Road, Richmond
273-1121
A flat course in good condition. One
of the few public courses where you
can book a tee-off time. Par 70, 5800
yds.

Mayfair Lakes Golf Course

5460 No. 7 Rd., Richmond
276-0505
Beautifully laid out brand new
course. Very good facilities and
restaurant. Par 72, 6225 yds.

Peace Portal Golf Course

16900 – 4th Ave., Surrey
538-4818
Off Highway 99 before the American
border, about an hour's drive from
the city. Established in 1928. Heavily
treed, undulating fairways. Nothing
but raves about this course. Par 72,
6440 yds.

PRIVATE CLUBS

Many private clubs accept guests ac-
companying members. Most also
have reciprocal privileges, whereby
you will be admitted if you are a
member of another bona fide club.
You must have a membership card
and/or a letter of introduction from
your club pro. Phone first for
confirmation. The best private
courses are:

Capilano Golf and Country Club

420 Southborough, West Van
922-9331
Fairly rigorous course, with a breath-
taking view. Par 72, 6274 yds.

Shaughnessy Golf and Country Club

4300 S.W. Marine
266-4141
Very prestigious and very busy.
Must be with a member to play. Par
73, 6320 yds.

Marine Drive Golf Club

7425 Yew and 57th
261-8111
Par 71, 6112 yds.

Point Grey Golf and Country Club

3350 S.W. Marine and Blenheim
266-7171
Par 72, 6260 yds.

Two good private clubs in the Lower
Mainland are open to the public on a
limited basis:

Seymour Golf and Country Club

3723 Mount Seymour Parkway,
North Van
929-5491
Open to the public on Mon and Fri,
call to book a tee-off time. Par 72,
5972 yds.

Pitt Meadows Golf Club

13615 Harris, Pitt Meadows
465-4711
Open to the public on Mon, Thurs
and Fri, and after noon on Tues, Sat,
Sun, and holidays. Par 72, 6342 yds.

PITCH AND PUTT

Eighteen holes of golf the quick way with a short fairway. Four public pitch and putt courses are centrally located; all rent clubs.

Queen Elizabeth Pitch and Putt
Queen Elizabeth Park
Cambie and 33rd
874-8336

Rupert Park Pitch and Putt
3401 E. 1st near Rupert
253-2530
Open April to Oct.

Stanley Park Pitch and Putt
Stanley Park
681-8847
Use the Beach Ave. entrance

Ambleside Pitch and Putt
1201 Marine, West Van
922-3818
Open March 1 to the end of Oct.

HIKING/ MOUNTAINEERING

The Federation of Mountain Clubs of B.C. offers courses in all levels of mountaineering and rockclimbing, and leads backpacking trips into the interior of B.C. If you're interested only in a day trip, the federation can provide you with a list of companies that offer shorter guided hikes. Call 737-3053. See also Parks/Beaches/ Gardens.

HORSEBACK RIDING

Alpine Riding Academy
3170 Sunnyside, in Anmore
469-1111
Trail rides are an hour to all day long in the valley and mountains around Buntzen Lake. Reservations are a must.

Tall Mountain Riding Stables
1301 Lillooet, North Van
(across from Capilano College)
980-0299
Rides in Mt. Seymour Park range from one hour to all-day trips with a saddle bag lunch provided. Overnight trips, which can include hunting and fishing, are also arranged. Ponies are available for children.

Golden Ears Riding Stable
23103 – 136th Ave, Maple Ridge
463-8761
Hourly and daily rentals, guided or unguided. Trail rides in nearby Golden Ears Park. Special rates for children.

Mustang Stables
22947 – 132nd Ave, Maple Ridge
467-1875
Horses rented by the hour or by the day for unguided trips only. The guide will escort you to Golden Ears Park, then you're on your own.

Southlands is a major equestrian centre and one of the most unusual neighbourhoods in Vancouver. Unfortunately, there are no rentals, but there is a lot of four-legged activity to watch. The centre of the community is:

Southlands Riding Club

7025 Macdonald and 53rd
263-4817

The club's focus is on English-style riding. It has indoor and outdoor riding areas for horse shows and stages a Mock Hunt in Pacific Spirit Park on New Year's Day.

HORSE RACING

From April to Oct thoroughbred horse races are run at Exhibition Park, at Hastings and Renfrew. Post time is 6:15 on Wed and Fri; 1:15 on Sat, Sun and holidays.

Brunch is served on Sun at noon in the clubhouse. To reserve a table on the clubhouse Table Terrace or in the dining room, phone 254-1631. Book several days in advance for tables on Fri and Sat. In the dining room you view the races only on closed-circuit television.

The rest of the year, from Oct to April, the action moves to the Clover-

At the edge of the city, Southlands is an oasis reminiscent of the quiet English countryside.

dale Fair Grounds at 176th St. and 60th Ave. in Surrey for harness racing. Race time is at 7 on Mon, Wed and Fri; 1:15 on Sat and Sun. Call 576-9141 for more information.

THE CLOVERDALE RODEO

An explosion of excitement every May during the Victoria Day long weekend. It's the second largest rodeo in western Canada and the sixth largest in North America, with prize money big enough to attract top cowboys from all over the continent. The events include calf roping, bronco riding, steer wrestling, wild cow milking, street dances, parades, pancake breakfasts, rides and a midway.

PROFESSIONAL SPORTS

Vancouver is not a town for spectator sports. Its residents are too busy jogging, skiing, or sailing to spend time cooped up in an enclosed stadium, and so professional sports end up being victims of low attendance.

HOCKEY

In 1968 Vancouver was able to enter the National Hockey League. The Vancouver Canucks played their first season two years later to near-sellout crowds. They lost more games than they won for the first 12 years, but the fans were always there. In 1982 the Canucks made it to the Stanley Cup finals, and the fact that the New York Islanders took the cup hardly mattered to the frenzied fans awaiting their heroes at the Vancouver Airport. The Canucks have been in a slump lately and a new management team was imported from the Philadelphia Flyers to get them to the top of the league. For information on the Canucks, call 254-5141.

FOOTBALL

The B.C. Lions have had a rocky history. They finished their first season in 1954 winning only one game. After eight more tough years they were finally in the Grey Cup and won it in 1964. The glory was short-lived, and by the end of the next season they were again in last place. The Lions play all their games in the B.C. Place Stadium downtown. Their season starts in June and runs until late October. For information on the Lions, call 681-5466.

BASEBALL

Do you have fond memories of sunshine, hotdogs, and Sunday afternoon baseball? Catch the Vancouver Canadians of the Pacific Coast League at the grand old Nat Bailey Stadium from April to Sept, on Sun afternoons and weekday evenings. The highly popular Canadians are a cult in Vancouver and their games often sell out, so arrive early. Tickets are available at the door. The stadium is at Ontario and 29th, on the east side of Queen Elizabeth Park. Phone 872-5232 for times or check the newspapers.

TICKETS

Tickets for professional football, hockey and other sports events can be purchased from Ticketmaster outlets, which have branches at all Eaton's and most Woodward's stores, and at the information booths of major malls. Or you can order your tickets by phone (280-4444) and charge them to Visa, Mastercard or American Express.

RIVER-RAFTING

If the daredevil in you wants to try whitewater rafting, companies in Vancouver organize trips that will take you through Hell's Gate, the Washing Machine, Devil's Cauldron or Jaws of Death. The Thompson and Chilliwack are known for frothing whitewater and the Fraser for whirlpools and waves. Fraser River trips are also more historical. Some trips use motorized rafts; on others you must row – it depends on the river.

You must transport yourself to a

Fred Skolovy

meeting place in the area, a one- to three-hour drive from Vancouver. Rain suits are provided but it's a good idea to bring a change of clothes.

In addition to the excitement of whitewater, overnight trips usually include camping under the stars, swimming, fishing, bonfires and salmon barbecues.

Hyak Wilderness Adventures
734-8622

Offers trips ranging from one to three days on the Thompson or Chilliwack rivers. A scenic float trip (no whitewater) is also available for the less daring.

Kumsheen
1-800-482-2269 toll free (B.C.)
Lytton, B.C.

Canadian River Expeditions
738-4449

Specialize in scenic float trips with no whitewater.

Old-time baseball at Nat Bailey Stadium with the Vancouver Canadians.

SAILING

CRUISE AND LEARN

If you don't sail and want to, you can learn while visiting Vancouver. Several sailing schools offer a cruise-and-learn vacation, a five-day trip around the Gulf Islands on boats that are 8 to 10 m (30-40 ft.). For about $650 you get sailing instruction, food and a berth. Trips run regularly from May to Oct. with four students and an instructor. An advanced version is sometimes offered. Considering the amount you could spend on hotels, restaurants, and entertainment, this course offers a unique combination of sun, salt water, new territory and new skills. The bonus is finishing with a Canadian Yachting Association Certificate.

Westcoast School of Seamanship
1618 Duranleau
Granville Island
684-9440

Pacific Quest Charters
1521 Foreshore Walk
Granville Island
682-2205

Cooper Blue Orca
1818 Maritime Mews
Granville Island
687-4110

Bluewater Adventures
202-1676 Duranleau
Granville Island
684-4575

Sea Wing Sailing School
1815 Boatlift Lane
Granville Island
669-0840

Setting sail off Jericho Beach into the waters of English Bay.

DAY CRUISES

West Coast School of Seamanship offers a low-cost day trip (no instruction) to Bowen, Gabriola or Thetis Island every Saturday for $60. Six people per boat but you don't have to be part of a group.

During the summer, West Coast also has 3-hour trips in English Bay on smaller sailboats. They leave daily at noon, 3 and 6 from Granville Island and cost $25.

CHARTERS

If you are an experienced sailor you can rent a sailboat for a half-day, day, evening or longer. Please note that sails are prohibited in False Creek and the maximum speed is five knots. The companies listed above will arrange charters, with or without a skipper.

SCUBA DIVING

Divers in British Columbia encounter an incredible range of marine life: 180 varieties of sponges, sea stars, anemones, corals, seals, sea lions, killer whales, the largest octopus species in the world, wolf-eels, crab, abalone, snails, prawns and over 325 varieties of fish.

Around Vancouver most scuba diving is done in Howe Sound and Indian Arm. Both are steep-sided inlets formed by glacial activity. Indian Arm is at the east end of Burrard Inlet, and Howe Sound is the Horseshoe Bay region and beyond.

No diving is allowed in Vancouver Harbour between Lions Gate Bridge and Second Narrows Bridge. Permission is necessary to dive in the outer harbour, but it is just a matter of a phone call to the Vancouver Port Corporation at 666-2405.

If you plan to dive a lot in British Columbia, purchase a book called *141 Dives in the Protected Waters of Washington and British Columbia* at one of the major dive shops (listed at end of this section under Rentals). Another excellent publication is *The Divers' Guide to Vancouver Island.*

WHERE TO DIVE

If you wish to dive with your own group, here are some suggestions for day trips. Because of the rugged, vertical shores, accessibility is a problem. All the spots listed here have shore access and are rated for beginners as well as advanced, except where indicated.

Whytecliff Park

This area has the only underwater reserve in the province. Follow signs to the park from Horseshoe Bay. The area around the marina is closed to divers from April 1 to Sept 30 due to heavy boat traffic, but other areas in the park are open.

Lighthouse Park

The park is about 9.5 km (6 mi.) past Park Royal Shopping Centre, and the entrance is off Marine Dr. in West Vancouver. A half-hour walk takes you from the parking lot to the shore. Lighthouse Park has been described as the richest dive in Vancouver. For intermediate and advanced divers.

Porteau Cove

This popular spot is a good place to meet other divers around a beach fire at the end of the day. On Highway 99, 24 km (15 mi.) past Horseshoe Bay, you will see an arched sign over the road saying "Porteau Camp." About 1.5 km (1 mi.) ahead is parking and beach access. Porteau Cove is a provincial marine park and has new facilities such as an artificial reef made from old ships' hulls, a wreck of a minesweeper, a campground, showers and a boat launch.

Tuwanek Point

Lots of underwater life here, but be careful of the many small boats in the summer. Tuwanek Point is on the Sechelt Inlet. Follow signs to Porpoise Bay Provincial Park from the town of Sechelt. Tuwanek Point is about 6.5 km (4 mi.) past the park.

Cates Park

This park is at the mouth of Indian Arm. Access is via the Dollarton Highway, 5 km (3 mi.) past the Second Narrows Bridge, very close to the city. You must phone the Vancouver Port Corporation (666-2405) for permission to dive. Park near the dock west of Roche Point and dive about 180 m (200 yds.) out to the rocky reef. For intermediate and advanced divers.

Howe Sound

Because of silt from the Fraser River, mountain runoff and high plankton levels, diving in Howe Sound can be less than exhilarating. Visibility is reduced in the summer, especially near the surface, but from late fall to spring the water is usually clear.

Gulf Islands

If you are willing to travel farther, diving in the Gulf Islands is spectacular. Try Beaver Point on Salt Spring. Take the ferry from Tsawwassen to Long Harbour on Salt Spring. Follow the signs to Fulford Harbour. Just before the town, take Beaver Point Rd. for 9.5 km (6 mi.) to Ruckle Park. Park at the end of the road and walk 800 m (875 yd.) to the shore. Dive in the bay if you are a beginner, or at the point if you are experienced.

RENTALS

These stores all rent equipment by the day, and some even rent personal gear such as fins and masks to divers from out of town. You will need a 6-mm (¼-in.) neoprene wet suit in B.C. waters. The dive shops frequently organize trips for the day, weekend or longer, as well as night dives. Occasionally, boat charters are available. For visitors, the stores will arrange whatever is necessary – air, transportation or diving partners. Most trips are geared to beginners and intermediate divers. Proof of diving certification and tank inspection is necessary to obtain air.

Diver's World

1523 W. 3rd near Fir
732-1344

Diving Locker

2745 W. 4th near Macdonald
736-2681

Adrenalin Sports

1512 Duranleau, Granville Island
682-2881

SKATING

Skate outdoors on the lower level of **Robson Square** from Nov until early March, but bring your own skates.

The rink at the **West End Community Centre** (Denman and Nelson) is open Oct through March, evenings and weekends, and rents skates. Phone 689-0571.

At **Britannia Community Centre** (Napier off Commercial Dr.), the rink stays open all year and will also rent skates. Phone 253-4391 for public skating times.

SKIING

You name it, Vancouver's got it! There's handy, effortless skiing at Grouse, Seymour and Cypress mountains, about a half-hour drive from downtown, and world-class skiing in the Whistler-Blackcomb

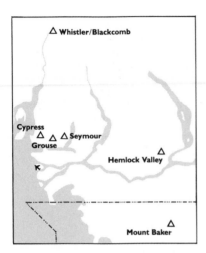

Whistler/Blackcomb

Cypress
Grouse △ △ △ Seymour

Hemlock Valley △

△
Mount Baker

area, a couple of hours away. Take your pick.

DOWNHILL SKIING

Whistler

Vertical drop: 1530 m (5020 ft.)
Base elevation: 652 m (2140 ft.)
Lifts: 3 triple chairlifts, 1 quad express, 6 double, 2 T-bars, 2 gondolas (one high-speed); capacity 23,850 people per hour
Runs: 96 runs, longest 11 km (7 mi.)
Terrain: 25 per cent novice, 55 per cent intermediate, 20 per cent expert
Average snowfall: 1140 cm (450 in.)
Snow reports: Vancouver 687-6761, Whistler 1-932-4191
Facilities: A whole village supplies anything a skier could want: instruction, helicopter skiing, cross-country (unlimited terrain, rentals, instruction), paraskiing, snowmobiling, telemarking and two mountain-top restaurants. Dual-lift tickets may be purchased that allow access to both Whistler and Blackcomb lifts.

Book accommodation through Whistler Resort Association (Vancouver 685-3650, Whistler 1-932-4222).
Getting there: Whistler is 120 km (75 mi.) north of Vancouver on Highway 99, a spectacular road, but keep your wits about you as it can be hazardous. Chains are often mandatory.

There is daily train and bus service to Whistler from Vancouver.
Comments: Whistler, along with its neighbouring mountain, Blackcomb (see following), can only be described in superlatives: the largest ski area in North America, the longest ski season in western Canada, etc. Basically, the best skiing around. The season runs from late Nov to May.

See also Excursions from Vancouver (Whistler).

Blackcomb

Vertical drop: 1609 m (5280 ft.)
Base elevation: 675 m (2215 ft.)
Lifts: 4 quad-expresses, 5 triple chairlifts, 1 double, 2 T-bars, 1 handle tow
Runs: 85 runs, longest 11 km (7 mi.)
Terrain: 20 per cent novice, 55 per cent intermediate, 25 per cent expert
Average snowfall: 1145 cm (450 in.)
Snow reports: Vancouver 687-7507, Whistler 1-932-4211
Facilities: Instruction, rental and repairs, three restaurants, plus all the facilities in neighbouring Whistler Village. Dual-lift tickets available for access to both Blackcomb and Whistler. Cross-country unlimited.
Getting there: Same as Whistler.
Comments: The highest lift-serviced vertical drop in North America and the largest glacier

Grouse Mountain

Grouse Mountain offers skiing half an hour away from downtown Vancouver.

summer skiing operation. No other resort on the continent offers skiing on two superb mountains beside each other, and most skiers are hard-pressed to say which mountain they prefer; both have thousands of enthusiastic fans. Winter season and hours are the same as Whistler, but Blackcomb now offers summer skiing on the Horstman Glacier, serviced by a new T-bar. Summer skiing is 8-4 daily.

See also Excursions from Vancouver (Whistler).

Grouse Mountain

Vertical drop: 365 m (1200 ft.)
Base elevation: 885 m (2900 ft.)
Lifts: 2 aerial trams to ski area, 4 double chairs, 2 T-bars, 3 rope tows, 1 hand tow
Runs: 13 runs, longest 2.5 km (1.5 mi.)
Terrain: 30 per cent novice, 50 per cent intermediate, 20 per cent expert
Average snowfall: 487 cm (192 in.) with snow-making equipment

Snow reports: Vancouver 986-6262
Facilities: Rentals, instruction, cafeteria, dining room, night skiing (till 11), ski check.
Getting there: Grouse is 12 km (7.5 mi.) north of Vancouver, a 15-minute drive from downtown via Lions Gate Bridge and Capilano Rd.

Public transit goes to Grouse from downtown. On Georgia St. catch the #246 Highland bus westbound, and at Edgemont and Ridgewood transfer to the #232 Grouse.
Comments: Grouse is most often used by people who want to learn to ski after work, and there are many ski school programs. (The brilliant chain of lights to the north of the city that can be seen year-round is the arc lighting from the ski runs.)

Mount Seymour Provincial Park

Vertical drop: 365 m (1200 ft.)
Base elevation: 1010 m (3313 ft.)
Lifts: 4 double chairlifts, 1 double rope tow
Runs: 25 runs, longest 2.4 km (1.5 mi.)
Terrain: 40 per cent novice, 40 per cent intermediate, 20 per cent expert
Average snowfall: 355 cm (140 in.)
Snow reports: Vancouver 986-3444
Facilities: Instruction, rentals, day lodge, cafeteria, night skiing (every night until 10 PM), snowshoe and cross-country rentals and instruction, no accommodation in park.
Getting there: Mount Seymour is 16 km (10 mi.) north of Vancouver. Take the right turn-off after Second Narrows Bridge and follow the signs. Accessible by car only.
Comments: A family and learn-to-ski area. Beginner's cross-country trails that are marked but not groomed.

Cypress Park

Vertical drop: 520 m (1700 ft.)
Base elevation: 926 m (3038 ft.)
Lifts: 4 double chairlifts, 2 rope tows; 5200 people per hour
Runs: 18 runs, longest 3.2 km (2 mi.)
Terrain: 20 per cent novice, 40 per cent intermediate, 40 per cent expert
Average snowfall: 355 cm (140 in.)
Snow reports: Vancouver 926-6007
Facilities: Day lodge, cafeteria, 26 km (16 mi.) of cross-country trails, rentals, instruction, lounge, no accommodation.
Getting there: Cypress is a 30-minute drive from downtown Vancouver, 16 km (10 mi.) away. Go over the Lions Gate Bridge and take the Upper Levels Highway west.
Comments: Biggest vertical drop of the three North Shore areas.

Hemlock Valley

Vertical drop: 348 m (1142 ft.)
Base elevation: 1006 m (3300 ft.)
Lifts: 1 triple chairlift, 2 double, 1 tow; 4200 people per hour
Runs: 19 runs, longest 1.6 km (1 mi.)
Terrain: 30 per cent novice, 45 per cent intermediate; 25 per cent expert
Average snowfall: 500 cm (197 in.)
Snow reports: Vancouver 520-6222
Facilities: Rentals, instruction, day lodge with cafeteria, restaurant, night skiing on Sat, accommodation at Hemlock Resort (1-797-4411) near lifts, 30 km (19 mi.) of cross-country.
Getting there: Hemlock is 125 km (78 mi.) east of Vancouver, 27 km (17 mi.) off Highway 7 near Harrison Hot Springs. Take chains.
For bus information call Hemlock Resorts.
Comments: Not a huge mountain, but good dry powder. Season is from mid-Dec to mid-April.

Mount Baker
(In the U.S.A.)

Vertical drop: 460 m (1500 ft.)
Base elevation: 1310 m (4300 ft.)
Lifts: 1 fixed quad, 6 double chairlifts, 2 rope tows
Runs: 26 runs, longest 3 km (2 mi.)
Terrain: 30 per cent novice, 50 per cent intermediate, 20 per cent expert
Average snowfall: 1900 cm (750 in.)
Snow reports: Vancouver 688-1595
Facilities: Instruction, rentals, cafeteria, daycare, no accommodation on mountain.

Getting there: Mount Baker is 120 km (75 mi.) south of Vancouver, a two-hour drive. Take Highway 99 south to Highway 542, then go east. Or take Highway 1 east to Sumas exit, then go south. Take chains. Car access only.

Comments: Although Mount Baker is in the United States, it is a popular destination for skiers from Vancouver. "Baker is the undisputed king of snowfall ... the quality ranges from west coast cement to bottomless powder." The season is long, usually until mid-May. Baker is run by the U.S. Forest Service and is not a resort, so amenities are few. Accommodation is limited; book well in advance or go for the day. Sometimes closed midweek; phone for dates. Canadians may want to consider extra medical insurance when skiing at Baker.

CROSS-COUNTRY

There are some cross-country ski areas within reach of Vancouver in the Lower Mainland. The three that are well groomed, well marked and provide the best skiing are Cypress, Whistler and Manning.

The season for cross-country skiing generally runs from the beginning of Dec until the end of March.

Cypress Provincial Park

The closest to Vancouver, Cypress is on the North Shore and has 27 km (17 mi.) of short trails, of which 5 km are lit for evening skiing. Hot food is available at Hollyburn Lodge. It is busy on weekends because it is so close to the city. For a snow report, call Vancouver 925-2704.

Whistler

There are two cross-country areas adjacent to Whistler Village. The best is the Lost Lake network, 15 km (9.5 mi.) of set trails. A daypass lets you take advantage of warming huts, trail maps and meticulously groomed trails. A free and more informal cross-country area is the golf course that occasionally has about 6 km (4 mi.) of set trails. These areas would appeal to beginners or those interested in a workout rather than a wilderness experience.

For back-country skiing try: Cheakamus Lake Trail (a flat logging road not far from Whistler Village), the 14-km (9-mi.) Singing Pass Trail, and Callaghan/Madley Lake. For information or a cross-country snow report call 1-932-6436 (seasonal).

Manning Park

The best cross-country area in the Lower Mainland is at Manning, where conditions compare favourably to those in Scandinavia. A variety of trails includes ten marked ones ranging from 4 to 58 km (2.5 to 36 mi.). Trails total 190 km (125 mi.), of which 30 km (18 mi.) are regularly maintained. The inland location means drier snow and plenty of sunshine.

It is a three-hour drive east of Vancouver, via the Trans-Canada Highway to Hope, then Highway 3 to Manning Park. Accommodation is available in cabins, chalets and at Manning Park Lodge, which has a cafe, dining room, and pub. Phone 1-840-8822 for accommodation and 733-3586 in Vancouver for a snow report.

RENTALS

Can-Ski Sportshop

569 Seymour near Dunsmuir
669-6333
1845 Marine near 18th St.,
West Van
926-7547
Downhill equipment only.

Carleton Cycle and
Outdoor Recreation
3201 Kingsway near Rupert
438-6371
Cross-country only, closed Mon.

Destination Ski Rentals

1550 Marine near McGowan,
North Van
984-4394
8173 Granville and 65th
266-1274
Downhill and cross-country, open
seven days a week.

Benno's Cross-Country Ski Rentals

1975 Maple at 4th, upstairs
738-5105
Cross-country only; lessons and
tours offered.

Sigge's Sport Villa

2077 W. 4th and Arbutus
731-8818
Cross-country only.

Grouse Mountain Ski Shop

6400 Nancy Greene Way,
North Van
984-0661
Downhill only, open days and
evenings, seven days a week, during
ski season.

Hollyburn Ski Lodge

Hollyburn Ridge, North Van
922-0825
Cross-country only.

Mount Seymour Ski Shop

Mount Seymour Parkway,
North Van
986-2261
Downhill and cross-country, open
seven days a week.

Recreation Rentals

2560 Arbutus at Broadway
733-1605

Sports Rent

1192 Marine Dr. at Pemberton,
North Van
986-1605
Downhill and cross-country. Open
seven days a week.

Precision Ski

1848 W. Broadway and Burrard
732-4368
No rentals, but high-tech tuning and
repairs. A computerized base resoler
restores skis to factory specifica-
tions.

SWIMMING

AT THE BEACH

The city has plenty of sandy beaches
that are good for swimming. The
water temperature is refreshing,
peaking at 21° C (70° F) in the
summer. The following beaches
have lifeguards on duty for June,
July and Aug:

Second Beach in Stanley Park
English Bay
Sunset Beach

Kits Beach
Jericho Beach
Locarno Beach
Spanish Banks

The **Polar Bear Swim Club,** organized in 1920, holds an annual Polar Bear Swim on New Year's Day in the icy winter waters of English Bay. Recently, there were 2250 registered swimmers, about 500 unregistered swimmers and many onlookers.

OUTDOOR SALT-WATER POOLS

Vancouver has two outdoor salt-water pools overlooking English Bay: at Kits Beach and in Stanley Park at Second Beach.

Kitsilano Pool
Kitsilano Beach
731-0011 (seasonal)
The Kits Pool is gargantuan, modern and heated to 26° C (78° F). Both small children and serious swimmers use this pool because its depth is graduated and it is so large. Open from Victoria Day (May 24) to Labour Day, Mon to Fri, 7 AM-8:45 PM; Sat and Sun, 10-8:45. Admission is $1.40 with discounts for families, seniors and children.

Second Beach Pool
Second Beach, Stanley Park
This pool is older than Kits Pool and is unheated. More suited to children than serious swimmers. Admission free.

OTHER OUTDOOR POOLS

Hastings Centre
2991 E. Pender at Renfrew
255-8912 (seasonal)

Kerrisdale Centre
5851 W. Boulevard and 42nd
261-8518

Mount Pleasant Centre
3161 Ontario and 16th
879-7315 (seasonal)

New Brighton
North foot of Windermere
298-0222 (seasonal)

Oak Park
990 W. 59th and Oak
321-2818 (seasonal)

Sunset Centre
404 E. 51st off Main
321-1616

MAJOR INDOOR POOLS

The two best indoor swimming facilities are the Vancouver Aquatic Centre in the West End and the University of British Columbia (UBC) Aquatic Centre. Both are Olympic-size pools with diving tanks, saunas, whirlpools, exercise gyms and toddler's pools. Both facilities are open late in the evening.

There are also two smaller indoor pools downtown operated by the YMCA and the YWCA.

UBC Aquatic Centre
University of British Columbia
228-4521
During the school year, there is public swimming on evenings and weekends. In June, July and Aug, also open to the public during the day. Phone to check times. Admission $2 adult, $1.25 child.

Vancouver Public Library

Vancouver Aquatic Centre
1050 Beach, south foot of Thurlow
665-3424
Sitting on the shore of English Bay.
Closed annually for maintenance the
last two weeks of Aug and the first
week of Sept. Public swim times are
irregular, so phone ahead. Admission $1.40 with discounts for seniors,
children and families.

YMCA
955 Burrard and Barclay
681-0221
Open to men and women at co-ed
swim times; there are some men-
only swim times. Out-of-town YMCA
memberships are honoured; day
passes for nonmembers are $6. This
allows full use of all facilities such as
the pool, sauna, whirlpool, massage,
drop-in fitness classes, weight room,
racquetball, handball and squash
courts.

Near the boats you can see the bobbing
heads of intrepid participants in this 1957
photograph of the annual Polar Bear
Swim.

YWCA
580 Burrard and Dunsmuir
683-2531
Women only. Out-of-town memberships honoured or day passes are
$6.75. You can then use the pool,
sauna, weight room or attend any of
the exercise or dance-fit classes.

OTHER INDOOR POOLS

Fees are charged at the city-run
pools listed here. Hours and facilities
vary, so call ahead.

Britannia Centre
1661 Napier near Commercial
253-4391

Kensington Centre
5175 Dumfries and 33rd
327-9401

Kerrisdale Centre
5851 W. Boulevard and 42nd
261-8518
This pool has a bubble over it in the winter but is an outdoor pool in the summer.

Killarney Centre
6260 Killarney and 45th
434-9167

Lord Byng School
3990 W. 14th and Crown
228-9734

Percy Norman
30 E. 30th and Quebec
876-8804

Renfrew Centre
2929 E. 22nd at Renfrew
434-4712

Templeton Park
700 Templeton and Adanac
253-7101

TENNIS

Vancouver is Tennis Town. The outdoor season runs from March to Oct, with the odd lucky day in the winter. Even 180 public courts are not enough, and you will probably have to wait on summer weekends.

OUTDOOR COURTS

With one exception, all public courts are outdoors, free and operate on a first-come, first-served basis. You'll find the most courts at:

Stanley Park
21 courts (17 by the Beach Ave. entrance, and 4 by Lost Lagoon at the foot of Robson). From April to Sept you can book a Beach Ave. court for a small fee. Call 688-8786.

Queen Elizabeth Park
33rd and Cambie
20 courts.

Kitsilano Beach Park
10 courts.

Jericho Beach Park
Five courts behind Jericho Sailing Centre.

Other public courts in pleasant surroundings are:

False Creek Community Centre
Granville Island
Three courts.

False Creek (residential area)
North of 2nd, foot of Heather
Five courts with a view from the top of a parkade.

Dunbar Community Centre
4747 Dunbar at 33rd
Six courts.

Rupert Park
Rupert and 1st
Four courts.

Almond Park
12th and Dunbar
Two courts.

Elm Park
41st and Larch
Two courts.

Tatlow Park
2nd and Macdonald
Three courts.

NIGHT TENNIS

The only lit public courts are on the Langara Campus of Vancouver Community College, on 49th between Cambie and Main.

INDOOR COURTS

University of B.C. Tennis Club

6184 Thunderbird Blvd. and East Mall
228-2505
Four courts under a bubble (must be booked) and 10 outdoors. Pay as you play.

Delta Airport Inn

10251 St. Edwards off Bridgeport
Richmond
276-1140
Book same day for indoor courts.

RENTALS

Goro's Sports Shop

1678 Robson near Stanley Park
682-7640
Rents racquets by the day.

Recreational Rentals

2560 Arbutus at Broadway
733-1605

WINDSURFING

Windsurfing schools operate at various beaches in town and will supply everything you need: instruction, board, wet suit and life jacket. The introductory rental-instruction packages vary from one to six hours, depending on the school. If you know anything about surfing or sailing you are one step ahead; but if not, the uninitiated can become competent after a few hours.

No sailboards are allowed at the mouth of False Creek between the Granville and Burrard bridges.

Windmaster

Denman and Pacific
(English Bay Beach House)
685-7245
Three levels of windsurfing instruction (including beginner courses) are offered in English Bay.

Windsure Windsurfing School

1300 Discovery
224-0615
Lessons are given near the school at Jericho Beach.

Windsurfing Shop

1793 W. 4th and Burrard
734-7245

Surf City

420 W. 1st and Cambie
872-8585

SECONDHAND EQUIPMENT

Cheapskates

3644 W. 16th near Dunbar
222-1125
A sporting goods consignment store. Apart from the things you would expect, like secondhand bikes and skis, you'll also come across gravity boots, picnic coolers, goalie pads and rowing machines – all at less than half of the price that you'd pay for new.

SHOPPING

SHOPPING AREAS **186**

ACCESSORIES AND EXTRAS **188**

ART SUPPLIES **188**

AUCTIONS, ANTIQUES AND ORIENTAL RUGS **189**

BOOKS AND MAGAZINES **189**

BOOKS (USED) **192**

CLOTHING FOR MEN **192**

CLOTHING FOR WOMEN **193**

MATERNITY WEAR **194**

CLOTHING FOR WOMEN AND MEN **194**

CONSIGNMENT CLOTHING STORES **195**

HOME FURNISHINGS **195**

KITCHENWARE **197**

MARINE SUPPLIES **198**

PHOTO SUPPLIES/FILM PROCESSING **199**

RECORDS **199**

SHOES, MEN'S AND WOMEN'S **201**

SOUVENIRS **202**

SPORTS EQUIPMENT **202**

FOOD STORES **202**
Bakeries, Granville Island Public Market, Cheese, Coffee and Tea, Delis and Gourmet Take-Out, Ethnic Foods, Fish/Shellfish, Meat

Bob Herger, Photo/Graphics

SHOPPING AREAS

ROBSON STREET

Robson is always bustling. The street is exactly what pedestrians relate to: many small stores and restaurants wedged in together. The sidewalk restaurants entice you to have a cappuccino in the sun and watch the crowds. Inside, restaurants have tables right by the windows because patrons don't want to miss anything happening on the street.

Many of the stores are chic if not downright exclusive. But even if you're not making purchases, Robson St. is still the most exciting street to stroll.

GRANVILLE ISLAND

Don't miss Granville Island for the dockside outdoor restaurants, the Granville Island Ferry, the Net Loft, the Kids Only Market, and most of all, the Public Market. It's a real

The Public Market and waterfront restaurants of Granville Island.

success story for the city of Vancouver. If you detest crowds, don't go near the place on weekends.

The Net Loft, a building across from the Public Market, is a collection of fascinating stores. You will find one of the best bookstores in town, the best native arts, great kitchenware, the city's only postcard shop, a handmade paper store, the best general arts and crafts shop in town, and more beads than you could ever use.

See The Sights and Shopping (Food Stores) for more details.

FOURTH AVENUE

The shopping area on Fourth Ave. stretches from Burrard to Alma. For yourself there are record stores, bookstores and clothing stores, and for your home there are shops selling glass, kitchenware, linens and everything for the bathroom.

You can eat bagels, drink espresso and indulge in chocolate. No shortage of good restaurants, either.

Because Kitsilano is very much a young with-it neighbourhood, there are an enormous number of sporting goods stores: you can get your skis tuned, find the fitness solution to your life, the perfect swim goggles, the latest Japanese bicycle or the gaudiest pair of jams.

WEST BROADWAY

From Trafalgar to Waterloo, West Broadway could be a normal neighbourhood shopping area, except that it's also the heart of the Greek community. As with most ethnic groups, they manifest themselves in restaurants and food stores.

CHINATOWN

Pender St. for two blocks east and west of Main is the centre of Chinatown, the second largest in North America. Keefer, east of Main, is bustling as well. Liveliest on Sundays. Don't miss dim sum — see Restaurants (Chinese). Also see Sightseeing (Chinatown).

SOUTH GRANVILLE

The shopping area on south Granville St. stretches from 7th to 16th Ave. Lots of Persian carpets, antiques, clothing, galleries and food stores. South Granville used to be an enclave of older and wealthier residents but has become very trendy. A recent rivalry over lavish storefronts and interiors in the neighbourhood has resulted in some wild commercial architecture.

KERRISDALE

Shop in Kerrisdale on 41st from Maple to Balsam, where you'll run into well-heeled, blue-haired ladies in pearls. Can be exclusive and expensive but has stores worth going out of the way for, such as Hager Books, Forster's Cheeses, Windmill Toys and Peterson's Shoes. Good bakeries, florists and a camera store.

GASTOWN

Water St. from Richards to Main is the heart of Gastown, and most stores are open Sundays in the warmer months. On the edge of Gastown, at Water and Richards, is The Landing, a collection of shops in a stately and recently renovated old Gastown building.

WEST TENTH AVENUE

This shopping area on West 10th at Trimble is near the University of British Columbia campus and has some first-rate stores: several women's clothing stores, Duthie Books, hi-tech furniture and lots to eat.

SHOPPING CENTRES

Two shopping centres, a bit different from most, are **Oakridge** (at Cambie and 41st) and **Park Royal** (on the North Shore just west of the Lions Gate Bridge). The completely renovated Oakridge Shopping Centre is the home of Woodward's (a high-quality B.C.-owned department store) plus Abercrombie and Fitch, and Marks and Spencer. Park Royal has three department stores, Woodward's, Eaton's and The Bay.

Both malls also have independent stores that are more exclusive than those in the average shopping centre.

Pacific Centre and **Vancouver Centre** are two downtown underground malls joining Eaton's and The Bay at Granville and Georgia.

ACCESSORIES AND EXTRAS

Beadworks
1666 Johnston, Granville Island
682-2323
One of the most unusual stores in the city. Hundreds of varieties of beads (bone, wood, ceramic, amber, silver, glass, etc.) with all the fasteners, wire, thread and helpful information you need to make any piece of jewellery. It's a snap to do especially because they have lots of finished pieces around for inspiration.

Gulliver's Travel Accessory Store
Sinclair Centre
757 W. Hastings and Granville
688-8810
If you have a secret passion for poking around hardware or stationery stores, you'll love Gulliver's. There are hundreds of quirky little gadgets, all to make the life of a weary traveller a little easier. Also in Park Royal North and Arbutus Village.

Martha Sturdy
3065 Granville and 15th
737-0037
Bold and dramatic jewellery, all designed by Martha Sturdy.

La Jolie Madame Lingerie
Pacific Centre, upper level
669-1831
Very feminine and pretty underclothes, lots of French lace and silk.

Satchel Shop
Pacific Centre, lower level
669-2923
1060 Robson and Burrard
662-3424
Superlative bags, small leather goods and luggage.

Zig Zag
4424 W. 10th and Trimble
224-2421
Loud and sassy store selling pop fashion accessories.

ART SUPPLIES

Associated Graphic Supplies
1321 Richards and Drake
685-1331
A small, friendly graphic and fine arts supply store, where people take the time to help.

Behnsen Graphic Supplies
1016 Richards and Nelson
681-7351
Large, modern graphic supply store with the largest selection in the city.

MacEwen Arts
560 Beatty at Dunsmuir
685-6920
A small, family-run store with a knowledgeable staff. The selection is not as broad as Maxwell's, but it's different and good. Seems like they're always having a sale.

Maxwell's Artists Materials
601 W. Cordova, CPR Station
683-8607
The largest art supply store in town. Particularly good range of papers and how-to art books, plus graphic supplies. In the old CPR station, now the SeaBus terminal.

AUCTIONS, ANTIQUES AND ORIENTAL RUGS

Main Street from 20th to 35th Avenue has many antique stores, generally with furniture from Britain. Near the corner of 10th and Alma are a few stores specializing in Canadiana. For oriental rugs, go along Granville St. from 7th to 14th Avenue.

Maynard's Auctioneers
415 W. 2nd at Cambie
876-6787
Home furnishings auctions on Wednesdays at 7 PM. Phone for times of the art and antique auctions that are held periodically.

Love's Auctioneers
1635 W. Broadway near Fir
733-1157
Auctions are held on Wednesdays at noon and 7 PM.

Artemis Antiques
321 Water in Gastown
685-8808
For precious and rare antiques from the 18th and 19th century Artemis can't be beat.

Jim Shockey Folkart Interiors
3715 W. 10th Ave. near Alma
228-1011
Specializes in folkart and Canadiana furnishings.

Old Country Mouse Factory
3720 W. 10th Ave. near Alma
224-8664
Refinished Canadiana pine antiques and reproductions.

Canada West
3607 W. Broadway near Alma
733-3212
Specializes in antique pine furniture.

Peter Tolliday Oriental Carpets
2312 Granville and 8th
733-4811
The leading dealer in oriental carpets, particularly old and antique carpets.

Persian Arts and Crafts
777 Hornby near Robson
681-4639
The name is misleading, as it goes far beyond arts and crafts; it has items like handcarved tables and impressive 100 per cent silk Persian rugs. The rugs are one of a kind, with the maker's wax identity seal hanging from them, a sign of quality.

BOOKS AND MAGAZINES

Ariel Books
2766 W. 4th near Macdonald
733-3511
Feminist books.

Banyen Books
2671 W. Broadway
near Macdonald
732-7912
Alternative lifestyles, eastern religion, yoga, nutrition, gardening, etc.

The Comic Shop, for kids, collectors and nostalgia seekers.

Blackberry Books

1663 Duranleau, Granville Island
685-4113
757 W. Hastings and Granville,
Sinclair Centre
685-0833
The Granville Island store is packed on weekends, partly due to the hordes at the Public Market but also because it's a darn good bookstore.

Book Warehouse

632 W. Broadway near Heather
872-5711
1150 Robson near Thurlow
685-5711
Discounted best sellers and a huge selection of bargain books. Open 10 to 10 every day.

Chief's Mask

73 Water near Abbott
687-4100
Books by or about North American native Indians.

Comicshop

2089 W. 4th near Arbutus
738-8122
New and used comics and sci-fi, probably the best this side of Toronto.

Duthie Books

919 Robson and Hornby
684-4496
4444 W. 10th and Trimble
224-7012
For general bookstores, the Robson and W. 10th stores have the best selection in town. The W. 10th branch is more academic.

Graffiti Books

3514 W. 4th near Collingwood
736-1131
Specializing in books for the visual and performing arts. Particularly good for graphic arts, music and film.

Granville Book Company

850 Granville near Robson
687-2213
Lots of traffic means things are often in disarray, but they do have books other stores don't. Excellent computer and sci-fi selection. Good place to kill time waiting for a movie to start. Open late seven days a week.

Hager Books

2176 W. 41st and Yew
263-9412
One of the best neighbourhood bookstores around.

Manhattan Books and Magazines
1089 Robson near Thurlow
681-9074
Excellent choice of discount books, also imported and domestic magazines. One of the few places to get the *Village Voice*. Large selection of books and magazines in French. Open seven days a week.

Pink Peppercorn
2686 W. Broadway at Trafalgar
736-4213
Nothing but cookbooks!

Siliconnections
3727 W. 10th near Alma
222-2221
Computer and business books.

W.H. Smith
701 W. Georgia, Pacific Centre
669-9311
Park Royal Shopping Centre South
922-0033
English chain with a British emphasis. Park Royal store is particularly good.

Sophia Bookstore
725 Nelson near Granville
684-4032
Books and magazines on and from Japan and the Far East.

Sportsbooks Plus
230 W. Broadway near Cambie
873-0230
Books, magazines and videos on every kind of sport.

Travel Bug
2667 W. Broadway and Trafalgar
737-1122
Excellent selection of travel books and some travel accessories.

University Bookstore
University of British Columbia
228-4741
One of the largest bookstores in Canada, but more like a department store – the space is shared with jogging gear and notebooks. Textbooks and trade books.

Vancouver Art Gallery Giftshop
750 Hornby and Robson
682-2765
Best spot for art books and magazines. Also cards, prints and design-oriented gifts.

Vancouver Kidsbooks
3083 W. Broadway and Balaclava
738-5335
The best assortment of children's books, run by a former librarian and current mom. Selection of board books for babies is excellent. Books, records and tapes, some in French.

White Dwarf Books
4374 W. 10th near Trimble
228-8223
Sci-fi and astronomy.

William McCarley's
213 Carrall and Water
683-5003
Books on architecture, design, and graphic arts. A small gallery is on the mezzanine.

World Wide Books and Maps

736 Granville and Georgia,
basement
687-3320
Maps and travel books, plus government publications.

BOOKS (USED)

Ashley's Books

3754 W. 10th at Alma
228-1180

Ainsworth Bookseller

321 W. Pender
682-2015

Bond's Book Shop

319 W. Hastings near Homer
688-5227

Colophon Books

407 W. Cordova and Richards
685-4138

William Hoffer Bookseller

60 Powell near Carrall
683-3022
Good quality used books, emphasis on literature.

Lawrence Books

3591 W. 41st at Dunbar
261-3812
May be the best used bookstore in town. Worth going out of your way for.

MacLeod's Books

455 W. Pender
681-7654

Octopus Books East

1146 Commercial near William
253-0913
Mostly used books, some new. Selected magazines you won't find elsewhere. Somewhat political, intellectual and esoteric.

CLOTHING FOR MEN

Edward Chapman

833 W. Pender and Howe
685-6207
Long-standing retail business dating back to 1890. Conservative selection of quality clothing, accessories and gifts. Specializes in British woollens.

Finn's Clothing

3031 W. Broadway near Macdonald
732-3831
2159 W. 41st near W. Blvd.
266-8358
Large selection with emphasis on quality dresswear. Store on 41st also sells women's clothing.

Mark James

2941 W. Broadway and Bayswater
734-2381
Business and fun clothes for young professional men. American and European imports at medium-to-high prices. Good range of accessories.

S. Lampman

2126 W. 41st near W. Blvd.
261-2750
Preppy sportswear and dresswear.

Harry Rosen
Pacific Centre, upper level
683-6861
Ivy league designer fashions: Calvin Klein, YSL and the like. Sportswear and dress-for-success clothes.

See also Clothing for Men and Women, below.

CLOTHING FOR WOMEN

Alfred Sung
1143 Robson near Thurlow
687-2153
Clean, simple and refined lines from Canada's top designer.

Enda B.
4346 W. 10th and Discovery
228-1214
Started out as a natural fibre store, and although it's loosened up that policy you won't find much polyester. Designer labels, large selection.

Laura Ashley
1171 Robson near Bute
688-8729
A British chain selling small floral print fabrics and romantic country-look fashions for you and your home.

Edward Chapman Ladies Shop
2596 Granville and 10th
732-3394
Traditional, tailored apparel. Other branches sell ivy league menswear.

Bacci Design
2788 Granville near 12th
733-4933
Casual European designer clothes for the ultra fashionable. Very expensive. Italian shoes also.

Margareta
948 Robson near Hornby
681-6612
Small, classy store with Regina Porter, Fenn, Wright and Mason, and the like.

Morgan
813 Hornby near Robson
688-7567
One of those small stores where you walk in and realize the buyer has exactly the same tastes as you; everything has a very particular style. Office clothes and some casual wear, mostly American designers.

Rodier
1025 Robson near Burrard
682-1155
Everything in this store has the Rodier label. Exquisitely well-designed clothing made in France or Italy, generally of cotton, linen, wool or silk.

Wear Else?
2360 W. 4th and Balsam
732-3521
789 W. Pender and Granville
662-7890
High-calibre store for the working woman, with sportswear, office clothes, evening wear and accessories. Prices medium to high.

MATERNITY WEAR

Allegra
805 W. Broadway at Willow
879-7443
The store is very small, but you will find style-conscious maternity clothes rather than pink smocks. Undergarments and sleepwear also.

CLOTHING FOR WOMEN AND MEN

Boboli
2776 Granville near 12th
736-3458
Hard to believe that clothes can get *this* expensive. Smashing storefront.

Knitwear Architects
1926 W. 4th and Cypress
736-4383
A unique concept, not really a wool store (not even a ball of wool in sight) but certainly for people who knit. They have about 25 sweaters on display, all their own designs. First you pick a style and then select the yarn from a sample chart and out comes the kit, ready to go. Styles (mostly for women, a few for men and children) are more up-to-date than at other wool stores. Yarns are cotton, wool, silk or mohair. If you're from out-of-town, get on the mailing list, they have a wonderful catalogue.

Polo Ralph Lauren
1123 Robson near Thurlow
688-7656
Men's, women's and children's clothing – traditional and expensive.

Ralph Lauren Country
375 Water at Richards
669-7656
The same Ralph Lauren quality but in denim, corduroy or plaid—the kind of clothes you'd wear if you lived in New York and were going for a weekend in the Catskills.

Leone
Sinclair Centre
757 W. Hastings and Howe
683-1133
It's impossible to talk about the clothes without mentioning the store. Leone is the most avant-garde (in the well-designed Italian way) retail space in town. It should be, they poured $4 million into constructing it. Small, ultra high fashion boutiques for men and women.

Club Monaco
1153 Robson near Thurlow
687-8618
Their preppy look can be enticing simply because the clothes are so well made and so reasonably priced. Men, women and children.

Marks and Spencer
Pacific Centre
685-5744
A British department store carrying the well-known St. Michael's line for men, women and children. Very conservative styles at low prices.

Holt Renfrew
Pacific Centre
681-3121
The upper level of this elegant department store houses sportswear, shoes and exclusive classic designs. Canada's Saks Fifth Avenue.

E.A. Lee
466 Howe near Pender
683-2457
Classic and traditional; plenty of navy blazers and grey flannel. Also men's shoes and some tailored women's fashions.

CONSIGNMENT CLOTHING STORES

Deluxe Junk
310 W. Cordova and Cambie
685-4871
A discount policy on anything that's been around for more than a few weeks (everything's dated) makes for some great bargains. Clothes are mainly '50s and '60s, all in good condition.

Ex-Toggery
6055 W. Boulevard
266-6744
Quality secondhand store in this up-scale neighbourhood spells bargains. Not high fashion, but some good basics. Also has samples.

Arthur's for Men
1864 W. 1st off Burrard
731-8656
Quality classic clothes, cleaned and pressed. Much cheaper than women's consignment stores.

Second Suit
1038 Davie near Thurlow
685-3388
Up-to-date used clothing, discounted samples and some new fashions for men and women. Geared to young tastes.

Turnabout
1553 W. Broadway near Granville (men's)
1545 W. Broadway near Granville (women's)
1208 Robson near Bute (women's)
733-5313 (office)
One of the better used-clothing stores with current fashions and higher prices than the others.

Value Village
1820 E. Hastings, near Victoria
254-4282
6415 Victoria and 39th
327-4434
Value Village is a department store full of secondhand merchandise. Mostly clothing (for the whole family), plus some home furnishings.

HOME FURNISHINGS
Yaletown is beginning to emerge as a spot for interior designers and furniture stores. Look on Mainland and Hamilton Streets from Davie to Smithe.

Artifax Design
3618 W. 4th near Alma
731-8066
Their aim is modern, inexpensive, design-oriented furniture. Some is locally made—a specialty is Canadian maple butcher-block. Also, grids, blinds, kitchen accessories, tableware, etc.

Country Furniture
3097 Granville at 15th
738-6411
Heavy pine furniture, rocking chairs and four-poster beds with country-look accessories. Prices are good and quality excellent.

Form and Function
4357 W. 10th and Trimble
222-1317
Small furniture pieces and accessories with an emphasis on design. An imaginative store selling stools, tables, chairs, rugs, blinds.

Ikea
3200 Sweden Way, south foot of Knight St. Bridge, Richmond
273-2051
Ikea provides low-cost furniture by getting you to pick items out of the warehouse and assemble them at home. The look is Scandinavian, modern and clean. Range of household accessories: sheets, fabrics, kitchenware, kids' furniture, rugs and lamps. In their famous ball room (literally filled with soft plastic balls), your children can romp and tumble while you shop. Family refreshments in the in-store Scandinavian cafeteria.

Industrial Revolution
2306 Granville and 7th
734-4395
A great selection of designer products for the home. Noted for their storage systems.

Inform Interiors
97 Water St. at Abbott
682-3868
Whatever is the latest in ultra-modern furniture design, you'll find it at Inform first. Furniture and light fixtures, imported or designed by the owner of Inform.

Jordans Interiors
1470 W. Broadway and Granville
733-1174
This is the best store if you are looking for that "polished designer look" in fine furniture and quality workmanship. Notice their lacquered furniture with the many layers of lacquer, and joinery without screws or nails. Interior design services as well as furnishings. Several locations.

Malacca Rattan Design
2301 Granville and 7th
732-8838
Fine wicker and rattan furniture, lamps, baskets, accessories, plus oriental carpets.

Metropolitan Home
446 Homer at Pender
681-2313
A store specializing in fifties furniture such as turquoise blue, kidney-shaped coffee tables and Naugahyde bar stools.

New Look Interiors
1275 W. 6th near Hemlock
738-4414
Good for Danish furniture, mostly teak and rosewood. Large showroom with modern sofas, carpets, lamps, console units and children's furniture at good prices.

Roche Bobois
1010 Mainland and Nelson
669-5443
If you fantasize about glove leather and down-filled sofas, go to Roche Bobois, one of a worldwide French chain of elegant, modern furniture stores. All the furniture is European and very expensive but of true quality.

Infoto/Patti Kuzmuk

KITCHENWARE

Basic Stock Cookware
2294 W. 4th near Vine
736-1412
Large kitchenware store with
complete selection plus coffee beans
and espresso bar.

Market Kitchen
1666 Johnston, Granville Island
681-7399
Small but very well-stocked kitchenware store across from the market.
Demonstration kitchen with lots of
cooking classes.

The avant-garde furniture at Inform is a
must-see if you're in Gastown.

Ming Wo
23 E. Pender at Carrall
683-7268
2170 W. 4th Ave. and Yew
737-2624
A large old cookware store in
Chinatown, jammed full of much
more than woks and cleavers – you'll
find tortilla presses, pasta machines,
soufflé dishes, etc. At Fourth Ave.
you won't find as much, but there's
an up-to-date choice of modern
kitchenware – just what you'd find in
the current issue of *Metropolitan
Home*.

Commercial fishing boats docked on False Creek near Granville Island.

Tools and Techniques
250 – 16th near Marine, West Van
925-1835
Big, bright and thorough, with a full range of cooking utensils, coffee beans and a demonstration kitchen.

MARINE SUPPLIES

Granville Island Marine Supplies
1648 Duranleau, Granville Island
681-6318
A large, friendly shop with a huge selection, particularly good for all-weather clothes and finishing hardware.

Kits Marine
1530 W. 2nd near Fir
736-8891
Limited stock but good prices, especially for hardware and teak. Skin diving and water-skiing gear, also life jackets for infants.

Marine Mail Order Supply
1368 W. Broadway and Hemlock
736-3565
Everything you could want at excellent prices in this no-frills store. Catalogue available for mail order. Staff is eager and informative.

Quarterdeck
1660 Duranleau, Granville Island
683-8232
375 Water near Richards,
in The Landing
683-7475
Books, charts, navigation instruments, tote bags, lanterns, brass-

ware, clothing and even canine life preservers.

Wright Mariner Supply
1533 W. Pender near Cardero
(at rear)
682-3788
A good selection of boating supplies, especially clothing and footwear at reasonable prices.

PHOTO SUPPLIES/FILM PROCESSING

ABC Photocolour
1618 W. 4th at Fir
736-7017
Best colour processing.

Kerrisdale Cameras
2170 W. 41st and Yew
263-3221
Local chain, but the main store has the largest selection and is the most service-oriented. New equipment, trade-ins, rentals, and a separate store (a couple of doors down) for darkroom supplies.

Lens and Shutter
2912 W. Broadway at Bayswater
736-3461
Excellent sales staff in this huge store. As with most camera stores in town, they will match competitors' prices.

Leo's Camera Supply
1055 Granville and Nelson
685-5331
A good place if you're looking for an obscure piece of equipment (and there's even more upstairs).

London Drugs
540 Granville and Dunsmuir
685-0105
1187 Robson and Bute
669-8533
Their camera department is the best for everyday low prices and sales. No darkroom supplies. One-hour photo finishing.

You can get film processed quickly at the following locations:

CP Foto
636 Hornby near Dunsmuir
681-7025

1 Hour Photo
Pacific Centre, upper level
681-2511

RECORDS

A & B Sound
556 Seymour near Dunsmuir
687-5837
A high-volume chain with a more daring selection than others. Often have loss-leaders on the current hits. Don't miss the extensive jazz and classical sections upstairs.

Banyen Sound
2669 W. Broadway and Trafalgar
737-8858
New age cassette tapes. Listening copies of everything in the store.

Black Swan
2936 W. 4th at Bayswater
734-2828
Specializes in jazz, blues, folk and some rock. Domestics and imports, new and used.

Collectors RPM

456 Seymour near Pender
685-8841

Best selection of vintage rock and roll and out-of print records. A Beatles specialist, with a Beatles museum upstairs full of paraphernalia and records.

D & G Collectors Records

3580 E. Hastings near Boundary
294-5737

Best place for vintage 45s (special orders taken). Heavy on rockabilly and country. New and used.

Highlife Records and Music

1317 Commercial near Charles
251-6964

Specializes in reggae, African, Caribbean and jazz, but you'll also find rock, folk, blues and country. A discriminating but not large selection. New and used.

The Beatles Museum shows all those old Beatles trinkets that are now collectors' items.

Magic Flute Record Shop

2100 W. 4th Ave. and Arbutus
736-2727

A well-stocked store selling classical records, CDs and cassettes.

Odyssey Imports

534 Seymour near Dunsmuir
669-6644

Almost exclusively high-priced British, Japanese and European imports, especially the latest British dance music. Also heavy metal. Lots of T-shirts, books and posters.

Sikora's Classical Records

432 W. Hastings
685-0625

The classical music specialists, new and used records.

Zulu Records
1869 W. 4th at Burrard
738-3232
Best independent rock record store
in the city. Lots of imports and used
records. Owned and operated by one
of the friendliest guys around.

SHOES, MEN'S AND WOMEN'S

Stephane de Raucourt
1024 Robson near Burrard
681-8814
European shoes and accessories for
women. High quality and fashionable, not to mention my favourite
shoe store.

Aldo
1016 Robson near Burrard
683-2443
Part of a Montreal chain; street-fash-
ion shoes for men and women.

Pegabo
1137 Robson near Thurlow
688-7877
Trendy quality shoes for men and
women, mostly from Italy.

Dack's Shoes
815 W. Pender and Howe
681-7049
High quality traditional men's shoes.

Ferragamo
918 Robson and Hornby
669-4495
Very expensive and very classic
Italian men's and women's shoes.

Freedman Shoes
2867 Granville and 13th
731-0448
One of the largest shoe stores in
town and one of the best. Fashionable shoes in the medium-price
range for men and women. Good
leather bags.

Ingledew's
535 Granville near Pender
687-8606
Conservative, quality dress shoes for
men and women in the medium
price range.

Peterson's Shoes
2179 W. 41st near Yew
266-5620
High-calibre women's shoe store in
Kerrisdale with spiffy Italian pumps.

Roots
Pacific Centre, upper level
683-5465
Shoes, bags, belts and leather
jackets in the Roots no-frills style,
which somehow always remains
fashionable. Quality Canadian-made
leather goods for men and women.

Sheppard Shoes
852 W. Hastings near Granville
685-0734
Name brands of quality men's shoes
plus Frye boots for men and women.

Walk with Ronsons
1015 Robson and Burrard
682-0795
Comfort is the key in walking shoes,
such as Rockports, and dress shoes.

SOUVENIRS

Maritime Museum
1905 Ogden and Chestnut,
Vanier Park
737-2211
A tiny gift shop with intriguing mementos of the briny West Coast. You will find framed prints, posters, model ships, books and marine post cards. A great place for a gift for Dad.

Museum of Anthropology
6393 N.W. Marine, UBC Campus
228-5087
It is difficult to call the objects in the Museum of Anthropology gift store souvenirs. It is full of exquisite crafts from the Pacific Northwest Indians and the best choice of books on the subject.

Science World
1455 Quebec,
near Terminal and Main
687-8414
This gift shop for kids is full of curious toys and gadgets, mostly with a scientific bent. There are inexpensive pocket telescopes, skeletons that glow in the dark, computer books, and many other weird and wonderful gifts.

Vancouver Aquarium
Stanley Park
685-5911
The Clamshell, the gift store beside the Vancouver Aquarium, has the largest assortment of quality souvenirs. A huge selection of West Coast nature books for children and adults, lots of toys, jewellery, Indian and Eskimo art, and the best Vancouver T-shirts.

SPORTS EQUIPMENT
See Sports/Recreation

FOOD STORES

BAKERIES

La Baguette et L'Échalotte
1680 Johnston, Granville Island
684-1351
French bakery and gourmet take-out selling baguettes, croissants and fancy cakes. Across from the Public Market, very busy on weekends.

Bombay Sweets
6556 Main and 50th
321-1414
Sleek new sweetshop making traditional Indian sweets from almonds, carrots, pistachios, coconut, etc. The carrot halvah demands a return visit.

Bon Ton
874 Granville near Smithe
681-3058
This European-style pâtisserie and tearoom has been around since 1931. Has the most decadent cakes in town. (The Diplomat, for example, is multiple layers of butter cream, pastry and rum-soaked cake slathered in more butter cream and nuts.)

Elsie's Bakery
1555 Yew near Cornwall
731-7017
One of the best all-round neighbourhood bakeries. Handy to Kits Beach. Great care with ingredients and preparation put Elsie's a step above. The coffee cake and bran muffins get my highest recommendation.

Ernie's Austria Bakery

2660 Alma near 11th
731-3010
This Kitsilano bakery has a well-de-
served, citywide reputation. How do
they make sourdough caraway rye
so much better than anyone else?
Bread arrives daily at 11 AM.

Keefer Chinese Bakery

217 Keefer near Main
685-2117
Being a particular fan of barbecued
pork buns (slightly sweet buns with
barbecued pork baked inside), one
day I bought a sample from each
Chinese bakery in Chinatown and
tried them all. The Keefer Bakery
won. Only 65 cents for this scrump-
tious snack. Their coconut buns and
tarts are also delicious. The three
other Chinese bakeries in this same
block are also good.

MacKinnon's Bakery

2715 Granville at 11th
738-2442
A wide range of bread, cookies,
squares and gooey cakes. I dare you
to walk by their window without
stopping.

Montreal Bagel Factory

2908 W. 4th near Macdonald
734-4525
The bagels are in demand, but don't
pass over the egg braid and pumper-
nickel breads, or the cinnamon buns,
or the walnut croissants.

Pâtisserie Bordeaux

3675 W. 10th and Alma
731-6551
Excellent croissants but it's really
the gateaux and tarts that win me

GRANVILLE ISLAND PUBLIC MARKET

The Public Market is the most
popular spot to buy specialty
foods and for good reason.
There is a huge array of quality
foods that most merchants take
great care to display well (even
making raw squid look
irresistible). It amazes me to see
people, obviously out for a
Sunday jaunt, leave empty-
handed. When I go to pick up a
dozen oysters, I end up with a
shopping bag full of things I
couldn't say no to.

The market is in a huge
building at the northwest corner
of the island and just outside the
market building are two
excellent food stores: a French
bakery and charcuterie named
La Baguette et L'Échalotte, and
a shellfish store, the Lobster
Man.

Crowds are thick and traffic is
heavy on Sat and Sun on the
small island. Parking can be a
gruesome experience.

Market hours in the winter are
Tues to Sat, 9-6. On holidays,
open Mon, closed Tues. In the
summer from Victoria Day (May
24) to Labour Day, open every
day.

over. They look fabulous and taste
even better. Reasonably priced, open
Sundays. Haven't had a thing I didn't
like. Very French.

A cheerful produce merchant at the Granville Island Public Market.

A FEW MARKET TIPS

● Shop weekdays instead of weekends.
● If you must shop on weekends, go between 9 and 10 AM or between 5 and 6 PM. Otherwise, grin and bear it.
● Once you are on the island, don't waste time looking for a parking spot close to the market – just take the first one you see. You will be, at most, a five-minute walk away.
● On weekends you can avoid the whole congestion problem by parking on 1st, 2nd or 3rd Ave. just east of Burrard. It's then a 10-minute walk.

A Sampling of Favourite Market Foods

● **Duso's** Sauce, a decadently rich cheese, cream and herb sauce for pasta.
● Cheese bagels from **Bageland.** A pastry in the shape of a bagel filled with sweet baker's cheese.
● Freshly squeezed juice from the **Juice Bar:** carrot, watermelon, hot apple-ginger, etc. Also the best salads.
● Turkey ham from the **Turkey Shop,** made of turkey but you'd swear it was ham.
● Coffee roasted-on-spot at the **Coffee Roaster.**
● A litre of freshly made fish stock from the **Stock Market.**
● French twist doughnuts from **Lee's.**
● Golden Mantle oysters from the **Salmon Shop.**
● Lox from the **Smoke House.**
● **Stuart's** 40 varieties of breads.
● Chocolate fudge from **Olde World Fudge.**
● The stunning display of pastries, breads, chocolates and take-out foods (such as boeuf bourguignonne or stuffed, deboned quail) at **La Baguette** just outside the market building.
● Cappuccino with almond syrup at the **Blue Parrot** espresso bar.

For information on the rest of Granville Island, see Sightseeing.

St. Germain Bakery
3246 Cambie near 16th
876-2188
In the Japanese way of improving
what someone else has done, we
have the St. Germain Bakery, a
Japanese French bakery. Their exquisite pastries are lighter and less
sweet than traditional French pastries and are edible works of art.

Uprising Breads
1697 Venables near Commercial
254-5635
A healthy, East End bakery run by a
workers' co-operative. Probably the
best whole-grain breads and some
great scones, muffins and carob
squares too.

CHEESE

Dussa's Ham and Cheese
Granville Island Public Market
688-8881
Fine French goat cheeses to hearty
Canadian Rat Trap Cheddar.

Forster's Fine Cheeses
2104 W. 41st, near East Boulevard
261-5813
Small store with an enormous array
of quality cheeses you won't find
elsewhere, and you can count on
freshness.

Tosi Italian Food Imports
624 Main and Keefer
681-5740
One of the more bizarre stores in
Vancouver – not only because it's an
Italian food store in Chinatown. The
place is not inviting; in fact, you must
ring to get in. Tosi is an importer-
wholesaler who does not really cater
to retail customers and his store
looks it. It's dark and old, but many

of the goods (olive oils, cheeses and
salamis) are half the going price.
Although the store looks decrepit,
the products are fresh and top
quality. Watch for the homemade
wine vinegar from wine-making
friends in the Okanagan.

COFFEE AND TEA

Aroma
2294 W. 4th Ave and Vine
736-1412
Fresh, quality coffee, an extensive
selection of coffee-brewing equipment, especially espresso machines,
and a small espresso bar.

Starbucks
See Restaurants (Espresso Bars).

Torrefazione Coloiera
2206 Commercial and 7th
254-3723
Spartan, East End Italian coffee store
with some of the best coffee around.

DELIS AND
GOURMET TAKE-OUT

Bread Garden
1880 W. 1st off Burrard
738-6684
812 Bute near Robson
688-3213
Luscious desserts, healthy salads
and entrées such as chicken pie,
vegetable torte or frittata. Eat in or
take out. See Restaurants (Espresso
Bars).

Dussa Delicatessen
4125 Main at 25th
874-8610
Easily the best European-style deli in
town; too bad it's not in a handier
location. Still, it isn't that far away,

and you know it's worth it as soon as you walk through the door. Several fine homemade salads, lots of sausages and cheeses at low prices, and a few baked goods.

Dussa's is in the middle of a row of secondhand furniture and antique stores running from about 19th to 30th. You could start at 19th Ave. and browse through antique stores. Pick up a picnic lunch at Dussa's and continue antique shopping up to 30th, then walk west a couple of blocks to Queen Elizabeth Park for lunch.

THE 50th PLUS ANNIVERSARY OF THE NANAIMO BAR
(or a second in your mouth and a lifetime on your hips)

Sooner or later you will undoubtedly run into a deadly delectable called a Nanaimo Bar. It consists of a chocolate shortcake bottom, a layer of sweet, sweet butter cream, then a thin layer of creamy chocolate – and a million calories.

It supposedly appeared in 1936 when the *Vancouver Sun* published a recipe called Chocolate Fridge Cake. Ten years later the Harewood Ladies Society in Nanaimo published the same recipe but called it a Nanaimo Bar. And now 50 years later you'll find it in every second restaurant and bakery in town. But then, if you travel east, you'll come across the Saskatoon Bar and the New York Slice looking suspiciously like our Nanaimo Bar. . . .

La Baguette et L'Échalotte
1680 Johnston, Granville Island
684-1351
You will find everything for an elegant French meal except the bottle of Nuits St-Georges. There are mousses, pâtés, quality cheeses, main courses (stuffed deboned quail, for example), breads, pastries, cakes and chocolates.

Lazy Gourmet
2380 W. 4th and Balsam
734-2507
I never get past the counter with the mocha cheesecake, toffee bars, dream bars, blueberry and cornmeal muffins, sticky buns and the like. So I often miss the seafood quiche, the spinach-and-feta pie and the chicken pesto – and end up with two desserts. There are a few seats by the window if you're lucky.

Leslie Stowe Fine Foods
1780 W. 3rd and Burrard
731-3663
A top-notch caterer has opened a retail food store selling exquisitely prepared take-out dishes (grilled swordfish with caper dijon sauce for example) and specialty packaged foods.

Max's Delicatessen and Bakery
3105 Oak and 15th
733-4838
A good spot to get together a picnic lunch or a quick dinner. Knishes, blintzes, salads, cheeses and sausages, but don't miss the cream cheese with lox and the chopped liver. Good greengrocer next door to complete the picnic. Open late seven days a week.

Stock Market
Granville Island Public Market
687-2433
A brilliant concept carried out perfectly. Originally the idea was to sell soup stocks by the litre (beef, chicken, fish, vegetarian, Chinese, duck, etc.). Then came sauces: satay, black bean, fruit, béarnaise and more. Then a dozen different salad dressings, pasta sauces, salsas, vinegars, mustards, jams, jellies and chutneys. Three different soups every day to be taken home or eaten there.

The thing that I find so amazing is that they produce *everything* out of their 28 m² (300-sq.-ft) stall at the market. The place is truly a wonder. (Oh, I should mention the breakfasts. This may not appeal to everyone, but check it out if you're attracted to Sunny Boy Cereal – a hot 7-grain cereal – topped with chunky home-made apple sauce and surrounded by cream.)

ETHNIC FOODS

Asian (Chinese, Indonesian, Japanese and Thai)
Excellent selection of seasonings, spices, sauces, cookbooks, fresh noodles and produce at the South China Seas Trading Company stall, Granville Island Public Market.

Chinese
In Chinatown on Pender and Keefer, one block east of Main.

East Indian
Shop on Main St. from 48th to 51st Ave., and at Patel's on Commercial Dr. and 6th Ave.

Greek
On W. Broadway from Macdonald to Trutch, especially Parthenon Foods.

Italian
On Commercial Dr. a few blocks north and south of 1st Ave.

Japanese
Powell St. from Jackson to Gore, and the Japanese Food Centre at 349 E. Hastings near Gore.

Kosher
Small selection at Kaplan's near 42nd on Oak, and Leon's at Oak and 21st.

Mexican
The only store that sells exclusively Mexican food products is Que Pasa on Cambie near 17th.

FISH/SHELLFISH

Fujiya Fish and Japanese Foods
453 Powell and Dunlevy
251-3711

Lobster Man
1807 Mast Tower, Granville Island
687-4531

Longliner Sea Foods
Granville Island Public Market
681-9016

Olympia Oyster and Fish
1094 Robson at Thurlow
685-0716

Salmon Shop
Granville Island Public Market
669-3474

Seven Seas
2344 W. 4th near Vine
732-8608

MEAT

Jackson Meats
2214 W. 4th at Yew
733-9165

RB's Gourmet Butchers
Robson Street Public Market
1610 Robson at Cardero
685-6328

Tenderland Meats
Granville Island Public Market
688-6951

Wettig's European Meats and Sausages
1474 Marine, West Van
922-7232

LOCAL SEAFOOD

You've got your flatfish – sole or flounder, a delicate whitefish served in thin fillets.

Lingcod, which comes in fillets or steaks, is available any time of the year, but is best in the winter.

Lean firm halibut steaks are best from May to September.

Thick red snapper fillets are around any time.

You've also got a choice of five kinds of salmon: sockeye (which usually ends up in a tin), pink, chum or the prized chinook and coho. Big salmon harvests are in the summer and fall.

Pacific mackerel is an oily fish with a distinctive flavour.

Steelhead trout, similar in taste to salmon, is best in winter.

Clams harvested locally are either littleneck or butter.

Mussels are becoming respectable and often wind up steamed in restaurants.

Dungeness crab, usually weighing only a pound or two, stalk the local waters year round.

Alaska King Crab, with legs 60 cm (2 ft.) long, is brought in fresh, Aug to Nov, from the Queen Charlotte Islands in northern B.C.

Shrimp and prawns, 5 to 20 cm (2 to 8 in.) long, are in season year round.

Sea scallops from the north coast are available all year, and the tiny, delicate bay scallops are fresh in winter.

The large Pacific oyster, which was imported from Japan in 1912, now is the most popular commercial oyster. You'll be offered them raw, stewed, baked, barbecued, smoked, pan-fried and deep-fried.

WITH THE KIDS

KIDS AND ANIMALS 210

DAY TRIPS 211

MUSEUMS 214

BABY-SITTING 214

ENTERTAINMENT 214

RESTAURANTS 215

SHOPPING 216
Clothing and Shoes, Consignment Shops, Toys, Furniture, Books

Many of these activities are not just for kids and so are described in more detail in other sections.

KIDS AND ANIMALS

Maplewood Children's Farm
405 Seymour River Pl., North Van
929-5610
Maplewood is a 2-ha (5-acre) petting farm of barnyard animals run by the North Van Parks Department. It is larger than the petting farm in Stanley Park, less busy and has more animals. Picnic spots. Open Tues to Sun, 10-4. Closed Mon unless it's a holiday. Admission $1 child, $1.50 adult and $4.50 for families.

Drive over the Second Narrows Bridge to North Van and take the Deep Cove/Mount Seymour exit; you soon cross Seymour River Place. Two B.C. Transit bus routes pass right by the farm: #212 Deep Cove and #211 Seymour.

Richmond Nature Park
11851 Westminster Hwy., Richmond
273-7015
Richmond Nature Park is 40 ha (100 acres) of shrubbery and peat bog, with paths leading you on a nature expedition. The boardwalk around the duck pond is accessible to strollers and wheelchairs, and longer paths wind through the bush.

The Nature House, full of games and displays on natural history, is itself worth the trip. Picnic tables. Wear boots if it's been wet. The nature house is open every day from 10-4:30. Admission is free.

Drive south on Highway 99 and take the Shell Rd. exit, then go left onto Westminster Highway. There is public transit to the park, but it is long and involved. Call 324-3211.

Colbrook Trout Farm
13067 Colbrook Rd., Surrey
594-1865
Colbrook is an operational trout farm with six fishing ponds for children. The springfed ponds are in a natural setting, and each stocks a different size of trout. You pay $1.00/family for admission, bait and rods. You also pay for fish you catch according to size – a 25-cm (10-in.) fish is $2. Open all year on Sun only, 10-6.

Going south on Hwy. 99, take the King George Hwy. exit and drive north 3 km (2 mi.). Turn right onto Colbrook Rd., a gravel road, and go for 3 km (2 mi.). It's the first right after the train tracks.

Capilano Fish Hatchery
See Parks/Beaches/Gardens (Capilano Park).

Horseback Riding
See Sports/Recreation

Horse Shows
Southlands Riding Club (263-4817) at 7025 Macdonald and 53rd holds several shows from spring to fall. Call to find out about events.

Vancouver Aquarium
See Parks/Beaches/Gardens (Stanley Park).

Stanley Park
For animals, go to the zoo, the children's zoo and the pony rides. Lost Lagoon and Beaver Lake have lots of ducks, geese and swans, but please don't feed them bread – it's very bad for them. Bring lettuce or buy birdseed at the Lost Lagoon concession.

DAY TRIPS

Children and ducks at Lost Lagoon in Stanley Park.

Granville Island

Visit the Kids Only Market, the Public Market, the Maritime Market and Emily Carr College of Art and Design.

The Kids Only Market is in a refurbished two-storey building at the entrance to Granville Island. It is jam-packed with 20-odd colourful stores and lunch spots geared to those under 14. There's a children's bookstore, computer store, record store, clothing stores, and any toy or gizmo that a child would fancy. The Kids Only Market is very busy on weekends and very quiet during the week. Open every day in summer and Tues to Sun in winter.

Play at the Water Park and the Children's Adventure Playground (supervised daily from 10-6) near the False Creek Community Centre. The Water Park is a riot. It's a huge wading pool, at the centre of which are a revolving fire hydrant and hoses that kids can use to douse anyone in reach. The adventure playground has innumerable rope and log configurations and a water slide – a big improvement on monkey bars and asphalt.

You may also take the Granville Island Ferry to the Maritime Museum or to Sunset Beach in the West End. See Sightseeing (Granville Island) for other ideas.

Stanley Park

Besides the animals and aquarium listed above, there is a miniature train ride, pitch and putt golf, tennis courts, a playground with an old fire engine, picnic spots, totem poles and Indian dugout canoes, a kids' (aged 5-8) traffic school, bicycle paths

The Water Park on Granville Island provides hours of entertainment for kids, while parents can watch from the patio of Isadora's Restaurant next door.

(bicycle rentals are just outside the park), beaches and swimming pools. If it's warm, stop by the water adventure playground across from Lumberman's Arch. See Parks/Beaches/Gardens (Stanley Park) for more details.

Chinatown
Shop for paper kites, Chinese tops and chopsticks, and then try out the new chopsticks at lunch. Also see Sightseeing (Chinatown) and Restaurants (Chinese).

Playland
Exhibition Park
E. Hastings near Cassiar
255-5161
The rides and miniature golf are open weekends in the spring and every day in the summer. Hours vary, call ahead. Day passes are $16 for those over 4 ft. and $12 for those under.

The Royal Hudson
Ride a vintage steam locomotive up the coast. See Sightseeing (The Royal Hudson/M.V. *Britannia*).

Pedal Boats on Deer Lake
255-0081
Deer Lake is in Burnaby, a 30-minute drive from downtown. At the east end of the lake are boat rentals with pedal boats, canoes, rowboats, kayaks and small sailboats, as well as picnic tables, a sandy beach and a lifeguard. The only access to the east side of the lake is via Canada Way, Burris or Buckingham St. Even though it is a small, urban lake, it is citified only at one end; most of the shoreline is wooded and good for exploring by water. Avoid weekends if possible.

Canoeing at Deep Cove
Deep Cove is a small resort community on the North Shore accessible from downtown by public transit. Deep Cove Canoe Rentals will supply a canoe so you can paddle to the many islands and parks. See Sports/Recreation (Canoeing/Kayaking/Rowing).

Grouse Mountain Skyride/Mount Seymour Chairlift
See Parks/Beaches/Gardens.

Seymour Demonstration Forest
See Sightseeing (Special Interest Tours).

Berry Picking
Pick raspberries and strawberries from mid-June to mid-July. The U-Pick farms closest to Vancouver are near the Reifel Bird Sanctuary.

Check for U-Pick farms under Food Products in the newspaper want ads.

Pick blueberries from mid-July until Sept. Take the No. 5 Rd. exit from Highway 99, go south and turn on to Granville Ave. in Richmond, where the berry farms are. Phone the B.C. Blueberry Co-op at 520-5777 for details. Take containers.

Stern-wheeler Ride up Burrard Inlet

For this Harbour Ferries tour, see Sightseeing (Touring Vancouver).

University of British Columbia/Pacific Spirit Park

Walk through the forest in the park, or swim in the kids' pool at the Aquatic Centre, tour the dairy barns or see the dinosaur skeleton in the geology museum.

Also see Parks/Beaches/Gardens (Pacific Spirit Park), Sports/Recreation (Swimming) and Sightseeing (Special Interest Tours).

Lynn Canyon Park

Visit the ecology centre, go hiking and picnicking, and walk across the suspension bridge 72 m (240 ft.) above the rapids.

The park is accessible from downtown by public transit via the SeaBus and the #229 Phibbs Exchange/Westlynn bus. Everything in the park is free.

Lighthouse Park

The kids will love scrambling on the rocks near the lighthouse. See Parks/Beaches/Gardens.

Newton Wave Pool

13730 – 72nd Ave.
near King George Hwy.
594-7873

Body surfing in Vancouver?! Besides the wave pool with 3-foot waves, there are waterslides, a wading pool, exercise room, whirlpool, steam room, baby-sitting and coffee shop. You can also rent inner tubes, air mattresses and kick boards. Well worth the drive, phone for directions.

Power Plant

750 Pacific Blvd., foot of Robson
682-8770

Make your own 45 record! Small recording studio where you sing along with their pre-recorded music. $16 for one song including practice time.

Richmond Go-Kart Track

6631 Sidaway, Richmond
278-6184

The Richmond Track is an 800-m (0.5 mi.) asphalt track with lots of curves. No minimum age, but a minimum height is necessary to operate the go-karts. Open every day from noon to dusk, $7 for 12 minutes.

Drive south on Highway 99, take the No. 4 Rd. exit and go east on Westminster Highway.

Skiing

Preschool ski lessons are given on a register-in-advance basis at Grouse Mountain (downhill) and at Cypress (cross-country). Drop-in ski lessons for juniors are held on Grouse weekends and holidays. Call the Grouse Mountain Ski School (980-9311) for particulars.

You can walk right inside a beaver lodge in the Search Gallery of Science World.

Splashdown Park
943-2251
Twisting water slides – 120 m (400 ft.) of them – are the main attraction, but there are also hot tubs, patios for tanning, lawns for picnics, a snack bar, mini-golf, video arcade, volleyball, smaller slides for little kids and a toddlers' pool. The water is heated. (Even if the weather is marginal in town, it is always sunny in Tsawwassen.) Located on Highway 17 just before the Tsawwassen ferry terminal. Admission $12 for anyone over 11, with discounts for younger children and half days.

Sunday Afternoon Baseball
Combine a picnic in Queen Elizabeth Park with the last two innings of baseball at neighbouring Nat Bailey Stadium. The Vancouver Canadians games start at 1:30, and admission is free after the seventh inning (about an hour and a half later). Call 872-5232 for schedule.

MUSEUMS

Science World is Vancouver's only museum expressly for children. Kids also love the *St. Roch* (a restored two-masted schooner where you can walk right on board) in the Maritime Museum and Burnaby Village Museum. For more details on these and other museums, see Museums/Art Galleries.

BABY-SITTING
See Essential Information.

ENTERTAINMENT

Friday's edition of the *Vancouver Sun* lists kids' activities for the coming week in two columns: Children's World and Family Fun. Regular events are:

Imax Theatre
Canada Place
682-4629 (info)
280-4444 (tickets)
A huge five-storey screen shows adventure films: ride the Colorado River through the Grand Canyon, explore the mysteries of flight, or some such delight. Reserved seats.

Vancouver East Cultural Centre
1895 Venables and Victoria
254-9578
Live theatre or films Sat afternoons from Sept to March.

Museum of Anthropology
6393 N.W. Marine, UBC Campus
228-5087
Family events (often related to Indian culture) periodically scheduled on Sun afternoons.

VANCOUVER CHILDREN'S FESTIVAL

With luck, you'll be in town with kids for the Vancouver Children's Festival, held in May at Vanier Park. If so, take advantage of the topnotch local and international actors, mimes, musicians, clowns, storytellers, jugglers and puppeteers gathered solely to entertain young people.

Huge, colourful tents are set up at Vanier Park on the shores of Burrard Inlet, and events are staged for a whole week. About 200 entertainers come from B.C. and from as far away as New York, Portugal and Japan. An excellent detailed program, available at ticket outlets, describes the performances and the ages they appeal to.

Outside the tents, there is free entertainment – strolling musicians, mimes, jugglers and the clowns who delight in painting small faces.

Although the festival is well attended, some tickets are available the week of the festival. Tickets go on sale in March at Ticketmaster outlets. Once the festival starts, tickets are available on site.

If you can't get tickets for the event you have your heart set on, go anyway for the free on-site entertainment, the food booths, the museums and the sea. For more information call 687-7697.

RESTAURANTS

Chinese restaurants cater to families and so mess and noise are not usually a problem. See Restaurants (Chinese).

Chuck E. Cheese's
9898 Government Place, Burnaby
421-8408
Located off the corner of North Rd. and Lougheed Highway. Rides, video games, a ball room, games and clowns in a restaurant? No surprise from a place called Chuck E. Cheese's. The food is nothing special, pizza and hot dogs, but everything takes second place to the fun. Birthday parties are their specialty.

Isadora's
1540 Old Bridge, Granville Island
681-8816
Play area for kids inside the restaurant and out. See Restaurants (Breakfast/Brunch).

Nick's Spaghetti House
631 Commercial and E. Georgia
254-5633
Paper bibs and a children's menu in a big-happy-family atmosphere.

Old Spaghetti Factory
53 Water near Abbott in Gastown
684-1288
Old-time paraphernalia decorates the restaurant, including a vintage streetcar and silent movies. Children's portions.

The Kids Only Market on Granville Island has dozens of shops just for kids.

Tomahawk Barbecue

1550 Philip near Marine, North Van
988-2612
Mostly burgers (named after local Indian chiefs), hot dogs, sandwiches and big breakfasts – very good quality and reasonably priced. Full of Indian memorabilia, and kids are given a paper mask and headdress. Open every day for breakfast, lunch and dinner. See Restaurants (Breakfast/Brunch).

SHOPPING

CLOTHING AND SHOES

Bratz

2828 Granville and W. 12th
734-4344
Looking for designer clothes for kids? This is the place. The imported clothing is lovely but incredibly expensive.

Kids hair salon also in the store.

Gorton's Emporium for Children

Lansdowne Park Shopping Centre
5300 No. 3 Rd. near Westminster Hwy., Richmond
273-3899
A children's department store stocking clothing, toys, books, etc., even party supplies.

Isola Bella

5633 W. Boulevard at 40th
266-8808
Furniture in the shape of castles, palm trees or dinosaurs. Also clothing, everything imported.

Kiddie Kobbler Children's Shoes

Park Royal South, West Van
926-1616
Several locations, but Park Royal is

the best. Good basic selection of quality children's shoes. Knowledgeable staff make sure you get the right fit.

Peppermintree Children's Wear

4243 Dunbar and 27th
228-9815

The best kids' store in Vancouver. Fashionable, quality clothes, shoes and accessories from North America and Europe in the medium-price range. The friendly staff are all experienced moms with helpful suggestions. Kids' play area.

CONSIGNMENT SHOPS

Nipper's

5585 Dunbar at 40th
266-1454

Piggy and Bee

548 W. Broadway near Cambie
872-6009

Used and moderately priced new clothing for babies and toddlers plus some used furniture.

Dragon and Phoenix

6248 E. Boulevard near 46th
261-1317

This used clothing store is one of the few that has a kids' section. Emphasis on clothes for children 12 months and up, particularly preteens. Shoes as well as clothes.

See also Shopping (Consignment Clothing Stores/Value Village).

TOYS

B.C. Playthings

1065 Marine, North Van
986-4111

This toy store definitely warrants a detour. They have art supplies, books, preschool supplies, climbing equipment, puppets, puzzles, games and records. Wonderful English wagons and face-colouring crayons. An 80-page catalogue is available for $3. Marvellous staff.

Bears Toy Store

1459 Bellevue and 15th, West Van
926-BEAR

This store is so delightful you won't be able to tear yourself away. It is the home of over 1000 Teddy Bears, but all kinds of other toys too, mostly European, and a very good choice of dolls. All the toys on display are meant to be touched.

3-H Society Boutique

2112 W. 4th and Arbutus
736-2113

All the toys here are handmade, often by the homebound or handicapped, and they will custom-make toys according to your wants. Their old-fashioned rag dolls are magical.

Windmill Toys

2387 W. 41st and Balsam
261-2120

A large store carrying everything you could want. Several locations, but the Kerrisdale one is the best. The books and model sets are particularly good.

Imagination Market
528 Powell St. (east of Main)
253-1033
The perfect name for a perfect idea. It sells industrial cast-offs for next to nothing. Buy bits and pieces of brightly coloured paper, cloth, plastic, rubber and cardboard for kids' arts and crafts projects. This store has the potential to be a disaster area, but it is well organized and the staff are super friendly.

The store holds regular classes here (free drop-in classes every Sat and Sun afternoon) and all round town. Open Thurs to Sun only.

Einstein's
4424 Dunbar and 28th
738-3622
A wonderful store selling science-related toys, games and books. Phone about their classes.

See also Sightseeing (Granville Island, Kids Only Market).

FURNITURE

Ikea
Bridgeport and Knight
Richmond
273-2051
Vast selection of colourful contemporary furniture and accessories for the whole family generally at low prices.

Ikea's famous ball room is knee-deep in hundreds of soft plastic balls to jump, throw and bury yourself in. It's for kids 3 to 7 and is supervised. An outdoor playground has tire rides, a suspension bridge and all sorts of climbing contrivances. The cafeteria has kid-sized furniture and a menu for children that includes baby food.

Kids Furniture World
12680 Bridgeport Road, Richmond
278-7654
Specializing in pine, maple, and oak children's furniture. Near Ikea.

TJ's Kiddies Korner
3231 Fraser near 16th
876-8616
3331 Jacombs Rd. (behind Ikea)
270-8830
This one-of-a-kind store will buy back what your child outgrows. Consequently, they sell new and used articles. Best selection and prices on items like Strolee carseats and Perego strollers. TJ's also does repair work, sells parts and rents infant equipment.

Friendly Bears
4411 No. 3 Rd. (near Cambie)
Richmond
276-8278
Largest selection of kids' furniture with prices that are moderate to high.

BOOKS

Vancouver Kidsbooks
3083 W. Broadway and Balaclava
738-5335
The best assortment of children's books, run by a former librarian and current mom. Selection of board books for babies is excellent. Books, records and tapes, some in French.

EXCURSIONS FROM VANCOUVER

GULF ISLANDS 220
Ferries, Services, Where to Stay

GALIANO ISLAND 221
Tourist Information, Accommodation, Restaurants, Sports and Recreation, Scenic Spots, The Arts

MAYNE ISLAND 224
Tourist Information, Accommodation, Restaurants, Sports and Recreation, Scenic Spots, The Arts

SALT SPRING ISLAND 226
Tourist Information, Accommodation, Restaurants, Sports and Recreation, Scenic Spots, The Arts

WHISTLER 229
Getting There, Tourist Information, Accommodation, Restaurants, Sports and Recreation

BC Ferry routes in the Gulf Islands.

THE GULF ISLANDS

The Gulf Islands form a cluster between the mainland and the south end of Vancouver Island. The southern Gulf Islands are Galiano, Mayne, Saturna, North and South Pender, and Salt Spring. Spanish placenames come from Captain Dionysio Galiano who was the first to explore the area in 1792.

Because the only public access is by ferry, the islands are fairly undeveloped. In the fifties and sixties they were a community of artists, writers, retired people and others looking for an alternative style of living. Now, with increased ferry service, there are many weekend cottagers.

The climate of the islands, which is sunnier and drier than Vancouver, has always been an attraction – resorts were built on the islands even in the late 1800s.

FERRIES
BC Ferries travel to all the Gulf Islands. Most trips are milk-runs, stopping at each island. Consequently the two islands closest to Vancouver, Galiano and Mayne, have the shortest ferry trips – 50 minutes to an hour and a half. Ferry service from Tsawwassen is once to three times a day. Sailing to Salt Spring is a much longer trip, about two and a half hours from Tsawwassen.

The route to the Gulf Islands is one of the few for which you can make a car reservation, an absolute necessity for summer weekends and holiday weekends. Phone BC Ferries at 685-1021 for the schedule and 669-1211 for reservations. See also Getting Around (Ferries).

SERVICES
There are no banks on Galiano or Mayne but you will find a post office, gas station, liquour store, bakery, deli and small grocery stores. Salt Spring is much more developed and in the town of Ganges you'll find a supermarket, small shopping centre, and a Canadian Imperial Bank of Commerce and Bank of Montreal.

WHERE TO STAY
Accommodation on the islands is limited; don't count on finding a place to stay without a reservation, particularly on summer and holiday weekends. The **Gulf Islands Bed and Breakfast Registry** (539-5390) will book accommodation on any of the Gulf Islands. Even if you can't

Woodstone Inn/Pat Walker

get a reservation, you can still see a lot on a day trip.

Most places will pick you up from the ferry if you are coming without a car. Request this when making your reservation. Prices for high season range from $55 to $125 and many places require a three-day minimum during this time.

You will find a choice of accommodation including a room in a private house (an informal bed and breakfast), bed and breakfast in a large Victorian house that caters to several guests, rustic cabins, modern rumpus-room style cabins, and classy inns, any of which might be by the water.

GALIANO ISLAND

Galiano is a skinny island that is 26 km (16 mi.) long. The resident population is about 800, most of

A stroll away from the Woodstone Inn is a marsh lush with bird life. The inn provides gum boots, binoculars and bird books.

whom live at the south end. The logging giant MacMillan Bloedel owns about half of the island.

TOURIST INFORMATION
A tourist booth, at Sturdies Bay near the ferry dock, keeps sporadic hours but is generally open in the summer when the ferry lands. Throughout the year you can write to the **Galiano Island Visitor's Association**, Box 73, Galiano, B.C. V0N 1P0 or phone 539-2233.

ACCOMMODATION
For rural sophistication try the **Woodstone Country Inn** (539-2022); **Sutil Lodge** (539-2930), a charming 1928 lodge on Montague

Country lanes through thick coastal rain forest on Galiano Island.

Heather Frankson

Harbour; **Penny's Cottages** (539-5457) and **Madrona Lodge** (539-2926), family-style west coast cottages; **Tall Trees** (539-5365) if you want to be pampered in a very private waterfront B&B; **La Berengerie** (539-5392) for a modest, B&B above one of Galiano's best restaurants; **Bodega Resort (539-2677)**, Galiano's dude ranch; and **Holloway House** (539-2581), bed and breakfast in a large log home.

RESTAURANTS

La Berengerie (539-5392) has a warm and cozy country-style dining room. The $18 fixed-price, four-course menu varies but leans towards continental. You'll generally find local specialties such as salmon and local produce. Arrive early for an aperitif on the porch. Frequent live dinner music such as classical guitar. Must book in advance.

The **Woodstone Inn** (539-2022) is open to nonguests for dinner. The dining room is the most formal on Galiano. Request a table by the window looking out on a lovely meadow. The fixed-price menu changes daily, four courses are $19.50 and a lighter two-course meal (your choice of which two) is $13.50. Entrées one night were roast duck with plum sauce or poached salmon with shrimp Pernod butter. Reservations a must.

Lony's Cozy Cafe at the Market (539-2505) is probably the best place on the island for a family dinner at reasonable prices. The menu changes every day but regular items are steamed scallops and grilled salmon, lamb and chicken. Lunch is soup, sandwiches and pizza. The decor is rustic with large tables, a fireplace and a deck. In the summer the cafe is open for lunch and dinner daily and for Sunday brunch. In the winter lunch is served, Mon to Sat; dinner, Fri to Sun; and coffee and dessert on week nights.

The **Hummingbird Inn** (539-2022), generally known as the pub, serves simple food: burgers, chowder, fish and chips, etc. Often crowded in the evenings. Open every day for lunch and dinner. Occasional live entertainment, usually a guitar-playing local. The Hummingbird operates a bus, the only one on the island, that goes from Montague Harbour (for campers and boaters) to the pub. During the summer it leaves Montague Harbour on the hour starting at 5:00 PM.

SPORTS AND RECREATION

Bicycling on Galiano requires stamina; the island is long and hilly and you may find yourself walking up some hills. The narrow winding roads have no paved shoulders so it is imperative to ride single file. Bikes can be rented at **Gulf Island Kayaking** (539-2442), **Matthew Schoenfeld** (539-2806) and **Blue Moon Rentals** (539-2954).

Two **campgrounds** with a total of 39 sites are located in **Montague Harbour Provincial Park**. You must hike to one of them while the other is accessible by car. It is first come, first served, and it can be difficult to get a spot during the summer or on long weekends. There are no RV hook-ups on the island.

In Canada the beach below the high tide line is public property. Because tides are much lower in the summer, it is possible to camp on the beach. Campfires are prohibited in the summer because of drought conditions.

No experience is necessary for guided kayak trips from **Gulf Island Kayaking** (539-2442) ranging from 3 hours to 5 days. Kayak and canoe rentals also.

Fishing gear and bait are available at **Galiano Garage** (539-5500) in Sturdies Bay. For fishing charters call **Bert's Charters** (539-3181) or **Fish and Ships** (539-2532).

The **Galiano Golf and Country Club** (539-5533) was established in 1975. The licensed clubhouse serves breakfast and lunch. It is par 32 over 9 holes, 1996 yds.

Bodega Farm (539-2677) has guided **horseback riding** trips for $10/hr on 40 km (25 mi.) of scenic trails with 360° views.

Every day during the summer Tom Hennessy, owner of **South-wind Sailing Charters** (539-2930), sets sail on his 14-m (46-ft.) catamaran for a four-hour cruise. Catamarans are fast and smooth and have plenty of flat deck space so are very safe for children. You will sail to a bird sanctuary and stop at a sandy beach on Salt Spring Island for a picnic supper. Costs a very reasonable $30. A variation of this trip is available as a $140-day trip from Vancouver. A 6-seater seaplane leaves from downtown Vancouver and flies to Montague Harbour where you can board directly onto the catamaran. After the supper cruise you fly back to Vancouver. Southwind also charters boats with or without skippers and offers regular sailings between Montague Harbour and Ganges (the village on Salt Spring Island) and can accommodate cyclists.

The Gulf Islands are probably the most popular **diving** destination in southwestern B.C. Air is available at Madrona Lodge (539-2926) and at the Alcala Point Resort (539-5720).

Galiano Resort (539-5252) in Sturdies Bay has a **tennis** court available to the public.

SCENIC SPOTS

By Galiano standards it's a long drive to the northern tip of the island at **Coon Bay**, but the beaches here are perhaps the best on the island – sandy or smooth sloping sandstone rock.

Montague Harbour Provincial Park is the site of 3000-year-old Indian middens that are still visible in the cliffs by the shore. An island/peninsula juts out of the park into the harbour; at low tide you can walk

Montague Harbour on Galiano Island.

around on the beach or take the path up above at high tide.

Galiano Bluffs Park was bequeathed to the people of Galiano. You can drive, via Burrill Rd. and Bluff Rd., to the top of the bluffs through stands of old-growth fir and cedar and arrive at views of Victoria and the American San Juan Islands. There are also hiking trails in the park.

Bellhouse Park, also a legacy to islanders, is a good picnic spot. It has picnic tables and good views of Active Pass and the Mayne Island lighthouse. Access is by Burrill Rd. and Jack Rd.

THE ARTS
The **Dandelion Gallery** in Sturdies Bay exhibits local painting, sculpture, glass, jewellery and photographs and sells books written by Galiano Islanders. Open every day in the summer and every weekend the rest of the year.

The **Galiano Gardens Theatre** stages good amateur productions. It is an outdoor theatre and sometimes even serves dinner. The theatre is on Pattison Lane just off Porlier Pass Rd. Look for posters in Sturdies Bay or ask about the current show at the tourist information booth.

MAYNE ISLAND

Compared to long narrow Galiano, Mayne is small and compact – you can drive anywhere in about 10 minutes. While Galiano is covered with forest, Mayne is much more pastoral. It has even fewer tourist amenities than Galiano. Don't go expecting much choice in restaurants or accommodation; the charm of Galiano and Mayne lies in the beaches and tide pools, the birds, seals and sea lions, the coast forests and the slower pace of life.

TOURIST INFORMATION
Pick up the indispensable map produced by the islanders that is available free on the ferry and at any store on Mayne. Not only will it help you getting around but it lists all the services and attractions on the island. In high season tourist information is available at the museum in Miners Bay. During the year write to **Mayne Island Chamber of Commerce**, Box 160, Mayne Island, B.C. V0N 2J01.

ACCOMMODATION
Fernhill Lodge (539-2544) has six rooms decorated in historical themes; **Oceanwood Country Inn** (539-5074) is genteel with French doors, chintz and afternoon tea; **Blue Vista Resort's** (539-2463)

Oceanwood Country Inn

cabins are the best bet for family accommodation; and the **Root Seller Inn** (539-2621) is a friendly country bed and breakfast that is popular with hikers and cyclists.

RESTAURANTS
Fernhill Lodge (539-2544) has built its reputation on historical dinners. Depending on the day of the week, the chef may be serving for example, a Cleopatra Dinner, a Chaucer dinner or a Roman dinner. The Crumblehumes research these historical meals, make a few adaptions for the twentieth century and serve dishes like red snapper with plums, coriander and wine (apparently a favourite of Cleopatra's), leek and walnut soup or a Chaucerian salmon with thyme sauce. These menus are rotated with a contemporary farmhouse menu. Reservations are a must.

Oceanwood Country Inn sits on 4 ha (10 acres) of wooded waterfront property. It has a lawn for croquet, a sauna and an outdoor hot tub. A small conference room, living room, library chockablock with books and magazines, and a games room with bridge tables (where afternoon tea is served) are all for the use of guests.

Oceanwood Country Inn (539-5074) is open to nonguests for dinner and Sunday brunch. Dinner is a fixed price $20 meal (brunch is $10) that is seasonal and focuses on local products. One fall menu offered beet and orange soup, warm scallop salad, roasted chicken with roast garlic and ginger-pumpkin soufflé. All wines are from the west coast. Book in advance.

Springwater Lodge (539-5521) serves pub food – burgers, sandwiches and fish and chips – but it's well done and when you eat in the sun on the deck overlooking Miners Bay, it's even better.

SPORTS AND RECREATION

Although Mayne is not flat, it is one of the easier islands to **bicycle** around. The island is compact and roads form convenient loops. Rentals are available at **Active Pass Auto Marine** in Miners Bay (539-5411).

Bait and licenses are also available at **Active Pass Auto Marine** (539-5411) and at the **Trading Post** (539-2214), both in Miners Bay. The best spot for summer **salmon fishing** around the islands is in Active Pass, the body of water separating Mayne and Galiano.

Island Charters (539-5040) will arrange **sailing** charters on their Saturna 33 sailboat for a half day, day or overnight. They will pick you up or drop you off at one of the other Gulf Islands.

A public **tennis** court is behind the firehall on Felix Jack Rd. off Fernhill Rd.

SCENIC SPOTS

It is about a two-hour hike to **Edith Point** round trip from the end of Edith Point Rd. You can walk along the cliff overlooking the water or if the tide is out, along the beach. The path is steep in parts. At the point there are smooth sloping sandstone rocks for sunbathing.

Mount Parke is a 12-ha (31-acre) wilderness park and the highest point on the island. Access is off Village Bay Rd. and you can drive part way up the mountain. Views of Vancouver, Active Pass and Vancouver Island are almost 360°. There is an unmanned satellite radar station on the top which monitors ship traffic in Active Pass.

St. Mary Magdalene Church, built in 1898, is one of many fine Victorian buildings on Mayne.

Stately old houses of the same era are in Miners Bay and Georgina Point Rd. You can glean a little of the history of the island from the old cemetery beside the church. Across the street a stairway leads down to the beach.

The **Active Pass Lighthouse**, built in 1885, at Georgina Point is open to the public every afternoon from 1-3. The grassy grounds are perfect for a picnic. This is a good birdwatching spot, particularly in winter, and there are many tidal pools along the sandstone shore.

The beach at **Bennett Bay** is very popular and is the warmest for swimming because it is so shallow. Mount Baker in Washington State is in the distance.

THE ARTS

Several artists and craftspeople open their studios to the public daily in the summer and on weekends during the rest of the year. Check the map published by the islanders for locations and times. The **House of Taylor** (539-2431) in Miners Bay is an excellent gallery of local arts and crafts.

Mayne Island Little Theatre stages amateur productions in spring and fall; watch for posters.

SALT SPRING ISLAND

Salt Spring is very different from the other Gulf Islands. It is the largest, most populated (7000 residents) and most developed. Unlike the others, Salt Spring has a real town, even a shopping centre, two banks, a newspaper, over 40 B&Bs and more real estate agents than you'd care to see in one place. Other singular features are the several small lakes

Dick Tipple

which provide warm swimming spots and the 14 briny springs at the north end of the island which gave the island its name.

The first settlers on Salt Spring were black Americans fleeing slavery in 1857. The island started and developed as an agricultural community and is now famous for its Salt Spring Island lamb.

TOURIST INFORMATION

Tourist information is available all year (though hours are sporadic) from the Travel Infocentre at 121 Lower Ganges Road in Ganges or during the summer at the Travel Infocentre at the Fulford Inn at Fulford Harbour. You could also write to the **Salt Spring Island Chamber of Commerce**, Box 111, Ganges, B.C. V0S 1E0.

The Gulf Islands are considered one of the best sailing areas in the world.

ACCOMMODATION

Of the many B&Bs on Salt Spring, some recommended ones are: **The Old Farmhouse** (537-4113), **Southdown Farm** (653-4322), **Weston Lake Inn** (653-4311), **Captain's Passage** (537-9469), **Ellacott Farm** (653-9502) and **Siddlesham House** (653-9232). B&B accommodation for families can be found at **Spring Thicket Farm** (537-5417), **Trincomali Vista** (537-2098) and **Applecroft** (537-5605).

Cabins can be rented on the sea or by a lake at: **The Last Resort** (537-4111), **Booth Bay Resort** (537-5651), **Cedar Beach Resort** (537-2205) and **Spindrift** (537-5311).

A quiet cove in the Gulf Islands where you'd find playful harbour seals.

The most deluxe and expensive accommodation is at **Hastings House** (537-2362), an elegant and gracious inn.

Rates for B&Bs during high season range from $55-90 for a double, cabins are a little more and Hastings House could set you back over $300.

RESTAURANTS

My favourite place to eat is the **Vesuvius Inn** (537-2312), both for its very good pub food and the spectacular setting on Vesuvius Bay. Other good casual restaurants are **Lulu's** (537-2331) for Mexican food; **Seaside Kitchen** (537-2249), known for its fish and chips and wonderful view; the **New Deli Cafe** (537-4181) and the **Chatterbox Cafe** (537-4127). **Hastings House** (537-2362) and the **Bay Window** (537-5651) are both formal restaurants with

traditional menus – where you might try some local seafood or famous Salt Spring Island lamb.

SPORTS AND RECREATION

Rent bicycles or sign up for a guided **bicycle** tour at **Island Spoke Folk** (537-4664). Rentals are also available at the **Salt Spring Marina** (537-5810) and **Western Cyclogical** (537-4411). If you're heading out on your own, remember that the north end of the island is flatter.

Arrange **horseback rides** through **Salt Spring Trail Rides** (537-5761).

Canoes, kayaks and small power boats are for rent at the **Salt Spring Marina** (537-5810) in Ganges. They also have a full service scuba shop.

Four public **tennis** courts are on Vesuvius Rd. near North End Rd.

The **Salt Spring Island Golf and Country Club** is a 9-hole, par 72 course that is open to visitors all year. It is across from the tennis courts.

SCENIC SPOTS

Beaver Point in **Ruckle Provincial Park** is an exquisite picnic and hiking spot: smooth rocks sloping into the water, arbutus trees on the point and small pebble coves for beachcombing. Trails are suitable for family hiking. Ruckle Park is also an historic site. The Ruckles were one of Salt Spring's first farming families; their home and outbuildings are still standing in the park and are identified by plaques.

Mount Maxwell is not the highest point on the island but it has a viewpoint that you can drive to and a network of easy trails.

Beddis Beach at the end of Beddis Road is wide and sandy and is good for sunbathing, birdwatching and beachcombing. Other beaches are at Beachside Drive on Long Harbour, **Saint Mary Lake**, **Booth Bay** via Baker Rd. and **Drummond Park** at Fulford Harbour.

THE ARTS

Volume II (537-9223) is a small but first-rate bookstore in Mouat's Mall in Ganges. Also at the mall is **Pegasus Gallery of Canadian Art** (537-2421), the best gallery on the island. During the summer artists sell their work daily at **Artcraft** in Mahon Hall in Ganges. The **Salt Spring Festival of the Arts** with music, theatre and dance is held in July. Watch for posters or inquire at the Travel Infocentre.

WHISTLER

Until 1977 Whistler townsite was a garbage dump. In just over a decade it has become a major international ski resort. And in the last few years Whistler has developed its summer-

The shoreline of much of the Gulf Islands is either steep cliffs or this smooth sandstone. Odd formations have been sculpted by thousands of years of hammering by the sea.

time facilities to the point where soon there will be no off season. However summertime at Whistler is not just for adventurous outdoors types. In addition to mountain biking, paragliding or heli-hiking, Whistler now offers one summer festival after another. There's Mozart, jazz, country and blues, Vancouver Symphony Orchestra concerts and daily street entertainment.

GETTING THERE

Whistler is 120 km (75 mi.) north of Vancouver on Hwy. 99, an hour-and-a-half drive. The winding mountain road can be dangerous in the winter. Snow tires are mandatory and chains are sometimes necessary. Call the **Dept. of Highways** (660-9775) for road conditions. Car rentals are available at Whistler through **Budget** (932-1236) and **Avis** (938-1331).

Throughout the year there is daily train (**BC Rail**, 984-5246) and bus service (**Maverick Coach**

Lines, 255-1171) from Vancouver to Whistler. During ski season the bus service increases and includes service directly from the Vancouver airport (**Perimeter Transportation,** 261-2299).

The train trip is much prettier but the schedule lacks flexibility – there is only one train. The station is a few miles out of town; a waiting shuttle bus transports train passengers to the village but you have to take a cab back. Whereas the bus to and from Vancouver drops you off and picks you up right at the village. The best idea would be to take the train up and one of the buses back to Vancouver.

TOURIST INFORMATION

A tourist information booth is on the highway at Lake Placid Road, 3 km (2 mi.) south of Whistler. Another booth is at the front door of the Conference Centre in the village. You can also call the **Whistler Resort Association** (932-3928 in Whistler or 685-3716 in Vancouver) for general information. To book accommodation call them at 932-4222 in Whistler, 689-3650 in Vancouver, 628-0982 in Seattle or toll free in the other states at 1-800-634-9622.

ACCOMMODATION

Accommodation at Whistler falls into three groups: high-priced luxury hotels, mid-range condominium hotels and pensions. Off season rates apply generally Nov, Dec and Apr (also Jan at some places). During high season minimum stays of three nights are required when making a reservation. The Whistler Resort Association (see phone numbers above) will book accommodation for you.

The best hotels, the **Chateau Whistler** (938-8000) and the **Delta Mountain Inn** (932-1982), will cost you an arm and a leg (nothing is cheap at Whistler) unless it's off season. The lobby of the Chateau is fabulous: huge stone fireplaces, comfy overstuffed wingbacked sofas, handmade Mennonite rugs, antique pine furniture and Canadiana folk art. Stop by for a look or a drink in the lobby bar even if you're not staying at the hotel. During high season prices start at about $200 for double rooms.

Because the entire townsite was built after 1977, many of the mid-range hotels are more or less the same age and style. Most rooms have been planned for skiers and have kitchen facilities and sleep at least four people. These rooms often show the wear of intense use. Book through the Whistler Resort Association (see phone numbers above).

The third group, the pensions, are Bavarian chalet style and are usually run by Austrian, German or Swiss Canadians. They are in large houses with half a dozen guest rooms and private family quarters. The pensions are in residential areas rather than in the village, although many are only a 15-minute walk away. If you are coming without a car, the innkeepers will drive you to and from the ski lifts. In the evening you could walk or take a cab to a restaurant. Hearty breakfasts are included and many rooms have private baths. Pension rates are more or less the same, about $100 for two in high season and $70 off season. Pensions are a great deal because along with comfortable accommodation, you get affable and informative hosts and interesting breakfast companions, more likely from Boston or Berlin rather than Vancouver. The pensions are **Edelweiss** (932-3641), **Haus Heidi** (932-3113), **Chalet Luise** (932-4187), **Durlacher Hof** (938-1980), **Alta Vista** (932-4900) and **Carney's Cottage** (938-8007).

RESTAURANTS
All the best restaurants in the Whistler area are expensive; you'll easily spend $100 for two. If you want a good meal on a weekend during ski season, make a reservation a few weeks in advance.

Vancouver's Umberto Menghi operates three Italian restaurants in the area: **Il Caminetto** (932-4442) and **Trattoria di Umberto** (932-5858) in the village and **Umberto's Grill** (932-3000) at Whistler Creek, a couple of miles south. The **Rim Rock Cafe & Oyster Bar** (932-5565) near Umberto's Grill has a big reputation for seafood. **Val d'Isère** (932-4666), which is a little cheaper than the others, serves classic French food and is in the village.

Both restaurants in the Chateau Whistler are very good. In fact one of the them, **La Fiesta** (938-2040), a Spanish tapas bar, may be the only bargain in Whistler. The other Chateau restaurant is the **Wild-flower Cafe** (938-2033). Charmingly decorated with over 100 old wooden birdhouses, it offers lavish buffets for breakfast, lunch and dinner or a menu featuring foods of the Pacific Northwest. Two other top-notch restaurants are Japanese: **Sushi Village** (932-3330) and **Irori** (932-2221), both in the village.

If all you want is a decent burger or some pasta, try **Johnny Jupiter's** (932-3531), **Jimmy D's Roadhouse** (932-4451) or the **Original Ristorante** (932-6408), all in the village. **Citta** is a popular hangout for young people.

SPORTS AND RECREATION
You can either rent **mountain bikes** and set off on your own or join a group. Trails lead from the village to Lost Lake; you can get there and back in an hour. The Valley Trail, a 13-km (8-mi.) cycling and hiking trail will take you most of the day. South of the village the trail is paved and flat; northwards to Lost Lake it is a bit more of a challenge. Bikes can't be reserved so get there early in the day. **McConkey Sport Shop** (932-2311) and **Bikestop** (932-23659) are both in the village; **Whistler Outdoor Experience** (932-3389) is at Lakeside Park.

The other option is to join a bike tour. These can be two hours, all day or several days. Itineraries are geared to different levels of ability. A popular guided ride is The Descent where you take your bike up Blackcomb Mountain in the gondola and ride back down. Call **Lifestyles Adventure Company** (932-4264) or **Whistler Backroads** (932-3111).

Five lakes are within 5 km (3 mi.) of the village. **Whistler Outdoor Experience** (932-3389) rents canoes, windsurfing boards and laser sailboats at Lakeside Park on Alta Lake and at Alpha Lake Park. They also offer windsurfing lessons and short canoe trips. Kayak rentals and tours are available from **Whistler Kayak Adventures** (932-3111), north of the village on Green Lake.

It was **fishing** that attracted people to Whistler for decades before anyone thought of skiing. The

Louise Christie

five lakes and many rivers and streams surrounding Whistler still provide great trout fishing. Go to **Whistler Village Sports** (932-3327) for tackle, licences and information. For guided trips call **Green River Fishing Guides** (932-3474) or **Whistler Backcountry Adventures** (938-1410). Trips vary from half day to several days.

Arnold Palmer designed the **Whistler Golf Course** (932-4544), an 18-hole championship course adjacent to the village. 6100 yds. (whites), par 72.

If you want to hike on your own, you can take a lift up Blackcomb or Whistler where there are several trails or join one of the groups for a free guided mountaintop hike. Call **Whistler Mountain** (932-3434) or **Blackcomb Mountain** (932-3141). The Valley Trail, leaving in several directions from the village out to the five lakes, is good for family hiking.

Diamond Head Chalet, a way station for hikers, was built in the 1940s near Elphin Lakes in neighbouring Garibaldi Provincial Park.

For organized group trips, **Whistler Outdoor Experience** (932-3389) offers three half-day hikes: alpine, wilderness or a photo hike with a photographer.

Climbing specialists, **The Escape Route** (938-3338), will arrange equipment rental, instruction or guided trips.

You have the choice of a scenic **rafting** trip or whitewater. Trips vary from 2 hours to full days. Wet suits are included in the whitewater trips – a perfect thing to do if it's raining. Call **Sea to Sky Raft Tours** (932-2002) or **Whistler River Adventures** (932-3532).

Summer glacier **skiing** on Blackcomb (932-3141) usually lasts until Labour Day. There is also a

selection of skiing clinics and camps. For winter skiing see Sports and Recreation (Skiing). If you are an experienced skier, you could try a day of heli-skiing: four glacier runs on fresh powder – 3650 vertical meters (12,000 ft).

Four outdoor **tennis** courts are available at Myrtle Phillips Elementary School at the village. Courts are also located at Alpha Lake Park, Meadow Lake Park and Emerald Park. Several hotels have pay-as-you-play courts: Delta Mountain Inn, Chateau Whistler and Tantalus Lodge.

Crystal Lodge on top of Blackcomb has fabulous view looking back at Whistler Valley. In the summer it is a 45-minute walk from the gondola.

INDEX

Alcoholics Anonymous, 20
Ambleside Park beach, 102, 167, 169
Ambulance, 20
American Express, 22
Anthropology, Museum of, 84, 126-27, 214
Antiques, 189
Aquarium, Vancouver, 118-20, 202
Aquatic Centre: UBC, 181; Vancouver, 167, 182
Archives, City of Vancouver, 128, 131
Arriva restaurant, 59
ART GALLERIES, 135-38
Art Gallery, Vancouver, 134, 191
Arts Club Theatre, 141, 148
Art supply stores, 188-89
Auto clubs, 21
Auctions, 189
Auto racing, 154

Baby-sitters, 24
Bacchus Ristorante, 30, 44, 149
Back Alley Theatre, 141
Bakeries, 94
Ballet British Columbia, 146
Banks, 22-23
Barclay Hotel, 33
Bars, 89, 148-52. See also Clubs; Lounges; Pubs
Baseball, 171, 172, 214
Bayshore Hotel, 33
BCAA, 21
BEACHES, 180-81; Ambleside, 102, 167, 169; English Bay, 180; Jericho, 38, 84, 106, 156, 163, 173, 180, 183, 184; Kitsilano, 156, 167, 180, 181; Locarno, 106, 156, 180; Second, 116, 180, 181; Spanish Banks, 106, 156-57, 180; Sunset, 158, 180, 211; Third, 113; Wreck, 106
Beach House Restaurant, 116-17
Beatles Museum, 133-34

Bed and breakfast, 33, 34, 36, 39
Bicycling, 72, 100, 154-58
Bird sanctuaries, 110, 116, 210
Bishop's restaurant, 55-56
Blackcomb Mountain, 176-77, 231, 232, 233
Bloedel Conservatory, 109-10
BOATING: canoeing, 85, 158-60, 212; with children, 212; cruising, 160-61; emergencies, 20; instruction, 160, 172-73; kayaking, 85, 158-60; marine forecast, 160; marine supplies, 198-99; rentals, 85, 159-60, 161, 172-73; river-rafting, 171-72; sailing, 172-73
Bookstores, 189-92
Bowen Island, 76, 80, 106, 161, 173
Bread Garden restaurant, 23, 49
Breakfast/Brunch, 42-44
Bridges restaurant, 89, 149
Britannia, M.V., 89-91
B.C. Ferry Corp., 75-80, 84, 89, 220
B.C. Lions, 15, 171
B.C. Place, 10, 15, 133, 154, 171
B.C. Railway, 74-75, 91
B.C. Sports Hall of Fame, 133
B.C. Sugar Refinery, 98
B.C. Transit, 22, 68-72, 78
Buchan Hotel, 34
Buddhist temple, 134
Buntzen Lake, 123, 165, 169
Burnaby Village Museum, 132-33, 158, 214
Bus depot, 73
Buses, 68-70, 73, 78-79, 81, 89, 95-96. *See also* Bus Depot; SeaBus; SkyTrain
Butcher shops, 208

Café Fleuri, 28, 42
Cafe Mercaz, 61-62
Caffe Barney, 42
Calendar of events, 100

Camera stores, 199
Camping, 39-40, 158
Canada Place, 72, 98, 100, 155, 214
Canadian Museum of Flight and Trans-
    portation, 134-35
Canadians, Vancouver, 171, 214
Cannery restaurant, 48
Canoeing, 85, 158-59
Canucks, Vancouver, 15, 171
Capers restaurant, 43
Capilano Fish Hatchery, 102
Capilano River Regional Park, 102-3, 123
Capilano Suspension Bridge, 103
Carol ships, 100
CARS, 21; auto clubs, 21; on ferries, 77-78;
    parking, 74; racing, 154; rentals, 73-74;
    towing, 21
Cates Park, 175
Centennial Seawalk, 102, 167
Cheese stores, 205
Chartwell restaurant, 29, 44
Chesa Seafood House, 45
Chez Thierry restaurant, 57
CHILDREN, 88, 131-33, 134, 158-59, 209-
    18
Children's Festival, Vancouver, 100, 215
CHINATOWN: map, 92-93; restaurants,
    53, 65; shopping, 93-94, 187; sights, 52,
    84, 91-94, 103-4, 212
Chinese: Cultural Centre, 52, 93; festivals,
    100; food stores, 203, 207; people, 16,
    92-93; restaurants, 42, 50-55, 94
Chiyoda restaurant, 61
Christmas events, 100, 133
Classical music, 143-46, 220
CLOTHING STORES: children's, 216-17;
    men's, 192-93, 194-95; second-hand,
    195; women's, 193-95
Cloverdale Rodeo, 170
Clubs, 148-52. *See also* Bars; Lounges;
    Pubs
Coffee: bars, 49-50; stores, 205
Colbrook Trout Farm, 210
Comedy: clubs, 148; festival, 100
Commercial Dr., 72
Consignment stores, 195, 217
Consulates, 22

Crisis Centre, 20
Cruising, 160-61. *See also* Boating; Tours
    by boat
Currency exchanges, 22-23
Customs regulations, U.S., 22
Cypress Falls Municipal Park, 122-23
Cypress Provincial Park, 178, 179, 213

Danann Mondial Cafe, 43
Dance, 146
Days Inn, 31
Deep Cove, 159, 160, 212
Deer Lake, 158, 159-60, 212
Delicatessens, 205-7
Delilah's restaurant, 55, 56
Delta Airport Inn, 36, 184
Delta Place hotel, 29
Delta River Inn, 36
Dentists, 20
Dim sum, 53-54
Discos, 150-51
Doctors, 20, 22
DOWNTOWN: accommodation, 28-32;
    map, 69; restaurants, 65-66; shopping,
    186-87, 188
Dr. Sun Yat-sen Classical Chinese
    Garden, 84, 93, 103-5
Dragon Boat Festival, 100
Drugstores, 23
Dry cleaning, 25
Dundarave concession, 47
Dynasty restaurant, 51

East Indian: food stores, 207; people, 16;
    restaurants, 56-57
El Mariachi restaurant, 62
Emergency phone numbers, 20
Emily Carr College of Art and Design, 85,
    136, 137, 211
English Bay, 158, 167, 173, 184
English Bay Cafe, 49, 149
English Bay Inn, 33
ENTERTAINMENT, 139-46, 147-52. *See
    also* Bars; Clubs; Lounges; Pubs
Espresso bars, 49-50
Ethiopian restaurants, 57
Ethnic: food stores, 207; groups, 16, 91

FERRIES, 75-80, 84, 89, 220; maps, 77, 220. *See also* Granville Island Ferries; SeaBus
Film Festival, Vancouver International, 100
Film processing, 199
Fire Department, Vancouver, 20
Firehall Arts Centre, 141
Fireworks, 99
First Night, 100
Fish, 164, 207, 208
Fish Hatchery, Capilano, 102
Fishing, 162-65; with children, 210
Fish stores, 207-8
Fitness (aerobics, weights, jogging), 165-67
Fitness gear stores, 166
Flight and Transportation, Canadian Museum of, 134-35
Flying Wedge restaurant, 46
Folk Music Festival, Vancouver, 100
Food stores, 202-8
Football, 171
Foreign visitors, 22
Four Seasons Hotel, 29, 44, 149
Fraser River, 10, 12, 13, 72, 124, 154, 157, 165, 171
French: people, 16; restaurants, 57-58
Fresgo Inn, 43
Fringe Festival, 100

Galiano Island, 221-24
Galleries. See Art galleries.
Gallery Cafe, 45, 136
GARDENS: Bloedel Conservatory, 109-10; Dr. Sun Yat-sen Classical Chinese Garden, 103-5; Nitobe Garden, 108-9; Queen Elizabeth Park, 109-10; UBC Botanical Garden, 108-9, 122; VanDusen Botanical Gardens, 124
Gastown, 13, 96, 100, 187
Gastown Grand Prix, 155
Gay clubs, 152
Georgia, Hotel, 31, 149, 150
Golf, 16, 167-69
GRANVILLE ISLAND: accommodation, 35; bars, 89; bicycling on, 156; boating near, 85, 158, 161, 173; children's

activities, 88, 211, 212; events, 88, 100, 141; galleries, 85, 136-38, 211; getting to, 89; jogging route, 166; Kids Only Market, 186, 211, 216; maps, 84, 86; Public Market, 84, 85, 156, 203-4, 207, 211; restaurants, 43, 66, 89, 166, 215; shopping, 186; sights, 84-89, 97
Granville Island Brewery, 24, 88, 97
Granville Island Ferries, 88, 89, 130
Granville Island Hotel, 35-36, 150
Granville Island Public Market, 84, 85, 156, 203-4, 207, 211
Greek: food stores, 100, 207; people, 16; restaurants, 58
Greyhound, 73
Grouse Mountain, 105, 177, 180, 213
Gulf Islands, 10, 76, 77, 80, 108, 220-29; map, 220

Hamburger Mary's restaurant, 23
Harbour, Vancouver, 100, 130, 174; bicycling, 155-56; boating, 161; map, 97; tours, 97
Harbour Ferries, 91
Hastings Sawmill Store Museum, 106, 133
Helijet Airways, 81, 82
Hemlock Valley, 178
HIKING, 169; Buntzen Lake, 123; Capilano River Regional Park, 102-3, 123; Cypress Falls Municipal Park, 122-23; Grouse Mountain, 105; Lighthouse Park, 106-7, 123; Lynn Headwaters, 123; Mount Seymour, 107-8; Pacific Spirit Park, 122
History, 12-15, 96
Hockey, 171
Holidays, list of, 22
Home furnishings, 195-97, 218
Hon's Wun Tun House, 54-55
Horse: racing, 170; shows, 170, 210
Horseback riding, 120, 169-70
Horseshoe Bay, 10, 70, 76, 78, 79, 80, 161, 163-65
Hospitals, 20
Hostel, Vancouver, 38-39
HOTELS, 28-38; maps, 28, 69
Howe Sound, 90, 160-61, 163-65, 174, 175; map, 160

Imax Theatre, 214
Il Barino restaurant, 59
Indian. *See* Native Indian
Indian Arm, 159, 160
Indy Vancouver, 100, 154
Interpreters, 22
Isadora's restaurant, 43, 89, 166, 212, 215
Italian: food stores, 207; people, 16;
    restaurants, 59

Japanese: festivals, 100; food stores, 207;
    people, 16; restaurants, 42, 60-61. *See
    also* Japantown
Japanese Deli House, 45
Japantown, 16, 207; map, 92-93
Jazz: clubs, 148; festival, 100
Jericho Beach, 38, 84, 106, 156, 163, 173,
    183, 184
Jewish: food stores, 207; Hadassah
    Bazaar, 100; people, 16; restaurants,
    61-62
Jogging routes, 166-167
Johnson, Pauline, 116, 117, 118

Kaplan's Deli, 61
Kayaking, 85, 102
Kenya Court Guest House, 36
Kids Only Market, 186, 211, 216
Kingston Hotel, 32
Kingsway, accommodation, 37
Kirin restaurants, 51, 53-54
Kitchenware, 197-98
Kitsilano: accommodation, 35-36; map,
    128; restaurants, 66; shopping, 186-87
Kitsilano Beach, 156, 158, 167, 183
Kitsilano Pool, 156, 181
Korean restaurants, 62

La Grande Résidence, 38
Lake Union Air, 82
Landmark Seafood House, 54
LATE NIGHT SERVICES, 23, 47
Le Crocodile restaurant, 58
Legal services, 20
Le Meridien Hotel, 28, 149
Lighthouse Park, 106-7, 123, 174, 213
Limousines, 97
Lions, 118

Liquor stores, 24
Locarno Beach, 106, 156, 180
Lonsdale Quay Hotel, 37
Lonsdale Quay Public Market, 70, 72
Lost and found, 22
Lost Lagoon, 111, 116, 166, 210, 211
Lounges, 148-49. *See also* Bars; Clubs;
    Pubs
Lunch, 44-45
Lynn Canyon Park, 103, 213
Lynn Headwaters, 123

Malinee's Thai Food, 63
Manning Park, 179
Maplewood Children's Farm, 210
MAPS, list of, 7
Marathon, Vancouver International, 100
Marine: emergencies, 20; forecast, 160;
    supplies, 198-99
Marineview Coffeeshop, 46
Maritime Museum, 128, 130, 156, 202,
    214
Markets. *See* Granville Island Public
    Market; Lonsdale Quay Public
    Market; New Westminster Public
    Market
Mayne Island, 224-26
Meat stores, 208
METRIC CONVERSION, 22
Mexican: food stores, 207; restaurants, 62
Ming's Restaurant, 53
Motor vehicles. *See* Cars
Mountaineering, 169
Mount Baker, 178
Mount Seymour Provincial Park, 40, 107-
    8, 169, 178, 180
Movies, 140
MUSEUMS, 125-35, 202. *Also see* under
    individual names
MUSIC: classical, 143-46; folk, 100; jazz,
    100, 148; new, 145; rock, 151. *See also*
    Record stores

Naam restaurant, 23, 47
Nanaimo-Vancouver bathtub race, 99, 100
Nat Bailey Stadium, 171, 172, 214
Native Indian: galleries, 126-27, 137-38;
    history, 12, 113, 117, 128; people, 16,

118; restaurant, 64, 65. *See also* Anthropology, Museum of; Totem poles

New Westminster, 10, 13, 21, 72, 100

New Westminster Public Market, 72

Newspapers, 26

Newton Wave Pool, 213

NIGHT CLUBS, 147-52

Nitobe Garden, 108-9

Noor Mahal restaurant, 56-57

North Shore, 10; accommodation, 37-38; buses, 70; restaurants, 66; SeaBus, 70-72

Nyala Ethiopian Restaurant, 57

Oakridge Shopping Centre, 187-88

Observatory, Gordon Southam, 128, 130

O'Doul's Hotel, 32

Oktoberfest, 100

Olympia Oyster and Fish Co., 46

Opera, 145. *See also* Classical music

Opticians, 20

Orpheum Theatre, 141-42, 145

Ossu Japanese Restaurant, 61

Outdoor restaurants, 47-48

Pacific Centre, 8, 21, 188

Pacific Cinémathèque, 140

Pacific National Exhibition, 99, 100

Pacific Spirit Park, 120-24, 156, 170; map, 121

Pan Pacific Hotel, 29

Park Royal Hotel, 38, 149

Park Royal Shopping Centre, 15, 118, 187-88

PARKS: Ambleside, 102, 167, 169; Buntzen Lake, 123; Capilano River, 102-3, 123; Cates, 175; Cypress Falls Municipal, 122-23; Cypress Provincial, 178, 179, 213; Dr. Sun Yat-sen, 103-5; Grouse Mountain, 105, 177, 180; Lighthouse, 106-7, 123, 174, 213; Lynn Canyon, 103, 213; Lynn Headwaters, 123; Manning, 179; Mount Seymour, 40, 107-8, 169, 178, 180; Pacific Spirit, 120-24, 156, 170; Queen Elizabeth, 109-10, 169, 183, 214; Richmond Nature, 210; Stanley, 111-19, 123, 155, 166, 169; Vanier, 128-31, 156, 158, 167, 215; Whytecliff, 174. *See also* Beaches; Gardens

Passionate Pizza, 46-47

Pharmacies, 23

Phnom-Penh restaurant, 64

Pho Hoang restaurant, 64

Photo: galleries, 137; supply stores, 199

Piccolo Mondo restaurant, 59

Pink Pearl restaurant, 51

Planetarium, H.R. MacMillan, 128, 129, 156

Playland, 211

PNE (Pacific National Exhibition), 99, 100

Point Atkinson Lighthouse, 106-7

Poison Control Centre, 20

Polar Bear Swim Club, 100, 181, 182

Police, Vancouver, 20, 22, 134

Police Museum, Vancouver, 134

Pools, 181-83, 213, 214

Population, 14, 16

Port of Vancouver. *See* Harbour, Vancouver

Portuguese restaurants, 62

Post office, 23

Presentation House, 142

Professional sports, 171

Public transit, 68-73

Pubs, 150. *See also* Bars; Clubs; Lounges

Queen Elizabeth Park, 109-10, 169, 183, 214

Queen Elizabeth Theatre and Playhouse, 142

Quilicum restaurant, 64, 65

Radio stations, 25

Rafting, whitewater, 171-72

Raintree restaurant, 64-65

Rape Relief, 20

RCMP (Royal Canadian Mounted Police), 20

Record stores, 199-201

Reifel Bird Sanctuary, 110

RESTAURANTS, 41-66, 94; for children, 215-16; map, 65; 24-hour, 23

Richmond Nature Park, 210

River-rafting, 171-72

Riviera Motor Inn, 32
Road service, emergency, 21
Robson Square, 100, 134
Robson St., 84; accommodation, 32-33; shopping, 186
Rock clubs, 151
Rodeos, 170
Rosellen Suites, 33
Royal Hudson steam train, 84, 89-91, 102
Rubina Tandoori restaurant, 57

Sailing, 172-73
St. Roch, 130
Salmon, 118, 162-65; hatchery, 102. See also Fishing; Seafood
Sales tax, 23, 42
Salt Spring Island, 175, 226-29
Santa Fe Café, 55
Sawasdee Thai restaurant, 63
Scanwich restaurant, 43-44
Science World, 131-32, 202, 214
Scuba diving, 174-75
SeaBus, 70-72, 76, 154
Sea Festival, 99, 100
Seafood, 164; restaurants, 45-46; stores, 207-8
Seattle, 73, 82
Seasons restaurant, 48
Seawall, Stanley Park, 111-16, 155, 166
Seoul House restaurant, 62
Settebello restaurant, 48
Seymour Demonstration Forest, 98
Shaughnessy, 156
Shijo restaurant, 61
Shoe repairs, 25
Shoe stores: children's, 216-17; men's and women's, 201
SHOPPING, 185-209. See also Chinatown; Granville Island
SIGHTSEEING, 84-100
Simon Fraser University, 15; Art Gallery, 136; tours, 98
Simpatico Ristorante, 58
Skating, 175
Skiing: with children, 213; cross-country, 179-80; downhill, 105, 108, 176-79; map, 176; rentals, 180
SkyTrain, 70, 72-73

Southlands, 157, 169-70
Souvenir stores, 202
Spanish Banks beach, 84, 106, 124, 156-57, 158
Spanish restaurants, 63
Splashdown Park, 214
Sport B.C., 154
SPORTS, 153-84
Sports Hall of Fame and Museum, B.C., 133
Squamish, 10, 90, 100
Stadiums: B.C. Place, 133, 171; Nat Bailey, 171, 172
STANLEY PARK, 10, 84, 111-19; "Around the Park" bus, 70, 117; beaches, 113, 116, 180, 181; bicycling, 155; Children's Zoo, 117, 210; getting to, 111; history of, 14; Kids Traffic School, 117, 211; Lost Lagoon, 111, 116, 166, 210, 211; map, 114-15; miniature train, 117, 211; pitch and putt, 116, 169, 211; playground, 117, 118, 120, 211; restaurants, 116-17; seawall, 111-117, 155, 166; Siwash Rock, 113; Theatre under the Stars, 142; totem poles, 112; tourist information booth, 21; trees, 116, 123; Vancouver Aquarium, 118-20, 202; zoo, 117, 210
Starbucks espresso bar, 49-50
Steam clock, 96
Steveston, 100
Sunset Beach, 158, 180, 211
Sunset Inn, 34
Sun Yat-sen Garden, 84, 93, 103-5
Sushi, 60-61
Swimming, 116, 180-83, 213, 214
Sylvia Hotel, 35, 149
Symphony Orchestra, Vancouver, 141-42, 146. See also Classical music
Szechaun Chonqing restaurant, 52

Taxis, 74, 75, 81
Teahouse Restaurant, 48, 116
Television, 25-26
Tennis, 88, 117, 183-84
Thai restaurants, 42, 63
Theatre, 141-43
Theatre under the Stars, 142

Theatresports, 141
Third Beach, 113
Tickets, 140, 171
Tojo's restaurant, 60
Tomahawk restaurant, 44, 216
Topanga Cafe, 62
Totem poles, 112, 126, 130
Tourist information, 21-22
TOURS: by air, 94, 105; by boat, 95-96; by bus, 96; by car, 97; on foot, 96-97; nightclub, 151; special interest, 97-99; by train, 89-91. *See also* Sightseeing
Toy stores, 217-18
Trade and Convention Centre, Vancouver, 98
Trailer parks, 39-40
Trains, 74-75
TRANSPORTATION, 67-82
Transportation Museum, B.C., 133
Trees, 113, 116, 122-23
Triathlon, Vancouver International, 100
TRIUMF, 98-99
Tsawwassen, 10; camping near, 40; ferry terminal, 76, 77, 78; tourist information booth, 22
24-hour restaurants, 23
2400 Motel, 37

Universities. *See* Simon Fraser University; University of British Columbia
UNIVERSITY OF BRITISH COLUMBIA, 14, 106, 120, 213; accommodation, 38; Anthropology, Museum of, 84, 126-27, 202, 214; Aquatic Centre, 181, 213; bicycling in, 157; Bookstore, 191; Botanical Garden, 108-9, 122; Fine Arts Gallery, 136-37; map, 121; Nitobe Garden, 108-9; tennis courts, 184; tours, 98-99

Vancouver East Cultural Centre, 142-43, 214
Vancouver Museum, 128-29, 156
Vancouver Symphony Orchestra, 141-42, 146
Vancouver Trade and Convention Centre, 98

VanDusen Botanical Gardens, 124
Vanier Park, 128-31, 156, 158, 167, 215
Vassilis Taverna, 58
Vegetarian restaurants, 47
Veterinarians, 20
VIA Rail, 74
Victoria: by airplane, 81-82; by bus and ferry, 73; by car and ferry, 76-79
Vietnamese restaurants, 42, 64

Walking tours, 96-97
Walter Gage Residence, 38
Waterfront Theatre, 143
Water parks, 88, 113, 211
Weather, 16-17
Wedgewood Hotel, 30, 44, 149
West End, 8, 13, 99; accommodation, 33-35; map, 71; restaurants, 66
West End Guest House, 34
Westin Bayshore Hotel, 33
West Vancouver, 10, 89, 102; buses, 70. *See also* North Shore
Whales, 79, 119
Whistler, 176, 179, 229-33
White Rock, 21, 70; accommodation, 40
Whytecliff Park, 174
William Tell restaurant, 56
Windsurfing, 184
Wine, 24; festival, 100
Won More restaurants, 52-53
Wreck Beach, 106
Writers Festival, Vancouver, 100

YMCA, 165, 182
YWCA, 31, 165, 182

Zoos: Children's, 117, 210; Maplewood Children's Farm, 210; Stanley Park, 117, 210. *See also* Aquarium, Vancouver